D1478278

LOSING AFGHANISTAN

"*Those who wonder how the international community failed so dramatically in Afghanistan need look no further. This selection of essays makes sombre reading. The differing points of view demonstrate the complexity of the challenge. Losing Afghanistan explores the arguments for and against intervention and highlights the difficulty of establishing unity of purpose and effort in such demanding circumstances. Above all, it poses a question: how can we in the West claim we know so much, yet demonstrate in Afghanistan that we understand so little?*"

GENERAL (RETD) SIR JACK DEVERELL OBE, FORMER
COMMANDER-IN-CHIEF OF ALLIED FORCES NORTHERN EUROPE

"*A wonderful book of insightful essays
on Afghanistan from an outsider lens.*"

EZATULLAH ADIB, HEAD OF RESEARCH AT INTEGRITY WATCH
AFGHANISTAN AND NATIONAL COUNTRY REPRESENTATIVE AT
THE WORLD ASSOCIATION FOR PUBLIC OPINION RESEARCH

"*The efforts to solve the immense and complex problems in Afghanistan may have often been misdirected, but failure was not guaranteed. Unfortunately, the peace negotiations, leading to the inappropriate haste of withdrawal, fatally undermined the population's confidence, catalysing the untimely collapse of the government. The strategic question posed by these brilliant essays is: how can the doctrine of liberal intervention be reframed to ensure the West intervenes overseas to manage future humanitarian calamities for reasons beyond just national security?*"

BRIGADIER (RETD) JUSTIN HEDGES OBE

LOSING
AFGHANISTAN

THE **FALL** OF **KABUL** AND THE
END OF **WESTERN INTERVENTION**

EDITED BY **BRIAN BRIVATI**

Biteback Publishing

First published in Great Britain in 2022 by
Biteback Publishing Ltd, London
Selection and editorial apparatus copyright © Brian Brivati 2022
Copyright in the individual essays resides with the named authors.

All the contributors to *Losing Afghanistan* are writing in their personal capacity and their views do not necessarily represent the views of the organisations they work for; nor does their presence in this volume constitute an endorsement by them or the organisations in which they work of the views of other contributing individuals and organisations.

ISBN 978-1-78590-731-9

10 9 8 7 6 5 4 3 2 1

A CIP catalogue record for this book is available from the British Library.

Set in Minion Pro

Printed and bound in Great Britain by
CPI Group (UK) Ltd, Croydon CR0 4YY

MIX
Paper from
responsible sources
FSC
www.fsc.org   FSC® C171272

This book is dedicated by its contributors to a number of different groups of people. To the women and girls of Afghanistan who have seen their dreams snatched away with the return of the Taliban. To the servicemen and women and their families who served in Afghanistan over the past twenty years in the NATO coalition and in the security forces of Afghanistan, and to the memory of all those who lost their lives.

> *The tumult and the shouting dies;*
> *The Captains and the Kings depart:*
> *Still stands Thine ancient sacrifice,*
> *A humble and a contrite heart.*
> *Lord God of Hosts, be with us yet,*
> *Lest we forget – lest we forget!*
> RUDYARD KIPLING, 'RECESSIONAL'

All proceeds from this collection will be donated to the Afghan Writing Project at Untold Stories which supports women writers in Afghanistan. Their first collection of stories, *My Pen Is the Wing of a Bird*, will be published in February 2022 by MacLehose Press, an imprint of Quercus Editions Limited.

CONTENTS

INTRODUCTION

___

BRIAN BRIVATI

Twenty-five minutes ago the guns went off, announcing peace. A siren hooted on the river. They are hooting still … We looked out of the window; saw the housepainter give one look at the sky & go on with his job … So far neither bells nor flags, but the wailing of sirens & intermittent guns.[1]

This was Virginia Woolf's diary description of Armistice Day, 11 November 1918, the end of the war to end all wars. In his chapter in this volume, the former Royal Marine Officer Graham Cundy describes the fall of Kabul in 2001: 'There was', he writes, 'little ceremony: the exchange of considerable amounts of US dollars and a handshake with Taliban commanders.' Also in this volume, the former Afghan Minister of the Interior, Masoud Andarabi, describes the fall of Kabul in 2021 at the end of the 'forever war': 'At noon, [the President] supposedly informed his chief of staff that he was going to take a nap. The chief of staff was in the dining room eating when he heard the helicopter. "What's going on?" someone asked. "The President's gone." President Ghani fled

Afghanistan and the Taliban walked back into Kabul. It remains unknown, at the time of writing, if any US dollars were involved, but neither bells nor flags featured on either occasion. There is a danger that, like that house painter in Bloomsbury in 1918, we too will only look up from our work for a moment to note this momentous event before returning to our daily lives. The purpose of this collection of essays is to make the case for *not* doing so. It is a plea that we should keep our gaze on the fate of the people of Afghanistan not only because this is a country of 38 million which is spiralling into economic collapse and famine but because the events in Kabul were made in Washington, London, Beijing and Moscow by action and inaction, by intervention and indifference. The title of this collection, *Losing Afghanistan*, implies that what has happened is a setback in an ongoing struggle. The nature of that ongoing conflict is seen differently by each of the writers in this volume. The aim has been to present a range of views and positions to embed the question of what happens next in the complexity of the kinds of decisions that need to be made and the choices future voters have to make in supporting those decisions or not. We sit at the end of a twenty-year cycle in which more of our politicians chose to act rather than not to act. We are now in an age of isolationism where many Western states choose inaction instead. The authors in this collection take different stances towards this debate and many of them offer vital insights into thinking about questions of intervention and non-intervention and the responsibility to protect.

Losing Afghanistan to the Taliban matters on an individual human and national level, on a regional level and on a global level. This collection is therefore divided into sections to reflect these different levels and the themes, challenges and lessons that cut across them. The group of writers assembled here do not have a single perspective on the ideological questions around liberal interventionism. They care about Afghanistan because it is their home or because they have lived, worked or researched the issues on which the fate of Afghanistan touches. The collection is divided into four sections: People, Neighbours, Forever War and Liberal Interventionism.

The chapters in section one, People, are written by Afghans (Mahmud Khalili and Masoud Andarabi) or by Westerners working in Afghanistan (Jill Suzanne Kornetsky and Hollie McKay) or focus on the impact on the Afghan people (Laura Cretney and Heather Barr). The focus moves out in the second section, Neighbours, to look at Afghanistan's neighbours from an economic perspective (Omar Al-Ubaydli), a comparative perspective (Haider al-Abadi), a regional perspective (Arun Sahgal and Shreyas Deshmukh) and a global perspective (Brian Brivati).

The final two sections of the book, Forever War and Liberal Interventionism, focus on the Western intervention in Afghanistan and the lessons that can be taken away from its ending. The views expressed range from those with a residual support for intervention (Graham Cundy) through to critical evaluations of the liberal interventionism (Jeremy Purvis and Stephen Gethins) to a perspective that is highly sceptical of military interventions (Paul Dixon). Between these poles, a range of analysis and explanation is offered on the context of the collapse and the extent to which it might have been predicted (Alia Brahimi and Safa Mahdi), on failures of intelligence and the conduct of the post-intervention nation-building project (Nick Fishwick and Philip Ingram) and a rarely told story of the efforts of winning hearts and minds carried out during the twenty-year mission by NATO TV (Thomas Dodd). Many of the themes, arguments and much of the historical resonance of the withdrawal is captured by Paul Cornish in his essay on the fall of Kabul and the evacuation.

At the beginning and end of the book there are two poems and between the sections there are human rights stories. The poems are by Masood Khalili and were translated by Robert Darr. The human rights stories linking the sections are designed to bring the reader back throughout the text to the position and the experience of the people of Afghanistan.

The overarching lesson of the Afghanistan intervention should be that before we begin to construct any policy, launch any war or risk lives, we need to be sure of what we are doing, why we are doing it and if the people to be 'protected' truly want it to happen. Especially if we have never seen war. Especially if we live and bring our children up in the relative peace and affluence of the West. If we are to bring force down on the heads of perpetrators of gross human rights violations, for example, then we need to acknowledge that the innocent will die as a result of that endeavour. This is not a pacifist argument. It is almost the opposite. I believe that there are just wars and there is an overwhelming case for intervention in states that are failing or have failed. When, in 2005, the UN unanimously passed the Responsibility to Protect Resolution, this represented the possibility of a better future in which the international community would intervene.

There is an extremely powerful pacifist position that holds that because of the inevitable innocent victims of any military action, we should stay out of the affairs of other states and never intervene with force. There is also a strong case, aspects of which are presented in many of the chapters here, that the failure to manage post-intervention politics means that even where we can achieve regime change by military action, we seem incapable of then building new nations. There is much wisdom in both pacifism and in the critique of nation-building as being an unachievable end product of intervention. However, the logic that led to the Responsibility to Protect Resolution still holds true. If we are not going to live in a world with first- and second-class citizens, the protected and the unprotected, then we need global institutions that embrace universalism. The root of universalism is equality: all lives are equal and all rights are enjoyed by all. This logic demands an international system that sees all citizens of all states as equally worthy of protection. If we can build an international community that bases its policies on the human implications of its actions rather than the implications for the competing and changing interests of the most powerful states, then perhaps the lessons of the Afghanistan intervention will have been learned. We can turn our gaze onto the consequences and the meaning of both action and inaction. We should not be frightened of intervening if we have the victims of our inaction at the forefront of our minds, but the sobering lesson of the past twenty years, and the reality of current geopolitics, is that the age of intervention is now over. We live in the age of isolationism. We face a deeply uncertain future. My hope is that the essays in this collection, with the variety of positions they represent and with the first-hand knowledge that they offer, will provoke a renewed debate on how, when or if intervention is ever justified. My belief is that they should settle the debate on our collective responsibility, after twenty years of involvement, not to walk away. Our strategic patience might have been exhausted but our humanitarian patience has to be renewed as we stand with the people of Afghanistan, whatever the nature of the regime that governs them now.

Brian Brivati
Kingston upon Thames
December 2021

THE TEXT OF HATE

جُنْگ نفرت

———

MASOOD KHALILI
(TRANSLATED BY ROBERT DARR)

A clamour arose when one of the Taliban, citing verses about 'enemies',
broke the tavern's gate and shattered the jar of wine and its full cups.

He is ignorant of the wise words of God-inspired authorities;
from a devil's text he shouts a stream of concocted litanies.

While he curses and maligns the Hindu and the Christian,
they both remain a thousand times more honourable than him!

The windows to knowledge have been shuttered to women and girls;
bound are their eyes and mouths! Bound their fine words of renown!

Take note of the vain, ignorant fool who argues without insight
that God created women to be lacking in honour and might!

Tell that ignorant fool that the peerless, Divine One
bestowed upon women strength and creative will!

To women God sent down verses of majesty and honour!
To you He stressed the duties of ablution and charity.

What entered you from Satan was supreme ignorance,
whereas God bestowed on women true beauty of character!

Masood Khalili is an Afghan diplomat, linguist and poet. He is the
author of *Whispers of War: An Afghan Freedom Fighter's Account of the
Soviet Invasion*.

Robert Darr is a translator and interpreter of classic Islamic mystical
texts and the director of the Arques School of Traditional Boatbuilding in Sausalito, California.

ZARIFA:[1]
A POLICEWOMAN FACES
A DANGEROUS FUTURE

'All my hopes and dreams were destroyed after the Taliban takeover and since those moments, I don't feel safe, even in my own home.'

A FEMALE POLICE OFFICER DESCRIBES HOW HER
LIFE HAS CHANGED UNDER THE TALIBAN

Zarifa (a pseudonym) had a bright career ahead of her. A law graduate who had studied overseas, she had joined the Afghan police force, rising to become an officer. She studied on the side of her job and was in her final semester of a master's degree at a prestigious university. Now, she stays at home, and sees nothing but a dark future for herself and her female friends.

After the collapse of the government, she received a call from the Taliban, who asked her to return to her police job, promising her salary would be paid from Qatar. But on returning to work, she found a different situation. Zarifa commented:

> When I got back to my office after the takeover, there was chaos. Some of the equipment had been broken. We were all frightened

3

to see a Talib as our new manager with long pyjamas and a turban. I could not face it and went to the washroom and cried.

Her family feared for her safety, worrying she might be hurt, killed or kidnapped by the Taliban, and asked her to stay home. Zarifa is now one among dozens of female police officers who have left the job and are living with no income, some previously the sole breadwinners for their families. 'All my hopes and dreams were destroyed after the Taliban takeover and since those moments, I don't feel safe, even in my own home. I think they will come and will kill me,' said Zarifa.

She added:

> When we joined the police during the previous government, it was still taboo for our families and community for women to join the army. But we fought hard for it and gained recognition and attitudes were slowly beginning to shift. We've lost everything in a matter of days and weeks.

Zarifa now stays at home, depressed and dealing with anxiety. She feels women like her have lost twenty years of progress and hard work. She hears stories of friends who have been arrested by the Taliban in the Barchi area in Kabul, but has no idea what has happened to them, making her all the more nervous for her future.

Some of her friends decided to leave Afghanistan and fled to neighbouring countries such as Iran and Pakistan. Somaya, Zarifa's friend, was a member of the national army forces and a fellow police officer. Somaya, her mother and two younger sisters each paid 20,000 Afghani to a smuggler for a dangerous four-day journey through the Chaman border, and now live illegally in Pakistan. 'Even here I don't feel safe. I can't go to immigration to register and can't go to the embassies as I fear we will be arrested. I have seen them deport over 270 families back to Afghanistan,' said Somaya in a message to Zarifa.

A friend and former colleague, Aliya Rayesi, who was head of Herat Prison, had also been asked to return to her job but has disappeared, with no news on her whereabouts or safety.

With bad news from friends, family and former colleagues, Zarifa sees little hope, concluding, 'I don't see any physical or mental safety for my friends in Afghanistan, or those who have fled to Pakistan. We have no future.'

PEOPLE

CHAPTER 1

WHAT NOW? THE FUTURE IN AFGHANISTAN

———

JILL SUZANNE KORNETSKY

A nation of 35 million people is hanging on to existence by a thread. Twenty years of reconstruction, aid, development and economy building, in one of the largest multinational assistance platforms the world has ever seen, is about to end in a widespread famine.

Closures of roadways around the country as districts and provinces fell (or were handed over) to the Taliban in advance of President Ghani's resignation and the fall of Kabul reduced normal flows of staple goods from July 2021. On 15 August, those flows stopped almost entirely. While local wholesalers around the country began this new era with sacks stacked to the roof, in the absence of reliable road transport, those stocks will not last long. In the meantime, prices have doubled and tripled for a population already struggling pay cheque to pay cheque, or out of work entirely.

Access to savings held within the local banks, or funds transferred in from abroad, was restricted initially to $200 per week, and later increased to $400 per week, an amount greater than the former monthly salary of a police officer or street sweeper.[1] While frustrating for some, this amount, which is based on my personal experience of people buying groceries in Kabul at the time of writing, is sufficient for food and other routine expenses for an Afghan family, mathematics which will not help when the supply of distributable cash is depleted entirely (a point quickly approaching as Western Union cash transfers are no longer being disbursed), in a country where perhaps 1 per cent of merchants have some ability to accept credit cards or electronic transfers.

Unemployment prior to the fall was somewhere between 11 per cent[2] (a serious underestimate repeated by many sources) and more than 40 per cent, up from 25 per cent in 2015.[3] Elsewhere the *employment* rate is listed as 41.5 per cent in 2020, down 2 per cent from the previous year.[4] Now add to those numbers the 300,000 members of the Afghan National Defense and Security Forces (ANDSF) unemployed overnight, the 220,000 teachers whose salaries were delayed for months before August, the more than 20,000 health-care workers both unpaid and unsupplied, the tens of thousands of national employees of demobilising development projects and any Afghan working for the 100,000 Afghans who have already left, many of whom had the business resources or personal funds for large support staffs. The numbers of people with gainful salaries in Afghanistan has fallen off a cliff. Day labourers (identifiable by the wheelbarrows they push) have taken to the streets in slow marches to protest their own hunger. Most of the newly unemployed weren't earning much more than a living wage before, and they have no savings to fall back on.

The informal internally displaced people (IDP) camps throughout

Kabul and other major cities have taken people out of homes and left them in uninsulated tents with insufficient blankets and winter clothing to bear the cold, and with little money to afford enough wood or charcoal from a fuel seller to cook with, let alone enough to heat a tent with. Cooking, for many, won't be an option anyways, as they will struggle to afford even $0.12 for a piece of Afghan bread, let alone $1.20 for a kilo of beans or $5.88 for a kilo of meat. Many of those everyday Afghans who used to give small change to beggars outside their car windows will likely have to resort to begging themselves, but there are fewer employed Afghans to give their spare change, there is less spare change to share and the elites and the wealthy of the country are largely long gone. All the goodwill, hopes and prayers in the world won't put 100 Afs, or ten pieces of bread, in someone's hand.

The chaos and unpreparedness surrounding the evacuation process – within the Islamic Republic of Afghanistan government, inside the Islamic Emirate of Afghanistan (IEA or Taliban) government, within Afghanistan's diplomatic community and within the international military forces – itself have left the world shocked, and many Afghans inside Afghanistan despondent, panicked and with dreams for the future upended and uncertain. Social media and mass media remain full of 'disaster porn' – obsessed with viewer statistics and click rates; playing up the worst fears of Afghans at home and abroad; contributing to the panic, misinformation and psychological distress; and with an almost singular focus on continued evacuation and of course the finger-pointing.

The unpacking of all that went wrong in Afghanistan has begun, yet few of these efforts offer any practical solutions for the 35 million Afghans who never had a chance to leave and likely never will.

It is as if people believe Afghanistan, a nation and culture 5,000 years in the making, having outlasted the Moghul, Arab, Persian, Ottoman, British, Russian, NATO and US armies, in an endless string of direct and proxy warfare, will now upon the exit of the Western coalition simply fall into the earth or be sucked into a black hole. Afghans have long been forced to pick themselves up and use whatever resources remain to rebuild their society – the enormous and unexpected setbacks of summer 2021 are no different. What could and should be different is the position and obligations of the international community (IC) to ensure that Afghans aren't left worse off due to the past twenty years of our involvement, and that the slow but steady indicators of progress aren't erased entirely in the fog of failures and the imposition of IEA ideologies and restrictions.

There is, both thankfully and alarmingly, a very small window of time in which the IC can act to ensure against the complete breakdown of Afghanistan's economy and society. It will take a rapid and large-scale influx of basic humanitarian aid; coordination between reputable independent actors; stronger safeguards against parasitic and opportunistic behaviour than ever before; preparations for reducing dependency and increasing self-sufficiency at the family and community levels; and the recalibration of promises and expectations, including the scale, scope, objectives and focus of international programming. It will not be easy, and will require ongoing support, reduced dramatically as compared with the enormity of prior platforms, for some years to come. But it can be relatively straightforward, if broken into dependencies and discrete if overlapping and often concurrent steps.

FIRST THINGS FIRST: SURVIVAL

STEP ONE: WINTER IS COMING

As many as 4 million Afghans now reside in IDP camps throughout Afghanistan, leaving the comforts of home by fear or by force. The displacements continue with Taliban agents forcing ethnic minority Hazaras from their farms across the country, dispossessing them not only of house and home but also of any food and fuel stocks they had saved for winter, and most or all of the extra sleeping mats and blankets found stacked neatly in the corners of most Afghan homes for winter warmth. Millions more Afghans remain out of work or are newly unemployed. The normal social safety net of relying on extended family and friends to make it through the lean times is fractured: where extended families relied on the salaries of a few employed men, those breadwinners are now out of work; monied Afghans have left the country in droves, taking with them as many family members as possible, but leaving behind many more.

The almost singular focus of Afghans, the Afghan diaspora and the IC on frantic plans for evacuations has left anyone without the prospect of an exit in the lurch. For some, remittances from abroad at $200 or $400 per week will keep them afloat; for others, no such lifeline exists. Immediate food aid is needed for half or more of Afghanistan's population. Winter aid packages are needed for rural Afghans, those living in informal settlements from prior displacement and the IDP population. These should be delivered, without delay, and in an ongoing series of repeated material disbursements, by those organisations in Afghanistan with the best track records for efficacy, and the least evidence of corruption. Further support might come in the form of small monthly cash disbursements for those same populations, electronic transfers from the Afghan diaspora and individual donors abroad, or a system of credits with local distributors.

The second set of options will offer Afghan families more agency in deciding what they need the most at any given time, but will operate at lower levels of efficiency (the UN buying rice by the container-load means a drastic cost reduction over buying single sacks from local stores) and have the potential for abuse and misuse (the usual suspects finding ways to divert aid from the needy to their personal accounts).

In the short run, accidentally providing some food supplies directly to Afghans who can otherwise afford it will be cheaper than well-meaning private initiatives attempting to assume the duties of international NGOs (INGOs) and multilateral agencies like the UN from abroad, with little understanding of the day-to-day context inside Afghanistan, buying supplies at multiples of the actual costs and relying on unvetted local contacts to operate with integrity and not skim too much. Where possible, private initiatives should seek to bolster the activities of their chosen UN or INGO hunger agencies, rather than compete with them. Local NGOs with long histories of implementing projects in rural Afghanistan could be considered as implementing partners and force multipliers, with careful controls and independent monitoring by the public and donors to avoid the graft and waste historically pervasive when funders hand over responsibilities in local programming.

STEP TWO: FINANCIAL CRISIS AVERSION

Afghanistan is facing impending financial crises on multiple levels. The liquidity of the central bank is a well-known and publicised issue that will take significant time for the IC to work through in order to reach a systematic and regular solution. Valid concerns that the operation of Da Afghanistan Bank by the Taliban will provide easy avenues for the diversion of cash to terrorist activity remain and are being considered by the relevant authorities.

The Afghan people have a more immediate financial crisis – the ability to access funds in bank accounts and via remittances from abroad. Immediately upon the news that the Taliban was on the outskirts of Kabul, with the assumption that the banks would fall or close permanently or that the Taliban would drain cash reserves or even accounts, there was a rush to withdraw entire life savings in cash. Facing mobs of people looking to withdraw more cash than is held on hand at any branch location, the banks quickly closed and remained shut for more than two weeks. Reducing daily or weekly transaction limits to $200 initially was actually a smart move that likely extended cash liquidity in Afghanistan by weeks or months and continues to allow those with personal or remittance resources to access enough cash to cover daily expenses.

Without a bridging solution to ensure bank branches continue to have cash on hand for distribution, the risk of impending famine is multiplied. Even with a significant boost in food and winter aid distribution by the UN and INGOs, there is unlikely to be enough to reach every hungry Afghan man, woman and child. If and when those with access to some funds lose the ability to withdraw those resources in cash, they will quickly face the same hunger as Afghans with nothing. Wire transfers can be used to deal with issues like rent and internet bills, and phones can be topped up using online services, but Afghanistan's economy is largely cash-based. Without physical cash, civil society risks collapsing.

A patch or bridging solution needs to be found in the short term, and as quickly as possible. Considering the actors in play on the ground at Hamid Karzai International Airport (HKIA), it may mean asking the Qatari delegation to oversee limited cash shipments into Afghanistan – to be delivered directly to the central offices of the local banks (not Da Afghanistan Bank), in exchange for electronic value transfers to the issuer or issuers, or to be disbursed at the airport to the individual banks' armoured vehicle fleets and escorted to the banks. It may mean using private military contractors not affiliated with parties causing concern to the IC, or the Taliban, to execute similar missions to reach the banks directly. While the IC decides how to handle this problem for the long term, an equal or greater effort should be devoted to the patch solution, to avert disaster in Afghanistan in the meantime.

STEP THREE: PASSABLE ROADS AND SECURE GROUND TRANSPORT

The delivery of aid in Afghanistan has represented a small portion of the overall flow of goods into the country over the past twenty years. The US and NATO missions in Afghanistan provided some measure of security for overland traffic, including the perception thereof, which increased confidence, and allowed the local economy to grow. Afghan companies subcontracted to supply foreign forces with food services doubled their returns by opening up supermarkets in the major cities. Afghanistan is also considered a terminal or dumping market, where nearly expired goods, and surplus goods from elsewhere, end up – from Tesco groceries to South African Red Bull to Libyan Tide washing powder. The vastly improved roads and facilitation of trade expanded the variety of goods available locally, including foodstuffs, cleaning supplies, medicines, electronics, cosmetics and other essentials, far beyond what was happening in the '90s, providing the opportunity for small businesses – from wholesalers to corner markets – to open, survive and even flourish.

As Afghanistan is landlocked, and the expenses of air freight are restrictive for most local and locally oriented businesses, the flow of goods enters the country largely by road, from Iran and Pakistan. While this has historically included goods produced locally in those countries – particularly fruits, vegetables and staple carbohydrates – the Chabahar port in Iran, constructed for Afghanistan by India, and more so Pakistan's multiple ports, receive containers of sea freight to be transferred to Afghanistan by trucks. Fuel oil, gas and diesel also enter Afghanistan by road from refineries in the region. While demand for petroleum has dropped significantly, as the approximately 76,000 ANDSF vehicles[5] are largely parked, forthcoming issues of power supply from Tajikistan and Uzbekistan project an increase in use of generators to run homes, stores, hospitals and so on. In-country diesel reserves cannot last indefinitely.

Currently much of this overland traffic is suspended or extremely limited by a combination of border-crossing closures, uncertainty about the possibility of trucks being seized by Taliban forces en route, uncertainty about the ability of Afghan purchasers to remit payments for their goods from local banks and other factors related to uncertainty and risk. As the IC engages diplomatically with the Taliban, reopening roads and assuring non-interference with transportation should be at the top of the list of issues to be discussed.

This issue is not a social or political one, and so should not face the same levels of resistance as when engaging on women's participation and rights, cooperation on counter-terrorism and other topics of contention between the West and the IEA. Secure roadways, the free flow of essential goods and guarantees of safeguards against roadway seizure are critical and, in relative terms, low-hanging fruit to agree upon. It is imperative we start with survival – work on issues of justice can wait a few weeks or months – until after positive diplomatic engagement and careful cooperation has already begun, and the logistics of goods flows has been addressed.

STEP FOUR: CONTINUITY OF BASIC SERVICES AND THE LOCAL ECONOMY

As the flow of goods by road picks up again, reducing pressure for humanitarian aid by air from Qatar, Pakistan and elsewhere, the IC can help the Afghan people to achieve a return to some sense of normalcy. Medicines and consumables for health facilities can be delivered with the assistance of INGOs on the ground already active in the health sector, ensuring that hospital staff have the materials needed to serve their patients. Wholesalers in the local chowks (wholesale markets) can begin replenishing their stocks, which in turn will supply community dukons[6] (small stores). For those with access to even limited amounts of cash, this will reduce the numbers of Afghans facing starvation, and may delay the onset of impending famine.

Roadways aren't the only concern disrupting basic services. Salaries for healthcare workers and teachers need a workaround to ensure these essential public servants can be paid in ways immune to being skimmed by the IEA. The issue of appropriate access to schooling for female students must also be accounted for, whether that be through diplomacy and cajoling the Taliban to return to mixed-gender classrooms – an approach unlikely to yield positive results given its own ideology and the threat of losing forces to Daesh (ISIS-K) for demonstrating weakness on a hard-line issue – or through finding alternative solutions, including widespread free online platforms to replace in-person education, a solution which will not reach the most vulnerable without access to the internet or a computer, or, more ideally, through securing access to additional properties for all-female schools with all-female teachers. While the Taliban is occupying government facilities and many former offices of NGOs who have left the country or suspended operations, there are plenty of unoccupied offices in Kabul and elsewhere which could be secured by direct payments to the landowners, or by the Taliban offering locations it has seized, for use as girls' schools and additional healthcare facilities.

Much of Afghanistan's power supply has been provided by Tajikistan and Uzbekistan, paid for by Da Afghanistan Breshna Sherkat (DABS, the central power company) from electricity bills arriving at every electrified home or office on a bimonthly basis. While city power is irregular at best in Kabul, and sporadic at best in the provinces, it is affordable. The cost to run diesel-powered generators roughly triples or quadruples the cost per kWh – an amount too high for the average Afghan to afford with any regularity, and likely to increase as diesel prices rise with scarcity and without subsidisation by the IC. Working directly with the governments of the supplying countries to pay or guarantee Afghanistan's electricity bill is an easier solution than dealing with a total blackout and a sudden and massive dependence on generators countrywide. DABS continues to issue electricity bills, and banks continue to accept payments, so in time, DABS or the IEA will have to resume payments to Tajikistan and Uzbekistan – a temporary solution to keep the lights on will allow time for that process to be established and responsibility to be transferred.

Taken altogether, these first steps will avert a famine, allow locals to begin solving their own problems with their own resources, create a grace period on a potential nationwide blackout and restore or support basic and critical services like healthcare and education, at least temporarily, while more long-term solutions to these issues are negotiated and agreed.

A NORMAL(ISH) LIFE

STEP FIVE: STABILISATION OF COMMERCIAL AIR TRAFFIC

Commercial air traffic at the HKIA is essential for IC engagement in Afghanistan, as well as for any hope of a continued and robust evacuation effort for Afghans with appropriate documentation to exit. As of early October 2021, only charter and military flights through Pakistan, Qatar and Afghan airline Kam Air, as well as UN-operated flights, are coming and going from Afghanistan. This is sufficient to bring a limited number of foreign diplomats, aid workers, contractors returning to demobilise their operations, a few independent businesspeople and the Taliban leadership into and out of Afghanistan.

Numerous foreign-staffed NGOs, social entrepreneurs, aid workers and embassies cannot or will not re-engage without a functioning commercial airport and flights with open seats to be booked. The logistics of entering Afghanistan from Pakistan or Uzbekistan and travelling to Kabul by roadway are very possible, as evidenced by journalists and other foreigners who have already made the trip, but complicated, despite Taliban escorts who up to the time of writing have been friendly and professional in ensuring safe arrival. That said, the journey is not without inherent risks from provincial Taliban not falling in line with their own leadership, or because of an increase in robberies due to the desperation of hungry people or the sudden absence of law enforcement along the way. For many governments and INGOs, the overland routes are unacceptable, and they will not return in appreciable numbers without a functional HKIA.

The IC must work with the Qatari delegation running the HKIA, and the Taliban, to secure access to the airport, and obtain guarantees that the property will be guarded against attacks by Daesh or other insurgent groups. The costs of charter flights have increased around 500 per cent, purportedly due to steep increases in insurance rates for the planes themselves (as much as $400,000 per flight), an issue that can best be managed and negotiated with sustained efforts by the IC, and if necessary, the provision of alternative insurance products subsidised by the IC for a year or more, until normal operations change the risk calculations back towards previous levels, and confidence is restored.

STEP SIX: SELF-RELIANCE AND SELF-SUFFICIENCY

We must be careful not to give the impression that normalisation means a return to the enormous aid and development platforms of the past twenty years. It won't and, for many reasons, it shouldn't. While intended to rebuild Afghanistan and set it on the road to independence and economic growth, most in-country development projects have faced enormous levels of corruption, have been wildly ineffective and have served only to create a culture of dependency. The goals of normalisation here are to return the basic functioning of Afghanistan's society and economy, including with regard to banking, flows of goods, education, healthcare and the domestic production of staple foods and agricultural goods. From there, it will be up to individual Afghans and Afghan organisations to set a course for future business and economic growth.

Tens of thousands of Afghans employed by foreign-funded projects who have grown accustomed to salaries far larger than the local economy can possibly provide in the near term, without big-budget foreign projects, will have to recalibrate back to local levels, and consider how they can make enough to meet their basic needs under new circumstances. Afghanistan simply does not have the capacity or need for tens of thousands of office workers, as the majority of projects will not be continuing, and the largest native industries capable of employing large numbers of people are agriculture, artisanal and small-scale mining, and with material and technical support, medium-scale mining operations and manufacturing. In the immediate term, Afghanistan needs its farmers.

Agriculture has been the backbone of Afghan life and economy for centuries. Seventy-five per cent of Afghans rely on agriculture for their livelihoods,[7] a historical industry that should first be harnessed to reduce the likelihood of future food crises. The IC has invested heavily in agricultural improvements over the past twenty years, teaching more productive techniques and supplying seed stocks and saplings, improving yields and increasing exports. Many of these efforts, originally focused on increasing GDP and export volumes, can and should be reconfigured to focus on food security at the household and village levels first.

Agricultural extension farms, operated locally, can provide acclimatised seed stocks from seed farming, a variety of tested and hardy seedlings to be used in household kitchen gardening and saplings to plant food forests.[8] In time, as food security becomes more dependable, and the reliance on food assistance is reduced to manageable levels by local production, Afghans can turn their agricultural prowess back to export-oriented activities. For now, we need farmers and homesteaders growing, preserving and distributing foodstuffs through the local economy, allowing hunger organisations to begin sourcing locally, and refocusing ambitions and expectations inwards, on reasonable possibilities in the new context.

STEP SEVEN: ACCOUNTING FOR, AND EVEN HARNESSING, PURDAH

While it is impossible to say what the future will look like in some months or years, whether moderation can be encouraged in the IEA or not, girls need to be in school, the same as the boys. If this means 'separate but equal' for the time being, either for secondary schools or for all ages, it is better to accept and accommodate this new restriction, at least in the short and medium term, than to fight it. The alternative is to draw out the suspension of female education entirely, while attempting a diplomatic mixed-gender schooling solution that is unlikely to bear fruit. The IC subsidising separate facilities for girls' education, at market rates (around $100 per room per month or less) and not the ridiculous foreign contractor rates ($25,000 to $50,000 per month for a ten-room villa) of the past, will be an expense well invested, and a diplomatic headache left for another day.

The same can be said of women's training and workspaces. Female breadwinners in Afghanistan, including war widows and divorcees, especially those with minimal or no schooling, have relatively few options where they can earn a living and provide for their children and parents. Despite being hard workers, social restrictions mean many jobs are considered unacceptable for women to perform, while high national unemployment rates mean even if it might be acceptable for women, employers have plenty of men to choose from. Women are left to take on jobs as house cleaners for about $50 per month (one-quarter to one-half of what a man might expect for the same role) – barely enough to afford bread – while many others have no alternative but to beg on the streets or to engage in prostitution. All these options have become harder or impossible since the fall of Afghanistan.

There is a huge role for social enterprise to play here, even working within the strict rules of purdah, or gender separation. Many Afghan women are willing if not eager for gainful employment. There is an untapped labour force, in the millions, who would happily work for a fair day's pay – a salary of even $250 per month represents a three to five times increase over what they might make working locally, is enough to feed a family and is far lower than almost any other country can offer. It's more than the Afghan military and police were earning in a month. For those enterprises brave enough to create purdah-compliant, all-female workspaces in the Afghan context, there are both humanitarian and economic positives. It is possible to support any number of women and their families, while also making enough profit to ensure the operation is indefinitely sustainable. Engaging now with non-profit efforts designed to grow into benefit corporations or social enterprises in the future will help Afghan women to earn a decent living in socially acceptable spaces, allowing them to feed their families with dignified work.

SELF-DETERMINED LIVES

STEP EIGHT: RE-ENGAGE CIVIL SOCIETY ACTORS – EYES AND EARS ON THE GROUND

The fall of Afghanistan shocked the world, and left the Afghan people feeling abandoned, panicked, disenfranchised, betrayed and despondent. A group of 75,000 ideological Islamic warriors, spread across a territory the size of Texas, is holding a country of 35 million at bay using only the fearful memories of past and recent atrocities, and a nationwide paralysis caused by uncertainty. Much of the country has spent the months after the fall at home, waiting – waiting for the shoe to drop and widespread executions to begin, waiting for the resistance or the IC to come to the rescue, waiting for any kind of leadership to make the uncertain clear. A rich collective culture accustomed to solving problems by networking, sharing information and working together has largely fallen silent, aside from a singular focus on evacuation lists and visa applications.

Civil society in Afghanistan has benefited greatly from improved infrastructure, educational opportunities and access to social media. Independent and local journalism, despite being under constant threat of harassment, abuse, detention, torture, attacks and disappearance, has flourished over the past twenty years. Activists of every kind – from environmental to anti-corruption to women's empowerment – have embraced the rights set forth by international treaties (to which Afghanistan is a signatory) and, with the support of the IC, found the courage to organise around them. Chambers of commerce, agricultural collectives, community development councils, women's rights organisations, organisations supporting musicians and artists and more have popped up across the nation. These organisations and communities, once born, are difficult to eliminate. With some time and stabilisation, and some nominal but enthusiastic outside support, they will lead the efforts to keep Afghanistan from losing what has been gained, preventing it from sliding backwards in time.

Already these activists are reappearing in public; women and men standing together demanding the rights of girls to an education from primary school to university, bravely facing off against Taliban patrols, enduring beatings and being disbursed by warning shots. Still others remain hidden – millions of eyes and ears on the ground in Afghanistan, bearing witness to everything that is happening, but usure of how to re-engage with each other and the world. Efforts must be made to encourage those waiting for evacuation, or who have no hopes of it, to renew those connections and communications, albeit with caution. They have valuable on-the-ground information that the IC should be using to reproach the Taliban about broken promises, to identify Afghans especially at risk and locations where Taliban leadership has lost control of their foot soldiers, to facilitate evacuation of those under threat and to plan for the effective and informed re-engagement of aid workers and non-profit organisations in 2022. Appreciable progress on the preceding steps will give local Afghans the courage to re-engage.

STEP NINE: PREPARING FOR A CLEAN AND JUST FUTURE – TRANSITIONAL JUSTICE, TRCS, LUSTRATION AND BLACKLISTING

As progress is made on the previous eight steps, Afghanistan will see the IC re-engage with aid delivery, humanitarian programming and other non-profit efforts. For-profit efforts will follow as the world decides how to deal with sanctions and their application, and the inevitable taxation of business by a Taliban government. Unfortunately, those whose incompetence, self-interest and corruption can be directly tied to the fall of Afghanistan are already salivating at the prospect of continuing their old ways in future programming. They are giving interviews and writing social media posts, obfuscating their roles in bleeding the country dry, using all the right buzzwords, telling sympathetic stories to stifle questions and preparing themselves to slip back into positions of power. The world cannot fall for this again.

While non-profit interventions are limited or on hold, and flows of project money are essentially turned off at the main, it is imperative to engage in the various mechanisms of transitional justice, even if they begin remotely, from abroad. The formation of a truth and reconciliation commission (TRC) will allow generations of Afghans who have survived endless wars to begin the process of healing from the trauma of it all. It will also give an opportunity to compile lists of human rights offenders, corrupt officials and those with long histories of abuse of power. These grey lists should then be investigated independently to generate blacklists – effectively a process of lustration in absentia – for those who have feasted for too long at the table of impunity, and whom the world must not allow further opportunities to repeat their crimes.

27

Aid and development projects will return to Afghanistan, in some months or years, and when they do, these people will be at the front of the line, professing their devotion to Afghanistan and their obvious necessity to the project. Don't believe it. The time for believing suspiciously well-financed Afghans who say 'trust me' is over. The time for working with Afghans based on their knowledge of English and seemingly Western mindset alone is over. The time for giving those with past contracts, more contracts, despite their dismal rates of efficacy and sustainability, and questions about how much (not if, but how much) was skimmed off project activities should be long dead.

To re-engage in contract-delivered programming without a system of safeguards, and a commitment to smaller, more effective platforms with far better oversight and the willingness to pull the plug on questionable operations would only repeat the mistakes of the past. Instead, we must admit to those past mistakes, learn from them and do better moving forward. Everyday 'normal' Afghans know exactly who are the bad and selfish actors in their society – it is the time to ask them to tell us all about it, through confidential and secure channels, beginning remotely and abroad to keep people safe, identifying information out of the wrong hands, and to investigate those reports in an independent and impartial process, such as a TRC and its outputs.

Jill Suzanne Kornetsky is a Kabul-based scientist, social entrepreneur, consultant, researcher, analyst, guest speaker, guest lecturer, author, editor and company founder.

CHAPTER 2

SOMEONE'S GOTTA SAY IT: UNSPOKEN GROUND TRUTHS AND MISTAKES NOT TO REPEAT

JILL SUZANNE KORNETSKY

Over the next months and years we will see an unpacking of what went wrong in Afghanistan, in white papers, seminars, speaker panels and governmental hearings. There is certainly plenty of blame to go around for the kleptocratic ambitions, corruption, fraud and waste that pervaded a vast majority of programming in-country. Underlying the bulk of these shortcomings is the failure to execute critical thinking and to speak with blunt honesty and realism about the situation and conditions on the ground. The time has come for the death of the company line, 'All is well and this is definitely working.'

This isn't to say that there haven't been advances – there have. The past twenty years in Afghanistan have seen a degree of success in building infrastructure, hope and possibility: raising up thriving cities out of rubble; empowering and educating a generation, including girls; expanding healthcare, with midwives, vaccinators, hospitals and clinics; increasing social engagement and personal freedoms not seen since the 1970s; and enabling trade and commerce which has seen a wider variety of goods flow into, and finally begin to flow out of, Afghanistan. The Afghanistan of 2022 bears little resemblance to the Afghanistan of 1998. Unfortunately, these successes were undercut, and that hope snatched away, at every step, by a systematised pattern of waste, fraud, abuse, corruption and mismanagement, as well as programmatic, diplomatic and governmental failures.

Afghanistan – and the 35 million people who call it home – has not fallen off the earth. In the haze and chaos of evacuations, the instant information and propaganda flooding internet news and the unending 'disaster porn' of Afghan-related social media, this simple fact seems to be forgotten. Despite the levels of despair, fear and panic gripping it today, Afghanistan, and the Afghan people, will outlast the disappointments, hardships and shocks of the day as they have for five millennia. Another change in government, another injury to their culture and freedoms, another period of anxious uncertainty – but they will once again survive, recalibrate and undertake the difficult work of reweaving the fabric of their national identity and civil society under an imposed foreign regime. It will be unnecessarily difficult, and take at least another generation or two, but Afghans will carry on nonetheless. The indomitability of Afghanistan endures.

The international community (IC) has both a chance and an obligation to help Afghans through this new era. In a globalised world there is no longer an option to leave problems 'over there'; security threats are multinational, climate change knows no borders and the

Sustainable Development Goals are a collective global endeavour. Even if there was an option to isolate Afghanistan's problems within its own borders, promises have been made to Afghan allies by the IC to stand and work in solidarity with them, ensuring that things are better and not worse as a result of twenty years of IC interventions. This necessitates continued engagement and assistance.

Walking away now, rather than regrouping and re-engaging, better and smarter, has not only moral and ethical implications but also security-related consequences. Afghanistan needs continuing assistance from and engagement with the IC, in the form of: direct and immediate humanitarian aid; development support – in smaller, slower, sustainable and easily monitored chunks; sincere non-profit programmes leveraging local resources and knowledge for local benefit; and sustainable micro, small and medium enterprises, built to endure the intricacies and challenges of the operating environment.

It is imperative that, in re-engaging, the IC commits to not repeating the mistakes of the past. This will require the saying aloud of some difficult and largely unspoken realities, including but certainly not limited to: the problematic and counterproductive nature inherent in for-profit delivery of aid and development programming; the depth and breadth of corruption in Afghanistan, from the Afghan elites, the Government of the Islamic Republic of Afghanistan (GIRoA) almost in its entirety, power brokers and warlords, to foreign 'Afghan saviours' more focused on self-promotion and financial gain than the Afghan people; the criminal connections and activities of the political class and businesspeople; the disconnect between donor intentions and implementing partner actions, and those who facilitate or allow the disparity;

Great White Hope-ism; the development of a false Afghan culture, herein referred to as 'Afghans in Suits'; the ineffectiveness, fraud and corruption of subcontracted oversight; the formation of entire government bodies and departments, ticking boxes and projecting effectiveness at oversight and anti-corruption, while themselves being as corrupt as the bodies they oversaw; and unchecked rent-seeking behaviours all round, by parties both foreign and domestic.

'AFGHANS IN SUITS'

Afghanistan is a multi-ethnic society with a rich and complicated collective culture. While each ethnic group and province has their own nuances, taken as a whole, 'real' or regular Afghans are most often moderate to conservative Muslims, faithful but curious about other cultures and accepting of pluralism around them and warm and welcoming with a strong sense of hospitality, regardless of financial status. Afghans have survived countless natural and political disasters by working together, under the guidance of elder whitebeards, and putting the needs of the family, tribe or community above personal wants. It is the culture of these 'real' Afghans that keeps foreigners committed to helping the Afghan people, and staying for the long term, which is more or less a requirement to make effective and sustainable progress in Afghanistan.

'Afghans in Suits' is a blanket term for a new and artificial culture in Afghanistan. It doesn't require an actual business suit, and is in no way limited to men. Indeed, many 'powerful' Afghan women fit the bill, having risen to their positions through corruption, nepotism and even drug and sex trafficking proceeds, used to buy seats in government. Nor is a foreign education or even foreign citizenship any guarantee that an Afghan in a Suit will act right – degrees in Afghanistan, Pakistan and India can be purchased for the right price, without spending a day in class. An Afghan in a Suit, once in possession of such a credential, will leverage it to positions beyond their abilities and understanding, without consequence – as many or most of their colleagues are also faking it, those above them are too busy rent-seeking to care, and those below them are socially prohibited from speaking out against a superior, or simply waiting for their turn at the trough.

Disclaimer: Every Afghan man who owns a suit is not necessarily an Afghan in a Suit, while some wearing traditional clothes are. Just as every woman can't be assumed to be well intentioned, every man can't be assumed to have poor intent. Many mid- and lower-level government employees take the same positions as their civilian counterparts: the outrageous levels of corruption are immoral, un-Islamic, un-Afghan and would be the death of the GIRoA – which it was.

That said, the IC is currently engaging, featuring, holding up and praising all sorts of bad actors already outside Afghanistan's borders – former members of Parliament, ministers and ministry directors – who directly and openly engaged in the corruption that killed the 21st-century Afghan dream. Most of their supporters abroad probably don't know better and fell for the sympathetic stories that Afghans in Suits like to tell; this is no excuse. Bad behaviour in Afghanistan was no secret – some simple background research should have exposed them and eliminated these people from such opportunities and acclaim.

Afghans in Suits are the inevitable result of pouring hundreds of billions of dollars in contracts, on top of a culture of poverty and scarcity, without any semblance of appropriate controls or oversight. Afghan elites, for-profit foreign contracting and devel-opment firms, self-named 'halfghan' intermediaries, Afghan poli-ticians and parliamentarians (yes, including the women), warlords who accept foreign funds but decline to fight when it counts and those with signatory privileges in GIRoA ministries – from min-isters to visa clerks – all got their illegitimate pieces of the pie, without delivering the promised results, and completely devoid of consequences. Many are now on the speaker circuit, decrying the situation and using all the right buzzwords – corruption, women's rights, human rights, terrorism, sustainable development, sanc-tions – without their hosts properly digging into their professional pedigrees. The world seems to be trusting without verifying, again, and it's an embarrassing mistake.

Afghans in Suits have never heard a tragic story that they couldn't co-opt for personal financial gain, met a well-meaning but naïve foreigner they couldn't scam or manipulate, heard a buzzword they couldn't hammer on to remain topical, had a timeline that excuses couldn't be made to extend (at cost, of course), passed an oppor-tunity to produce a false receipt and pocket the difference, met a deadline or deliverable they couldn't either fake or blow entirely or encountered a destitute or persecuted Afghan whose situation they couldn't leverage for publicity or a buck.

Afghans in Suits are always keeping up with the Joneses. There is a constant drive to get more, have more, and to dress, act and live like the wealthy (and poorly behaved) foreign and domestic role models Afghanistan has had over these decades. They jealously seek any benefit they see another receiving. This can be seen in the ongoing civilian-driven evacuation effort in Afghanistan – with every depart-ing plane of at-risk individuals, those with long histories of graft and spoiled behaviour, and who are decidedly at less risk than most, are declaring, 'I deserve it more than them – get me on a plane now!' Afghans in Suits' most used strategy is to observe and replicate; they are great storytellers, recalling and parroting rhetoric proven in the past to loosen purse strings, engender sympathy or elicit favours. They will be the first to tell you they 'aren't like the other Afghans', and are 'Western-minded', though their behaviour suggests they think this means promiscuity, gluttony, self-indulgence and freedom to misbehave. They say, 'trust me' and 'believe me' a lot, and resort to emotional manipulation, when lying.

Like their misbehaved role models, Afghans in Suits conflate money, power and sex. Some add violence and sexual violence to the milieu. Afghans in Suits believe the accessibility of a woman signifies her availability for relations; why would a girl or woman who isn't seeking, or at least casually open to, sex be out in public interacting with them at all? Powerful Afghan men with one or more wives at home often need a few girlfriends, or bacha bazi (underaged 'playboys') too – how else will other men know his status and power if his sex life isn't obvious? Sexual harassment of women in the workplace – from hijab shaming to pressured flirtation, assumptions that every female business partner or assistant is an automatic 'girlfriend' and blunt requests for sexual favours – has remained common if not rampant, almost justifying fathers and husbands keeping their female relatives at home, for their honour and protection, thus reinforcing patriarchal systems of power, authority and abuse.

Afghans in Suits are ruining the party for everyone. Most have already left the country; the common people, and their true allies, hope they have left for good, and won't ever return.

OVERSIGHT: THE MEN, THE MYTH, THE MISSING MONEY

The Afghan oversight bodies tasked with managing and prohibiting the corruption – including the Independent Joint Anti-Corruption Monitoring and Evaluation Committee (MEC), the Administrative Office of the President and the National Procurement Authority – were staffed almost universally by Afghans in Suits. These agencies were among the most corrupted departments in the country – enabling and benefiting from the mismanagement, embezzlement and waste they were ostensibly formed to prevent. Each of these offices were whitewashed and box-ticked by a token foreigner, or dual citizen Afghan enabler, naïve or complicit, kept on staff primarily to legitimise their operation. Foreign commissioners of the MEC demanded to be paid in cash, to avoid reporting income at home, and paid funds designated for secure hotels to friends in town. Local management staff saw this blatant abuse, and knew they could get their cut too, without consequence.[1] They should thank the donors and the Afghan people for the homes they bought abroad with the funds they misappropriated.

Foreign oversight bodies tasked with the same responsibilities fared little better – official office visits occurring for one half day every few years, with oversight personnel otherwise restricted to secure compounds or operating from their home countries. Entire 'offices' went up in a day, complete with furniture, electronics and staff – a dog and pony show all-around to please the donors – only to be dismantled a day after the site visit was complete. Subcontractors engaged to monitor progress on behalf of funding agencies quickly learned that nobody was checking their work either, producing glowing, box-ticking evaluations and falsified field data[2]

36

– enough to keep everyone happy and the contract payments rolling in from abroad. They envied the money the Afghans in Suits had, and eventually joined with them in the fraud; a contributing fraud that ultimately proved fatal for the GIRoA government.

A WORD ON EVACUATIONS

The chaos of the US and NATO withdrawal and evacuation, between 15 and 31 August, has led to an equally chaotic continued evacuation by civilian efforts. With everyone's volume turned up to ten, it gives the impression that every Afghan is in imminent danger, that Afghanistan will shortly be sucked into a black hole and that we have days to weeks to accomplish the rest of the evacuation mission. For the most part, this is untrue.

The evacuation of the estimated 200,000 Special Immigrant Visa applicants and their families, as well as P1 and P2 visa applicants and other Afghans who qualify for a visa programme or humanitarian parole, is going to take years.[3] Not weeks or months... Years. In the rush to apply for programmes and get on lists to try to be first in line for the next departing plane, this timeline is being ignored. With the current food crisis, and a cold winter ahead, a focus on manifesting flights over all else is short-sighted. The evacuation is no longer occurring at more than 10,000 souls per day; it will now happen by the carload overland and by the planeload overhead. Until commercial air traffic to Afghanistan fully resumes, the evacuation engines can only move so fast. Many evacuees will not have the opportunity to leave before they run out of money for food. For those waiting to leave, and for those who will never leave, food and shelter are now critical issues which cannot be overlooked.

There are certainly populations at risk in Afghanistan today:

military translators, outspoken and well-known Afghan journalists (especially women), prominent Afghan National Defense and
Security Forces (ANDSF) figures, musicians, high-profile sports
figures (especially women), ethnic and religious minorities and a
few others. Eligibility for visa programmes is not a measure of risk
– the average Hazara villager is facing a far higher risk of abuse
or death, due to their ethnicity and Shia religion, than the average
office worker for a US-funded project. Translators, female judges,
members of the National Resistance Front of Afghanistan (NRF)
and those Afghans with whom individual Talibs have a specific and
personal grievance have been targeted and are certainly in danger.
It is important to note, however, that as each of these groups leaves
Afghanistan, and their exit is covered by news outlets, narratives
and self-assessment of risk by those left behind have begun to escalate and parrot.

Another difficult truth, which needs to be said, is that the world
is not prepared to evacuate every Afghan who speaks a foreign
language, has internet access, has a Western connection or worked
adjacent to foreigners and wants to leave. Well-meaning foreign
allies and internet friends are promising Afghans that they will be
able to leave and go to the West, without understanding the issues
of eligibility or the scope of the global refugee crisis – an unfair
and largely unkeepable promise. Current visa programmes are
not for economic refugees, but for those who meet certain criteria
of employment and risk. The flood of Afghans applying for visas
they are ineligible for, signing up for evacuation without a passport
or a visa, and entering their names onto the same lists over and
over is slowing down the pace of actual evacuations for the eligible
and high-risk. Afghans in Suits are demanding they get priority

regardless of risk, and in the flood of their repeated attempts, applications and submissions, actually at-risk Afghans will continue to lose their lives.

For Afghans not connected to the West, not former translators, not former judges who put Talibs and other violent men in prison, not in other high-risk categories and not with a personal grievance with a Talib, life has been quiet – dangerously hungry – but far quieter than life has been in a long time. An overstretched Taliban is struggling to keep the lights on, and their own foot soldiers in line. For the time being, the risk of widespread death squads committing genocide, and a wholesale destruction of infrastructure, akin to the 1990s, is low, and the IC is working to keep it that way. The evacuation of Afghan allies and high-risk humanitarian parolees must and will continue, long into the future. In the meantime, a population stressing itself into psychological problems and ulcers, or shelving basic survival activities to send mass emails, won't make it go any faster.

THE NOT-OMNIPOTENT TALIBAN

Afghans today are collectively feeling a sense of despair, shock, uncertainty and betrayal. In the course of just a week or two in August 2021, half a million Afghans were displaced from their homes, a million or more lost their sources of income and the ideological, authoritarian leadership of the Taliban is back in power. Supply chain interruptions have caused the price of staple goods to double or triple, for those Afghans with any money at all to buy them. Hunger is now a greater concern than terrorism, or even the threat of renewed persecution and targeted killings by the Taliban itself, in terms of loss of life in the near- and mid-terms.

The story, however, is not as simple as it seems. Afghanistan in 2022 looks nothing like Afghanistan in 1998: massive developments have been achieved – despite even more massive levels of corruption, waste, fraud and mismanagement – on a number of fronts. Afghanistan's population has tripled, with life expectancy up almost twenty years. Infrastructure has developed out of an assortment of rubble fields into ever-expanding cities; albeit while leaving far too many districts and villages out. Literacy rates have more than doubled, and 7 million or more Afghans regularly use the internet. With education, and access to information and communication, comes empowerment; the youth of Afghanistan today are more socially engaged and globally connected than ever before, and far less tolerant of blatant infringement on their human rights.

The Taliban, too, is different, for many of the same reasons. Political engagement and internet access has helped the Taliban to become more politically savvy. Propaganda – once limited to open radio communications in the field, overstating the status of a battle in progress to demoralise the enemy – has become more technological, appearing widely across social media, and in easily shared formats on messenger apps. This propaganda, bolstered by the disaster porn of Afghan-related social media, contributed to the fall of the country by demoralising the ANDSF and the civilian population against fighting back. The long negotiating process in Doha has exposed Taliban leadership to the comforts of opulence and convenience, and the dignity of having a seat at the table; while the old Taliban leaders might have blown up Afghanistan's airports to make a point, the new Taliban leaders find the hours-long ride from Peshawar over shoddy roads to be an unthinkably uncomfortable affair. Pakistani backing has allowed the Taliban to even enter Panjshir, the last bastion, something which had never happened during the last Taliban regime, before being pushed back out by the NRF.

That said, the Taliban is not all-powerful. In fact, it has already shown signs of internal divisions, disorganisation and unpreparedness to assume the responsibilities of governing or ruling. Its forces are composed of roughly 75,000 largely uneducated and rural foot soldiers, splintered into over a dozen internal factions by the successive killing of senior figures and the chaos of succession. Since the takeover of Kabul, there has been a new schism – between Qatari-leaning, marginally more moderate factions, and Pakistani-aligned, hardcore adherents to the ideology. The current line-up of ministers of the Islamic Emirate of Afghanistan (IEA) is as much a reflection of weakness as it is of power – with hardliners fearing loss of their manpower to Daesh (ISIS-K) if leadership is seen as too moderate and accommodating in the pursuit of IC support and humanitarian aid, some of the most extreme ideologues have been appointed ministers.

In an odd twist of fate, the Taliban IEA is now facing the challenges of keeping the lights on, while also facing at least two insurgencies – the NRF tenaciously holding onto Panjshir, as well as a gradual but deadly escalation by Daesh (ISIS-K). Even in Kabul, foot soldiers are nervous – fear can only keep a population at bay so long; with 75,000 against a population of 35 million, and 5 million or more of those being males of fighting age, the Taliban is severely outnumbered, with foot soldiers often assigned to places unfamiliar to them. There have been scattered reports of neighbourhoods fighting back against overreaching local Talib patrols, wiping them out entirely. Upon being shot at, post-takeover, on a

main road in Kabul, the fifteen to twenty fully armed Talibs ma-
terialising out of the bushes to pursue the lone shooter refused to
continue that pursuit down a dark alley.[4] Far from their provincial
territories, patrolling unfamiliar cities with little guidance, many
Talibs are uneasy if not frightened.

The Taliban didn't expect to take Kabul, and bear sole responsibility for governance, so quickly. While politically and diplomatically savvier than before, there is no real understanding of how to
govern a society with infrastructure, communications, electrifica-
tion and the internet. Previously high Taliban recruit salaries, up
to $1,200 per month or six times what the ANDSF was making,[5]
are now going unpaid; reports of the Taliban going door to door
to be fed are widespread. It may only be a matter of time before a
breakdown in the chain of command begins, with frustrated fighters losing their chance at paradise along with their fighting salaries.
Considering the financial motivation it took to cause a resurgence
in Taliban recruitment over the past few years, the peer pressure
keeping hungry Talibs on the job far from home cannot last indefinitely. The lifespan of this Taliban regime may be shorter than the
last.

Jill Suzanne Kornetsky is a Kabul-based scientist, social entrepreneur,
consultant, researcher, analyst, guest speaker, guest lecturer, author,
editor and company founder.

CHAPTER 3

FROM TALIBAN TO TALIBAN: CYCLE OF HOPE, DESPAIR ON WOMEN'S RIGHTS

HEATHER BARR

Secondary schools have reopened for boys but remain closed to the vast majority of girls.[1] Women are banned from most employment; the Taliban government added insult to injury by saying women in their employ could keep their jobs only if they were in a role a man cannot fill – such as being an attendant in a women's toilet.[2] Women are mostly out of university, and due to new restrictions it is unclear when and how they can return. Many female teachers have been dismissed.[3]

The policy of requiring a *mahram*, a male family member as chaperone, to accompany any woman leaving her home is not in place according to a Kabul official, but Taliban members on the street are still sometimes enforcing it, as well as harassing women about their clothing.[4] The Taliban has systematically closed down shelters for women and girls fleeing domestic violence.[5] Women's sports have been banned.[6]

The Taliban has appointed an all-male cabinet. It abolished the Ministry of Women's Affairs and handed over the women's ministry building to the reinstated Ministry for the Propagation of Virtue and the Prevention of Vice, which was responsible for some of the worst abuses against women during the Taliban's previous period in power from 1996 to 2001.[7]

This was the situation two months after the Taliban had regained control of the Afghan capital, Kabul, as the US and its allies departed, wrapping up their twenty-year engagement in Afghanistan's forty-year war.

Afghan women are fighting for their rights. They tried to negotiate with the Taliban, and when that failed, they protested.[8] The Taliban broke up their demonstrations, beating participants and the journalists covering the events, and then banned unauthorised protest.[9]

The US and the whole international community seem stunned and unsure of what to do. It forms a sadly perfect bookend to the days after the 9/11 attacks, when the US and its allies grieved and raged and then emphasised Taliban abuses of women and girls to help them build support for their invasion of Afghanistan.[10]

The US has long had an uneven – and self-serving – track record on defending women's rights abroad.[11] But the US is not alone in being unsure of what to do to protect the rights of women and girls under Taliban rule. Even governments priding themselves on their commitment to women's rights have struggled to find solutions. They have also struggled to make the rights of Afghan women and girls a top priority at a moment when troop-contributing nations are licking their wounds, and concerns about Afghanistan again becoming a host to international terrorist operations could over-shadow concerns about human rights.

HUMANITARIAN CRISIS

Taliban attacks on rights are not the only problem women and girls are facing. Afghanistan's economy is in free fall, set off by wide-spread lost income, cash shortages, rising food costs, being severed from global financial systems and an abrupt halt to the develop-ment assistance that made up 75 per cent of the previous govern-ment's budget.[12]

This crisis, like most humanitarian crises, will cause the most harm to women and girls.[13] Officials with the UN and several for-eign governments are warning of economic collapse and risks of worsening acute malnutrition and outright famine. Surveys by the World Food Programme (WFP) reveal that nine in ten Afghan families have insufficient food for daily consumption, with half saying that they ran out of food at least once in the previous two weeks.[14] One in three Afghans is already acutely hungry.[15]

In December 2020, the UN Children's Fund UNICEF had al-ready warned that an estimated 3.1 million children – half of Af-ghanistan's children – were acutely malnourished.[16] Other United Nations reports warn that over 1 million more children could face acute malnutrition in the coming year.[17] By mid-2022, 97 per cent of Afghans may be below the poverty line.[18]

Healthcare workers and teachers, many of them women, have not been paid for months, and the healthcare system is collaps-ing.[19] Where schools for girls are open, few students attend, out of fear that they cannot move to and from school safely, along with financial problems, and a sense of despair about their future. And unpaid teachers may or may not teach.[20]

WEAK INTERNATIONAL RESPONSE

Even as it became increasingly clear over the course of years that cheerful US and NATO statements about their progress in defeating the Taliban were papering over huge and growing cracks, few could imagine a Taliban return as abrupt as the one that took place in August 2021. Few would have predicted this level of humanitarian crisis and collapse of essential services within weeks of the end of a twenty-year military, political and development engagement by at least forty-two countries costing an estimated $2.3 trillion.[21]

The early weeks of resumed Taliban rule seemed marked by indecision and slow response by the international community, in spite of a G7 pledge on 24 August, following an emergency meeting, that 'we will work together, and with our allies and regional countries, through the UN, G20 and more widely, to bring the international community together to address the critical questions facing Afghanistan'.[22]

A special session of the UN Human Rights Council on 24 August produced no meaningful progress.[23] In September the UN Security Council renewed the mandate of the UN mission in Afghanistan but did not take specific steps to strengthen the mission's human rights work, which faced staffing gaps and problems after some workers left their posts or were evacuated.[24]

A subsequent meeting of the Human Rights Council produced agreement to appoint a special rapporteur on human rights in Afghanistan, with a mandate including monitoring and advocating for the rights of women and girls.[25] This is a less powerful mechanism than the fact-finding mission a broad coalition of human rights organisations had called for.[26] The resolution creating the role of special rapporteur provided the person with greater staffing resources than most special rapporteurs but did not accelerate the on-boarding process. Under the standard timeline, the rapporteur and their team won't be in place until mid-2022.[27]

An announcement by the International Criminal Court's prosecutor called into question the role that the body will play in protecting human rights in Afghanistan. The court's Office of the Prosecutor had been considering action in Afghanistan since at least 2007 and opened an investigation in 2020.[28] Alleged war crimes and crimes against humanity within the court's jurisdiction in Afghanistan include: attacks against civil servants including female officials; attacks on schools – particularly girls' schools; and rape and other sexual violence against women and girls. The investigation was suspended nearly as soon as it was opened, however, while the Office of the Prosecutor considered a request from the former Afghan government to defer to national proceedings.

On 27 September 2021, the prosecutor announced that he would seek authorisation from the court to resume investigations in the absence of any prospect of genuine national proceedings but would focus on crimes committed by the Taliban and Islamic State and 'deprioritize' other aspects of the investigation.[29] This approach sends a message that some victims in Afghanistan are more entitled to justice than others, and risks undermining the legitimacy of the court's investigation.[30]

There is significant variety in the views of key countries about engaging with the new Taliban authorities in Afghanistan. Regional politics are fraught and complex. China and Russia may see themselves as benefiting from a shift in global power dynamics due to the US defeat in Afghanistan, and they and others including

Pakistan and Qatar seem more ready than countries that contributed troops to engage with the Taliban. China, Russia and Pakistan were among only five countries that voted against the Human Rights Council resolution to establish a special rapporteur.[31]

'FEMINIST FOREIGN POLICY' AND THE TALIBAN

Women's rights activists have made important progress around the world in the twenty years since the Taliban were previously in power, from 1996 to 2001. These advances make the Taliban's violations of the rights of women and girls even more cruel and intolerable than they were in 2001 and should help to spur action by countries that have made progress to right these wrongs.

In recent years, several countries – including Sweden, Canada, Mexico and France – proclaimed that they have a 'feminist foreign policy'.[32] According to the Swedish government, a feminist foreign policy 'means applying a systematic gender equality perspective throughout the whole foreign policy agenda'.[33]

Feminist foreign policy is also a recognition that you cannot have human security when half the population is oppressed and living in fear. As Germany's foreign minister wrote in 2020, 'Numerous studies demonstrate that societies in which women and men are on equal footing are more secure, stable, peaceful and prosperous.'[34]

WHAT CONCERNED GOVERNMENTS SHOULD DO

How should a world increasingly embracing 'feminist foreign policy' respond to Taliban violations of the rights of women and girls in 2022?

The first step is to muster political will. Lack of political will may be a particular challenge in the wake of the withdrawal of foreign troops, but it is not a new problem. During the decades of international presence, troop-contributing nations paid lip service and provided funding towards women's rights, but rarely political capital, and over time the lip service and cash dwindled too.

In 2011, the *Washington Post* reported that efforts to support women's rights were being stripped out of US programmes, quoting an official who said, 'All those pet rocks in our rucksack were taking us down.'[35] In a disturbing indication of a lack of focus on women's rights, many government and aid organisations have in recent weeks sent all-male delegations to meet with the Taliban, undermining any efforts they are making to press for greater respect for women's rights.[36]

Then there is a need for the international community to reach as much consensus as possible about what the problems are and what should be done. There are signs that even countries that have been more open to engaging with the Taliban have been disappointed by their unwillingness to appoint an inclusive government and their violations of women's and girls' rights. The Taliban government excludes not only women but also religious minorities and most non-Pashtun ethnic groups.[37] Even China, Russia, Pakistan and Iran have all called for the Taliban to form an 'inclusive government'.[38] Pakistan Prime Minister Imran Khan has said that banning girls from education in Afghanistan would be 'un-Islamic'.[39] Qatar's foreign minister called the Taliban's ban on girls' education 'very disappointing'.[40]

The Taliban's unbending stance on the rights of women and girls is so extreme that this, and its opposition to an inclusive government, may drive broad concern about its actions and help the international community to build consensus about how to engage. The

US may not be the most able leader for this process and may prefer not to take the reins. Other countries and institutions – including countries that have pledged to have a feminist foreign policy, Muslim-majority countries and organisations like the EU – should consider taking on greater leadership than they have so far, in response to a weak response from the US.

Next comes the need for a plan. Whatever the plan is, it should avoid any actions that would worsen Afghanistan's deepening humanitarian crisis and disproportionately affect women and girls. There are signs of emerging agreement for humanitarian assistance and essential services, with the United Nations Development Programme having made arrangements to pay the salaries of healthcare workers on a temporary basis.[41]

But major issues remain unresolved, suffering from a lack of consensus by the international community, including how to respond to Taliban efforts to exclude women from working for aid agencies.[42] Female workers are essential to ensure that aid reaches women and women-headed households, so permitting female humanitarian workers to do their jobs is not setting a condition on humanitarian assistance so much as an operational necessity to be able to deliver that assistance.

The international community has struggled to identify what leverage they have that can be used to influence the Taliban. The situation has been complicated by opaqueness on the Taliban side. Governments and donors need to figure out what the Taliban wants from the international community, and how much, and where the Taliban is willing to compromise to get what it wants. And they need to identify what other pressures – including the demands of their own members and the risk of Taliban fighters defecting to the Islamic State – constrain the Taliban from compromise.

Equipped with this knowledge, the international community should recognise that almost every country on the planet – except six, conspicuously including the US, plus Iran, Palau, Somalia, Sudan and Tonga – has ratified the Convention on the Elimination of All Forms of Discrimination against Women (CEDAW).[43] Afghanistan ratified the convention in 2003. The convention requires countries to 'pursue by all appropriate means and without delay a policy of eliminating discrimination against women'.

This promise has not been fulfilled in any country; no country has achieved full gender equality and disparities in access to education and employment, wage gaps and failure to adequately respond to gender-based violence are common around the world. But even in that context, Taliban violations of the rights of women and girls are uniquely extreme. No other country openly bars girls from studying on the basis of gender. It is shocking to see a country intentionally destroy its system for responding to gender-based violence and dismantle institutions such as the Ministry of Women's Affairs that were designed to strengthen compliance with CEDAW.

The leverage the international community has to influence the Taliban needs to be deployed in defence of the rights of women and girls. Doing this will be a complex, difficult and long-term task. But as CEDAW members, and, in many cases, countries that used women's rights to sell a war and spent twenty years promising eternal solidarity to Afghan women and girls, the international community owes them this effort.

Heather Barr is associate director of the Women's Rights Division at Human Rights Watch.

CHAPTER 4

STOLEN PROMISES: THE US RETREAT AND THE AFGHAN DIASPORA

LAURA CRETNEY

'I didn't think that I would see the day that Afghanistan would be taken over and people would be fleeing for their lives and people would be hanging out of planes, and there would be children dying in the skies.'

GULWALI PASSARLAY, AFGHAN ACTIVIST AND FORMER REFUGEE

In 2021, Afghans around the world – Sunni and Shia; Pashtun and Hazara; parents and their children – looked on in shock and disbelief while their country fell to the Taliban. Some watched the BBC and CNN reports from their homes in cities like Harrow and Toronto, where some have resided since the 1980s and earlier. Others heard the news as they waited in informal settlements and camps in Pakistan, Iran and Turkey, many at the mercy of smugglers on the migrant route to Europe, their already uncertain futures becoming less certain by the day. Many received panicked text messages from family members in Afghanistan, terrified of what Taliban rule would bring and desperate to escape to join their loved ones overseas.

The rise of globalisation and the increased connectivity and movement of people it has brought have led scholars to furiously debate the concept of diaspora; what it means, who constitutes a diaspora, when and why. The field of diaspora studies has proliferated over the past thirty years and migration – whether fuelled by conflict, climate or capitalism – is quickly becoming the issue of our time. The fall of Afghanistan to the Taliban in the summer of 2021 has added a new dimension to these debates: what does it mean for a diaspora when the homeland no longer exists? For so many Afghans, the country they dreamed of one day returning to is no more. After decades of war, trauma, hope and heartbreak, Afghans have no government, no national anthem, not even a flag to call their own.

This chapter will explore the recent history of migration from Afghanistan, the majority of which has been driven by conflict and shaped by the flow of refugees. It will examine the formation of the Afghan diaspora since the Soviet invasion in 1979, highlighting the challenges Afghans have faced in their host countries and how they have mobilised in response to events back home. Finally, it will consider what the Taliban takeover of Afghanistan could mean for the millions of Afghans residing outside of their homeland during the years to come.

A CONFLICT-DRIVEN DIASPORA

The global Afghan diaspora as it exists today is predominantly shaped by the millions of refugees who have fled the country in multiple waves over the past forty years, beginning with the more than 5 million people who sought safety outside Afghanistan during the Soviet war of 1979–89.[1] As the fighting between the Soviet army and the Mujahideen rebels intensified, the majority of Afghan refugees settled in neighbouring Pakistan and Iran, with just a moderate number fleeing further afield to Europe. A second wave of refugees fled from 1996 onwards, when the Taliban took control of much of the country and established a ruthlessly repressive regime that enabled severe human rights violations, the worst of which were inflicted upon women and minority groups. A third wave of migration was initiated by the US war in Afghanistan from 2001 onwards, following the 9/11 attacks. Despite the huge numbers of Afghans who were repatriated – voluntarily and involuntarily – during this period, the failure of the US-led operation and the subsequent deterioration of the security situation created another wave of refugees, many of whom ventured further afield to seek refuge in Europe.[2]

Throughout each wave, the major driver of migration was conflict, although its manifestations have varied according to demographic and geographical factors. The Hazara community, for example, represent an ethnic and religious minority in Afghanistan and have faced persecution from the Taliban and other extremist groups such as the so-called Islamic State.[3] The flow of refugees to certain destinations including Australia has been dominated by Hazaras in recent years, many of whom have arrived on unscheduled boat journeys via Indonesia.[4] Afghans from the south of the country have faced violence, harassment and loss of land due to military operations and many communities have lived in fear of the danger posed by warlords and armed groups who have exploited the instability created by the war, leading many to flee across the border to Pakistan.[5]

According to the United Nations Department of Economic and Social Affairs, the total emigrant stock of Afghans – from various migratory waves – was 5.12 million in 2019. The overwhelming majority of Afghan refugees – as many as 85 per cent – are found in Afghanistan's neighbouring countries, with Pakistan playing host to the world's largest Afghan refugee population and Iran coming in second.[6] Significant communities are also present in European countries such as Germany and the UK, along with the US, Canada, Australia, India and the United Arab Emirates.[7] Turkey has also been a focal point of the migratory patterns of Afghan refugees, housing a sizeable community of thousands of Afghans since the 1980s and functioning as a transit country for thousands of those heading for various destinations in Europe.[8]

The United States is home to a somewhat surprisingly small community of Afghans given its crucial role in creating the conditions that led to the mass migration of refugees – just 132,000 in 2019. Even this community is relatively new, with 60 per cent having arrived after 2010.[9]

In Europe, Afghans have remained one of the largest groups of asylum seekers since the 1980s and their numbers grew continuously throughout the 2010s as the Taliban expanded its grip on the country.[10] From the late 1970s onwards, Germany became a key destination for Afghans and today their numbers are estimated to be a quarter of a million, representing the largest Afghan diaspora in Europe.[11] According to Dr Yahya Wardak, who runs AFGHANIC (an organisation supporting the integration of Afghans in Germany), the Afghan diaspora in Germany is a very heterogenous group, with the city of Hamburg playing host to more Afghans than any other European city.[12]

In the UK, meanwhile, Afghan migration has been a more recent phenomenon, occurring increasingly from the mid-1990s due to the relatively liberal immigration and asylum legislation of the time.[13] Afghan communities are present all over the UK in cities and boroughs such as Manchester, Birmingham, Bolton, Ealing and Harrow.[14] Other European countries with sizeable Afghan communities include the Netherlands, which is home to approximately 50,000 Afghans, and Denmark, with just under 20,000.[15]

CYCLES OF TRAUMA AND EXILE

The trauma experienced by Afghans who have traversed the migration routes from Pakistan, Iran and Turkey to Europe, usually at the mercy of people smugglers, is well documented. Refugees are known to have suffered imaginable violence and abuse during their journeys, enduring terrifying and traumatic experiences such as (land and sea) border crossings and, in many cases, arrest and detention at the hands of border security and local police in countries along the way. Unaccompanied travellers, particularly children, also suffer the trauma of losing their family support system while having to protect themselves from abuse and adjust to unfamiliar cultures.[16] But the trauma of being a refugee does not end upon arrival at the final destination: identity struggles, systematic discrimination, social exclusion and inter-generational traumas all occur frequently for Afghans in the diaspora.

While it is easy to use the label 'Afghan' to describe all those from Afghanistan, members of the diaspora often juggle multiple identities at once depending on demographic factors and the specific context of their migration. For example, an 'Afghan' in the diaspora might be 'northern' or 'southern', 'communist' or 'religious', 'Sunni' or 'Shia', 'Pashtun' or 'Hazara', and so on – and such descriptors are not limited to purely binary terms. Diaspora communities are heterogenous, fluid and often segmented depending on the specific situations of their individual members.[17] In some countries, such as Australia, the term 'Afghan' has become synonymous with the Pashtun ethnic group, while some people – particularly those from the Hazara ethnic minority – prefer to use the term Afghani or Afghanistani to differentiate citizenship from their ethnicity.[18]

One minority group that is often overlooked is the Sikh community – one of the smallest religious minority groups in the country. Sikhs fleeing Afghanistan are not only escaping the decades of violent conflict in the country but also persecution on the basis of their religion at the hands of other Afghans, including the Taliban. Sikhs in Afghanistan have at times been subject to physical and verbal abuse and have been treated as second-class citizens on the basis of their religion. Afghan Sikhs in London maintain links with one another and gather regularly in the Gurdwara in Southall. Although this helps them to maintain a connection to their Afghan roots and identity, living as a minority away from the homeland has left some Sikhs – particularly those growing up in the diaspora – feeling confused about their identity.[19]

Many – particularly younger, second- and third-generation – Afghans also face a struggle between their identity as Afghans and their identity as citizens of their host state, particularly in the West, where some young Afghans have described feeling pressure from their families not to 'Westernise'. Two young Afghan women described their feelings about what they refer to as 'culture shaming' during an episode of the *Chai Sabz* podcast released in August 2021. They discuss how their conservative Afghan culture collides with the cultures of their host states, Germany and the USA, explaining how family members have at times shamed them for having Western friends and leaving home to study. They highlight the impact this has had on their mental health, as well as mentioning that they have become distanced from some members of their family as a result.[20]

On the other hand, some members of diaspora communities have experienced a strengthening of their 'Afghan' identity as a result of living in an imagined community outside their homeland. This could be because the experience of being a foreigner can override ethnic and religious divisions, reinforcing commonality and creating a sense of solidarity among Afghans from all backgrounds. This might also be compounded by the policies of host states, which do not tend to differentiate between Afghan asylum seekers on the basis of ethnicity or religious affiliation.[21]

This is evident in the occurrence of marriages between Afghans in the diaspora that might not otherwise have transpired in the homeland, for example between different ethnic and religious groups. For some this is strategic, for the purpose of creating and strengthening ties and relationships in new communities and bringing families and communities together across traditional demographic divides. However, as a 2020 research paper showed, it can also bring past traumas back to the surface. Conflicts can re-emerge in the form of disputes and confrontations between family members, retraumatising those who fled the conflict and transmitting trauma intergenerationally to the married couple themselves, even if they did not experience the conflict directly.[22]

At times this happens as a result of current events in the homeland, which have the power to both unify and divide Afghans in the diaspora. A prime example of events in Afghanistan unifying Afghans in the diaspora was the brutal murder of 27-year-old Farkhunda Malikzada by an angry mob in Kabul in March 2015 after a confrontation with a local mullah, who falsely accused her of burning a copy of the Quran. Afghans in the diaspora gathered in European cities to express their outrage at Malikzada's killing in a show of unity that transcended ethnic, religious, political and generational differences. Yet some events can have the opposite effect, highlighting divisions and cultural contradictions and transporting conflicts from the homeland to diaspora communities. The case of Malikzada, for example, ignited debates within the Afghan community in Denmark that pitted older, more conservative Afghans against their younger and more progressive counterparts, creating tension within some families and communities.[23]

Aside from questions of identity and community, Afghans in the diaspora also face a number of systemic and structural barriers from the point of their arrival in the host land and throughout both their lives and the lives of future generations. Arriving at their destination brings with it a whole set of new challenges for refugees, beginning with the struggle to obtain asylum and therefore access key services and opportunities.

In Pakistan, Afghans suffer the consequences of public resentment that has built over time as a result of the continued waves of migration and the spillover of the conflict across the Afghan–Pakistan border. Once idolised by Pakistanis as Mujahideen heroes, today Afghans in Pakistan are negatively stereotyped in public discourse, blamed for crime, unemployment and violence, and arbitrarily arrested and detained.[24] Such perceptions are compounded by the short-term nature of humanitarian responses, which focus on providing emergency aid rather than a longer-term effort on development and therefore fail to create opportunities for Afghans in Pakistan to integrate and contribute positively to the host state.[25]

At a structural level, there is a huge disparity between the level of protection and treatment afforded to the 1.4 million registered Afghan refugees and the estimated 1 million unregistered Afghans in the country. While the legal status of registered Afghans is relatively secure, those who are not registered live in constant fear of being deported. According to a report by the Afghanistan Analysts Network, almost 52,000 unregistered Afghans were forcibly deported from Pakistan within a window of just ten weeks in 2015. The returnees were bundled into the back of trucks with people, suitcases and mattresses squeezed in around them and hastily decamped across the border.[26]

In Iran, fast-changing regulation and increasingly complex bureaucracy pose an enormous challenge for Afghans fleeing conflict. Since 2007, the Iranian government has also established 'No-Go Areas' for Afghans, preventing access for refugees to a number of locations and thus making it difficult for them to maintain jobs and send their children to school.[27] Meanwhile, similarly to Pakistan, the rights of registered versus unregistered Afghans differ significantly. Refugees who are granted Amayesh cards (which afford them residency rights) have access to protections and opportunities that those without cards do not.

The situation for Afghan asylum seekers in the West is not much better. The increase in nationalist rhetoric and the rise to power of anti-immigration political personalities and parties have led to the securitisation of asylum policies, to the extent that even the countries that had previously been the most friendly to refugees

– like the USA and Germany – are becoming increasingly hostile to asylum seekers.[28] The Trump administration's overhaul of the asylum system between 2017 and 2021 made it virtually impossible for refugees to settle in the United States. Meanwhile, Afghans in Germany often have to wait for years to access refugee status and the limited rights that come with it, according to Maria Hosein-Habibi, the associate director of the Association of Afghan Organisations in Germany (VAFO). This affects their ability to study, learn the local language and access the job market, thus effectively placing their lives on hold and at the mercy of the system.[29] In Australia, many Afghans waited years for visas, in constant fear that they would be deported back home.[30]

This harsh reception at the policy level is echoed across society in many Western host countries, particularly as the number of refugees has continued to grow in the past decade. Racism, xenophobia and fear of the Other have fed populist rhetoric across the West, with security concerns and counter-terrorism being used to justify hostility towards asylum seekers – Afghan and otherwise. As instances of violence and hate crimes against refugees and migrants rise, the victims are often unable to report them and seek justice due to their uncertain legal status. Meanwhile, the media focuses on militaristic images of sea crossings and border controls, telling a Eurocentric story that ignores the homeland conflict and traumatic journeys many have experienced to get there.[31] Western governments have even embarked on information campaigns directly targeting Afghans and other nationalities in their homeland in an attempt to deter those considering making the journey.[32]

In Australia, the Afghan community are often associated in public discourse with terrorism and religious militarism, rather than with the trauma and suffering they have experienced. Some Australian-Afghans have cited the need to be perceived as a 'model minority' community due to the increase in racism, hostility and discrimination towards migrants and refugees.[33] The same appears to be true in the UK. In an interview with the author in November 2021, British-Afghan activist and former refugee Gulwali Passarlay spoke of feeling like he didn't belong – neither in his homeland nor in his host country:

> We feel alienated, we feel unwelcome, we don't feel we belong. We lost Afghanistan and now we've lost Britain because of Brexit and the far-right-wing agenda … I've been here for the last fourteen, fifteen years and I still don't feel like I belong here, even though I've become a citizen and a British passport holder. And I don't feel like a citizen of Afghanistan either, I'm like a citizen of nowhere … In Britain, the hostility towards migrants and refugees, and particularly from the government, has been making it worse.[34]

Public resentment towards refugees has also given governments impetus to deny many claims of asylum and pursue repatriation policies that see vulnerable Afghans sent back to the homeland, at risk of violence and persecution once again. In Europe in particular, governments have increasingly denied access to Afghans, leaving many stranded in camps and at border crossings. In 2016, the European Union signed an agreement with the Afghan government allowing for the unlimited deportation of Afghans, leveraging EU funding to force the Afghan government into compliance. Many who are forcibly repatriated try to leave again, while others are vulnerable not only to the threat of armed groups like the Taliban but also to drug addiction and the lure of criminal activity.[35]

Such threats are further compounded for minorities like Afghan Hazaras and Sikhs, who become instant targets for violence on their return. The case of Afghan Sikh refugee Baljit Singh clearly exemplifies this. Singh was deported to Afghanistan by the British government in 2010 but he was imprisoned on arrival for eighteen months without a conviction, although he was informally accused of falsely claiming to be Afghan. He suffered physical and verbal abuse in prison, including having boiling water thrown at his face. After months of appeals, the UK allowed him to return, but many refugees from minority groups are not so lucky.[36]

Such cases highlight a troubling contradiction that has emerged over the past decade in British policy (and is echoed across other Western countries), whereby Afghanistan has been deemed safe enough by the Home Office to deport refugees, yet not safe enough for the Foreign Office to remove travel warnings for tourists, businesspeople and diplomats. Many European countries, in fact, continued to deport Afghans right up until the day Kabul fell to the Taliban, maintaining that Afghanistan was safe enough.[37]

MOBILISING FOR THE HOMELAND

Diasporas are often overlooked as actors with power to shape events in the homeland, particularly during cycles of conflict. But the Afghan diaspora is a prime example of the impact communities – both real and imagined – located outside the homeland can have on homeland politics and the lives of their fellow citizens, at home and abroad.

Throughout the recent years of conflict in their homeland, and especially over the past ten years, Afghans in the diaspora have mobilised in a number of ways to shape events in Afghanistan and support the Afghan people. This has occurred most significantly in the form of economic remittances, which are sent both formally and informally. According to the World Bank, as much as $5.8 billion was formally remitted to Afghanistan between 2008 and 2020. This continued throughout 2020, despite the economic effects of the Covid-19 pandemic, with $788 million remitted during that year alone, contributing a hugely significant 3.9 per cent to GDP.[38] In an interview with the author, British-Afghan Gulwali Passarlay alluded to the sense of responsibility driving this phenomenon: 'Afghans support their families back home. It's for their relatives, they send money back home ... I have friends who work two shifts to provide for their families.'[39]

Aside from their direct economic influence, diasporas also represent a huge (and often untapped) resource for the development of the homeland, given their unique potential to transfer knowledge and skills, provide and support humanitarian interventions and engage in entrepreneurial activities that can boost the homeland economy. The Afghan diaspora in European countries like Germany and the Netherlands have been particularly active in forming organisations and networks for developing the homeland. Such organisations are primarily focused on health, education and humanitarian relief, particularly in response to disasters and emergencies, cooperating with local and international partners on the ground. Their work represents a much-needed contribution, after years of conflict have seriously deteriorated these key development areas.[40]

Another key humanitarian contribution that many Afghan diaspora organisations have made in recent years has been to the safety and protection of newly arriving refugees. Dr Yahya Wardak is an Afghan-German who runs the organisation AFGHANIC, which supports the integration of Afghan refugees in Germany on top of providing key development assistance on the ground in Afghanistan.[41] Similar organisations exist in the UK, such as the Afghanistan and Central Asian Association (ACAA), founded by British-Afghan former refugee Dr Nooralhaq Nasimi, who arrived in the UK in 1999 in the back of a refrigerator container. ACAA works with Afghans and Central Asians in the UK, providing support and services such as English language classes, employment workshops and women's support groups for those living away from their homeland. They also conduct visits and outreach to families and individuals in detention.[42]

Another way in which the diaspora have mobilised in response to the situation in Afghanistan in recent years is through voluntary repatriation for the purpose of participating in politics and development in the homeland. Many positions in the post-2001 government of Afghanistan were occupied by Afghans from the diaspora, who had developed relevant experience and expertise during their time outside the homeland.[43] Many were motivated by a sense of solidarity and responsibility to participate in the reconstruction of their country. Others were motivated by the opportunity for political influence and profit.[44]

In an episode of the *Afghan Affairs* podcast released in October 2020, host Said Sabir Ibrahimi and Afghan-American national security analyst Haris Tarin discuss this phenomenon. Tarin explains that he has witnessed a number of Afghans from the diaspora returning to Afghanistan for short periods of time to engage in development activities. They later return to their 'real homes' in Canada and the US where they now live, bringing the money they have earned back with them and buying large houses and fancy cars instead of investing it in Afghanistan.[45] Aware of this issue, many – particularly younger – voluntary returnees have sought opportunities to contribute to development through private companies and international NGOs, in order to avoid engaging with corrupt institutional structures.[46]

Others have engaged in artistic and cultural activities, often with a political or development focus. Fatimah Hossaini is an Afghan photographer, teacher and artist. She was born a refugee in Iran in 1993, after her parents had fled the violence of the Soviet war and the Taliban takeover, and grew up with a dream of returning to the homeland she still saw as hers. She moved to Kabul in 2018 to work as a photography professor at Kabul University, making the city her home and beginning to explore the country she had longed for throughout her life in exile in Iran. While she was there, she founded an organisation called Mastoorat, a platform and hub for artists and performers in Kabul. She also began work on her first book, featuring the portraits of Afghan women. Hossaini's art served the dual purpose of highlighting and celebrating the beauty of Afghan cultural heritage and the strength and diversity of Afghan women, while also offering a stark contrast to the narratives of Afghan society that usually appear in the international media, pushing back against orientalist portrayals of her country.[47]

Diaspora engagement in development, while hugely important, is not without challenges. In recent years, insecurity, corruption and a lack of local capacity and cooperation from the Afghan government have posed serious threats to the ability of diaspora-led organisations to deliver impact on the ground. This has been enough to deter some diaspora organisations from engaging in such work, while others have navigated this using their personal networks and contacts in Afghanistan.[48] Meanwhile, international governments and NGOs have also failed to capitalise on the development potential of the diaspora through policy and funding in a meaningful way, limiting their potential for impact. Governments, particularly in Europe, have instead focused on policies that stem the flow of refugees at their borders, as opposed to contributing to meaningful development that might deter many from making the journey in the first place.[49]

There has been a similar lack of attention paid by the international community to the potential for Afghans in the diaspora to contribute positively towards a political process. The often criticised lack of inclusion of the Afghan diaspora in political negotiations has arguably contributed to the failure of the American-led campaign in Afghanistan by omitting a key interest group.[50] But the lack of inclusion in homeland politics has not stopped some diaspora Afghans from engaging in the politics of their host countries. Peymana Assad arrived in Britain from Afghanistan as a refugee at the age of three. She is the first person of Afghan origin to be elected to public office in the UK, currently serving as a Councillor on Harrow Council, and is an active member of the Labour Party with widespread support from the British-Afghan community in Harrow.[51]

According to British-Afghan activist Gulwali Passarlay, the Afghan diaspora in the UK has seen a surge in engagement and unity over the past five years:

The Afghan diaspora was very inactive, or at least most of us were very inactive, but thankfully in the last five years or so, Afghans have become a lot more engaged and active within politics and within civil society here. We have a lot of Afghan societies at universities now and we've been fundraising for Covid. So, for example, there's a group called Afghan Charity. We raise money to support orphans and the disabled and people who are vulnerable in society. And there are ten to twenty Afghan societies, university societies. We have Afghan societies in most towns and cities now, like local community groups.[52]

The increase in diaspora activity in the UK – and elsewhere – could plausibly be linked to the proliferation of social media and online connectivity over the past decade, which has created new opportunities for diaspora communities. Cyberspace has created an opportunity for greater inclusion of Afghans in the diaspora in an imagined community, while also drawing public attention to the vulnerability of many Afghans in the UK. It has also allowed for the emergence of diaspora networks and organisations that exist only in cyberspace, for the purpose of providing information about events on the ground in Afghanistan and facilitating real action outside of the bounds of the internet.

Social media in particular has revolutionised the way in which Afghans outside the homeland keep in touch with loved ones at home.[53] In some ways, this can mitigate the trauma of separation experienced by many refugees. On the other hand, however, the constant news cycles and instant media updates facilitated by social media create an additional layer of trauma, meaning Afghans outside Afghanistan rarely have a break from the chaotic reality of life and war back home.[54]

THE HOMELAND HAS FALLEN

Sunday 15 August 2021 was a day Afghans will never forget. As pickup trucks rolled into Kabul and bearded men wielding AK-47s fanned out in the streets of their country's capital, Afghans around the world received panicked messages from terrified loved ones and watched, powerless, as their countrymen crowded around a packed airfield and fell from the sky after desperately clinging to the landing gear of Americans planes. The country they knew and loved from afar became unrecognisable and their hopes of return grew more distant than ever.

Afghans in Europe and the United States have described feeling frustrated, helpless, afraid, powerless, disappointed, angry, grief-stricken, numb. Heartbroken. Betrayed.[55] In an article written for *The Guardian*, Afghan-British refugee advocate Zarlasht Halaimzai wrote, 'The morning after the Taliban took over Kabul, I woke up to a suicide note that a woman in Kabul had sent to a WhatsApp group I was in. I am trying to be strong, she wrote, but I can't.'[56] For many of those who experienced the trauma of war and conflict-driven migration first-hand, they are now being re-traumatised as they watch what's happening in their country. They are re-experiencing the feeling of losing their country as the Taliban erase the progress that was made over the past twenty years.

Gulwali Passarlay said, 'The thing that really upsets me and most Afghans is we don't have a flag anymore, we don't have a country, we lost everything. People were able to dream, and people lost their dreams.'[57]

Writing for *The Guardian*, Zarlasht Halaimzai said, 'Witnessing the catastrophe in the ambiguous position of an Afghan outside

Afghanistan brought back all the feelings of fear and pain that I had felt as a child when my family feared for our lives.'[58]

Many former refugees who are safe in host countries abroad are now experiencing a sense of survivor's guilt, watching their fellow Afghans back home fearing for their lives and desperately trying to flee – most of them with no guarantee of safe passage or a better life on the other side.[59] When Kabul fell, many diaspora Afghans were consumed with supporting loved ones who had not managed to leave. Those with more public profiles were being called on immediately for interviews and comments by Western journalists – many of whom had actively ignored their article pitches on Afghanistan over the years previously. Gulwali Passarlay and Zarlasht Halaimzai were both flooded with requests for interviews from journalists in the West during the days after the fall of Kabul. Some journalists barely bothered to prepare, asking questions shrouded in racism and Islamophobia and treating them as spokespeople for Afghans everywhere, regardless of their personal experiences.[60]

The media's interest is already waning, it seems, just a few months after the Taliban takeover. Passarlay conducted between thirty and forty interviews during the days after Kabul fell. Three months later, he says, there is little interest in his insights from journalists. Social media appears equally disinterested in the new Afghanistan. In August, his story posts on Instagram were being seen by over 4,000 people. In November, the algorithm has decided Afghanistan is no longer trending: he is lucky if his stories receive 400 views.[61]

Passarlay is one of many Afghans who have been actively using their platforms and their connections, and recent events have somewhat unsurprisingly sparked an increase in diaspora engagement and mobilisation in response. According to Passarlay, Afghans in Britain have come together to condemn the US retreat in the homeland and subsequent UK government policy, particularly regarding evacuations and refugees.[62] In response to this uptick in mobilisation, one Afghan published an open letter in a diaspora-run publication called Afghan Eye, urging diaspora Afghans to tread cautiously when speaking and mobilising in response to the Taliban takeover. The letter calls on Afghans in the West in particular to avoid imposing their own understandings on the situation in the homeland, as these are a product of their experiences and education overseas and therefore not necessarily reflective of the views and most urgent needs of Afghans in the homeland.[63]

While the US retreat has had clear and concerning implications for the existing Afghan diaspora, arguably the most significant effect of the Taliban takeover is the new wave of diaspora Afghans it is creating. In August 2021, the UN estimated that up to half a million Afghans could flee across the border by the end of the year, which comes on top of the existing 2.2 million Afghans already living in neighbouring countries.[64] In November 2021, a BBC report by Secunder Kermani interviewed some of the many Afghans fleeing the country via the remote town of Zaranj, which is located near the Pakistan border and has become a hub for people smuggling. The Taliban profit from the smuggling activity, taking a fee for every pickup truck that leaves the town filled beyond its capacity with desperate people. In his video report, Kermani comments, 'The pickup trucks just keep coming ... At times it feels as if the whole of Afghanistan is trying to find a way out.'[65]

All this comes during a disturbing new era where refugees are increasingly being used as political pawns – as the ongoing situation on the Belarusian border with Poland clearly shows. The negotiations around which countries would resettle fleeing Afghans have taken place against the backdrop of growing hostility towards refugees and aggressive migration policies, particularly in Europe, shrouding the process in uncertainty. During the early days of evacuations, according to Zarlasht Halaimzai, some Afghans would take off on an evacuation flight with no idea where it would land – their destination would be negotiated while they were in the air. Many of those who were given a chance to leave were forced to choose between saving their own lives and remaining in Afghanistan with their families, adding yet another layer of trauma to the process. Halaimzai writes, 'Every time a plane took off from Kabul airport, it shattered a life and broke up a family.'[66]

Even for those who did have citizenship elsewhere, their evacuation was far from certain and the process filled with chaos and heartbreak. Many, like artist Fatimah Hossaini, had returned to Afghanistan despite having the right to reside elsewhere, hoping to contribute to rebuilding and developing their country. People like Hossaini now face the pain and devastation of leaving the lives they had been rebuilding.

It took Hossaini two attempts to secure a seat on a plane. The first time, she could not reach the airfield due to the crowds of desperate Afghans surrounding it, while the Taliban violently tried to push them back. The second time she was successful, although her hopes of making it onto a plane had been so low that she said to her friend upon leaving the flat they were sharing, 'I'll be back later when I can't get in. See you!' Hossaini made it onto a French evacuation plane, relying on the contacts she had made while exhibiting her artwork across European embassies. She arrived in Paris laden with just two small bags containing everything she could carry from the life she had been building in Afghanistan.[67]

For the political class who had profited from the endemic corruption in Afghanistan since the US invasion, however, it was a different story. Rumours whirred about politicians, including the President, arriving in private planes in Dubai, Europe and America with suitcases filled with millions of dollars in cash – although President Ghani has refuted this claim. The resentment felt among others in the diaspora is apparent, with British-Afghan activist Gulwali Passarlay saying:

> They need to be persecuted, they need to be brought before the International Criminal Court in The Hague for their crimes, because they are the people who have taken Afghanistan's wealth … These people are now safe and sound with their families and loved ones, and they have left Afghans in a situation where, I mean the UN has said that this is the worst humanitarian crisis of our time.[68]

HOPES OF RETURN

Despite the fact that many in the diaspora have spent their entire lives outside Afghanistan, their identity has been forged through their ties to the homeland, and many have spent years longing to return. 'It is where our parents grew up, it is where many of our family members live, and it is the label we carry with us whenever people ask, "Where are you *really* from?"', writes Froher Yasin, president of the Cambridge Afghan Society.[69] Many had planned to return once they reached a position when they have something to 'give back' to Afghanistan. Others were simply waiting until it was safe to do so.

Gulwali Passarlay was waiting until he finally received citizenship in the UK and could be sure that he would be able to return safely, without getting stuck in Afghanistan with no way out. Throughout his fourteen years in the UK as a refugee, he has dreamed of returning to see his mother again. It was his mother who forced him and his brother to leave, escaping violence and conscription in their hometown when he was just eleven. 'Whatever you do,' she said, 'don't come back.' He has waited painstakingly for the British passport that would allow him to travel safely back to see her. While in the UK, he has obtained two degrees, carried the Olympic torch, given TEDx talks, written a book, founded a community interest company and spoken at countless events all over the country on behalf of refugees. Yet the thing he always wanted more than anything was to be able to go home:

> I always wanted to go back, I wanted to become an Afghan ambassador, perhaps a member of Parliament, a parliamentarian, be a minister, deal with the refugee situation, the displacement, because I have a degree and I have a master's and I have world experience, I've travelled to many countries. I wanted to use my expertise and education in the right way.

Passarlay officially became a British citizen in August 2021 after waiting nearly fourteen years. The same month, the Taliban took control of Kabul. He doesn't know when he will see his mother again.[70]

Laura Cretney is a PhD candidate at Durham University researching the role of diasporas in homeland conflict. She is also the director of an Isle of Man-based consultancy offering insight and expertise for organisations working in the Middle East and North Africa.

CHAPTER 5

A FAILURE OF LEADERSHIP

———

MAHMUD KHALILI

Afghanistan has been a place of intrigue and mystery for a very long time. As far back as 300 BC, we can see Alexander the Great fight his way through the high mountains of Afghanistan, to get to India on the way to world domination. There is a myth about when Alexander was in Afghanistan. His beloved mother sent him a message asking why it was so hard to conquer such simple people. Alexander sent her soil from Afghanistan. When she examined the soil, all the men around her seemed to get into fights with one another. His mother sent him another message telling him that she understood his point.

Afghanistan has always seen war in its history. The mountainous geography made it easy for the country to be run by different tribal leaders. Each tribal leader could be autonomous to a large extent because of the distances between different groups due to the mountains and harsh winter climate. This is why it has always been so hard to contain Afghanistan, because you have to control all the tribal leaders first, which is not an easy task for any invading force.

History has shown that Afghanistan is not a place to conquer.

You have to have overwhelming force that you can sustain, other-wise at one point or another, Afghans will take the opportunity to start fighting back. The people of Afghanistan have always known that they have a strength that an occupying force will always take for granted: their determination to win no matter what the cost and time. When you don't care how long it takes to win a war, you will eventually be the victor.

During one of the two British Empire invasions, a battalion of British soldiers were retreating from Kabul when the Afghans at-tacked. It was a slaughter. The Afghans killed all the British soldiers, leaving one wounded. His name was Dr William Brydon. He was allowed to live. He got back to his headquarters, mortally wounded but still alive. Brydon got there just in time to tell them of the mas-sacre and to warn them to never go there again. Afghanistan is not an easy place to take over.

The story of how the Taliban has taken power starts in 1979 when the Communist government in Afghanistan decided to throw away the country's policy of non-alignment and invite the Red Army's troops in. This is the first example of an instance when a lack of leadership has brought us to this place in our history. Afghans secretly enjoyed financial and military support from both the US and the Soviet Union but always trod the line carefully to make sure that neither world power would be overly angry at this unoffi-cial policy. The Communist government of Afghanistan could have continued to enjoy its non-aligned status, but it chose to throw the country into war. It knew very well that the people would never accept an invading force, especially one that did not believe in re-ligion, but it went ahead anyway and allowed 150,000 Red Army troops to land in Kabul on Christmas Day in 1979.

Millions of Afghans have thought of what life would be like and how the destiny of the nation would have been altered if the government had not made the decision to allow the Red Army to enter Afghanistan. The people were poor but there was peace and stability. The neighbours respected Afghanistan as a modern and sovereign nation. Was it so important to take sides in such a world war when it was going so well?

The second example of a lack of leadership and vision was when the Mujahideen, or freedom fighters, who had stood up against the invasion, decided to win the war outright. They had a national movement to back them up. Young leaders from every part of the country had mobilised their people to fight and gain their freedom. They fought in the name of God, making it a religious war. It was the faithful against the faithless Communist Red Army. The lack of leadership was evident not in the fact that they resisted but that they kept fighting without negotiating a peace that could have been all-inclusive. It would be easier to go back to peace if there was a functioning government in place, with government workers, police, schools and everything else that comes with running a government.

At this time, another element entered the fray. Pakistan now had aspirations of strategic depth and used its proximity to Afghanistan to garner more influence, with the American government promising to distribute funds and weapons to the resistance groups. You have to remember that it was a Cold War, and the USA could not just publicly support the resistance. So, it gave billions of dollars in economic assistance and weapons to Pakistan. Pakistan, in turn, gave those to the resistance leaders who would be its puppets, giving the country influence in what happens in Afghanistan.

Pakistan had a plan to rule over Afghanistan so that it could put more pressure on the Indian government. Its goal was to get back Kashmir.

The Cold War situation did not allow for the USA to directly support the resistance, giving power to the Pakistanis. The US leadership did not care about what the Pakistanis did and the long-term repercussions it presented as long as they helped to defeat the Red Army in Afghanistan. The lack of leadership on the part of the Afghans who became Pakistani puppets was the start of a long and gruesome relationship that Pakistan would have with Afghanistan over the next forty years.

So, the brave people of Afghanistan fought against one of the superpowers of the world and they won. They beat the Red Army, which withdrew from Afghanistan in 1989. However, this left a great power vacuum, which was where the third example of a lack of leadership occurred. This instance was a great blow to the idea that any kind of peace might have had a chance of happening in Afghanistan, and, this time, the lack of leadership was demonstrated not only by the Afghans but also by the world, especially the USA. As soon as the Soviets withdrew, the United States and the rest of the world backed out and abandoned Afghanistan. They wanted nothing more to do with the country or the people who had just helped to give a decisive mortal blow to the Soviet Union.

The many Afghan factions fought from different parts of the capital city of Kabul. It was a brutal civil war that destroyed the city and killed thousands upon thousands of innocent civilians. A lack of clear leadership was evident as hundreds of rockets and mortar shells exploded throughout the city on a daily basis. Pakistan was the only country involved, and that was to serve its own interests, but where was the world? Why had they abandoned Afghanistan? Still no one can answer these questions.

The civil war went on. Around 1995, the Pakistani ISI (its intelligence agency), which was and still is the mastermind behind Pakistan's strategic depth policy in Afghanistan, understood that its puppets were not able to win against one of the main heroes of the Soviet war, Ahmad Shah Massoud, so it pivoted and shifted its focus. The ISI knew that it had thousands upon thousands of young Afghans in Pakistani madrassas or religious schools. It already knew who could be the leaders of this new group that would be known as the Taliban. The Pakistani ISI funded them, gave them weapons and a goal: go take Afghanistan and spread your brand of super-fundamentalist Islam. Do it for your God. Do it for your Prophet. The Taliban leaders went with it and by 1996 they had taken over most of the country.

Their masters, the Pakistani ISI, were happy. They were reaching their goal of strategic depth. The world was still in abandon mode. Only India supported the resistance, and that was it. Only one or two pockets of resistance remained and one of them was from the Panjshir valley where Commander Massoud was still resisting. First it was the Soviets and now it was the Taliban. He always said, 'They defeated the Soviets because they were invaders. They were not going to allow puppets of Pakistan to rule over Afghanistan.' They ruled over Afghanistan with an iron fist until 2002.

The world changed on a day that no one would ever forget, 11 September 2001. The USA could no longer stay silent and continue its policy of abandonment, which had come back to bite it in the backside. It was now in it for the long haul. It had been attacked for the first time on its own soil and who had done it? The Taliban? No, it was al-Qaeda and the leader, Osama bin Laden, was hiding in Afghanistan. This blow to America was not going to go unanswered. Sadly, Commander Massoud, the main resistance leader, had been assassinated by Osama bin Laden two days before the 11 September attacks on America.

Who did the US turn to this time? The Northern Alliance, the coalition of different ethnic groups that Commander Massoud had united in order to fight against the Taliban. The USA sent in teams of Special Forces and, with the support of the Northern Alliance troops on the ground, they started to laser target Taliban positions. By winter, the Taliban fighters had either been killed or fled back into Pakistan. The Northern Alliance took over most of the country. Afghans came back to their homeland. Afghanistan had been freed from the fundamentalist and oppressive ideology of the Taliban. The USA and the world promised to never abandon Afghanistan again and to stay until the Taliban was truly defeated.

In December 2001, the UN held a conference in Bonn, Germany, and invited the different players in Afghanistan. It was a peace conference and a victory conference. The world was present. The Northern Alliance were front and centre. Everyone was happy. The only group of people who were not included in this conference was the Taliban. This might be controversial to some but in my opinion, this was another instance where Afghanistan and even more so the world had no vision or leadership. The Afghans might not have known what was needed for a sustainable peace but the world's great minds should have known. The inclusion of the Taliban in one way or another would have maybe paved the way for it to not keep fighting. Maybe it would have allowed it the space to let bygones be bygones, but this did not happen, and the Taliban was brushed aside as the loser of the war.

The next twenty years would be a roller-coaster ride. A presidential structure was set up with the President having the most power. A free-market system was established to support the new Afghan economy and billions of dollars started to be pumped into the country. Immediately, salaries went through the roof, people started to reconstruct their lives and homes and everything seemed to be going in the right direction. This is where I think there was another leadership failure, which affected what was going to happen over the next twenty years.

Afghanistan was a really poor country. It did not have a highly educated society and there was very little skilled labour. The creation of a free-market system was a big mistake in my opinion. It led to those in power having the opportunity to establish a highly corrupt system. This was ignored by the world so that Afghanistan could be helped to get on its own feet. But a corrupt system and one that feeds even more corruption because of the market system would never be good in the long run. The leaders of the world should have thought of a better way to improve the standards of living in the country in an organic way and not just because billions of dollars were at hand to be spent.

For instance, salaries were equivalent to those in the United States, but people would have been just as happy with salaries that were less. This would mean that the price of living would stay low and that people would not become used to such high salaries that were inflated. Eventually what happened was that the money dried up and people didn't know how to continue. Another system should have been set up in order to allow the slow increase of people's standards of living and spending.

The lack of leadership was evident on both the Afghan and US sides. The Afghan President, his Cabinet minister, police, military men and many others were used to corrupt money, and it is never good for leaders to be able to be bought by anyone. The United States could have clamped down on corruption from the beginning, by not allowing big contracts to be given to any government official who took bribe money or who did not complete government contracts consistently over a long time. Everything was up for grabs and the so-called Afghan leadership did everything it could to keep getting rich.

The Pakistani ISI did its best to have as many Afghan politicians and security personnel in its pocket as it could. Every government that wanted some kind of influence in Afghanistan paid bribe money to these supposed leaders. If you are owned by everyone, then how can you even think to serve a country, to bring peace and to make sure that the people have a bright future? You can't. This was one of the main factors in the failure of leadership. Corruption destroyed any chance we had to really fight the Taliban – and the Pakistani ISI and the Taliban used this to their advantage.

The people kept hope alive that one day the world and their so-called leaders would bring peace. So, they ignored the corruption, but year after year, things kept getting worse and worse. When I talk about corruption in the system, I only mean those who had real power, not the youths who worked in the ministries, the secretaries, the advisers or those who just went along with what their elders or those in power were telling them to do. Most young Afghans hated that they had such a highly corrupt leadership, but what could they do?

Afghans started schools and universities. They started clinics and hospitals. Young women created art and music. Young men became business owners of all different kinds. They not only rushed towards government jobs but carved a new way. The government didn't pave the roads in most residential parts of the capital and so people from one locality pooled money together to have their street cemented. This happened in most cities across the country. People did not have any faith in their government because they only saw it as corrupt and power-hungry. They had seen first-hand the lack of leadership and its negative effects.

Both Afghan Presidents played ethnic politics which only gave more space for the Taliban to grow and become stronger. President Karzai started it by telling the West to not attack the Taliban as much because they are all Afghans and that we Afghans could fight the war on our own. Ethnicity was a major factor because the Taliban were and are mainly Pashtuns. The Presidents were of the same ethnic group and so they gave less value to actually fighting the war. Ethnic politics demonstrates a direct lack of leadership. When a leader stops having a vision for the whole country, for every ethnic group, then how can he be a national leader and how can he be fair towards all peoples in his country? He can't.

The United States also fell into the ethnic politics game that is played in Afghanistan. Maybe they didn't do it intentionally but nonetheless it did happen. How? By appointing an Afghan as the special representative of the USA to Afghanistan, they inadvertently got involved in the ethnic politics of the country. This was especially the case because Khalilzad, the special representative of America for twenty years, also had ethnic politics on his mind. He was often soft on the Taliban, talking about how it had changed and how it had a new, softer ideology, which we all knew was a total fabrication.

Not many people knew this, but Khalilzad also had aspirations to one day become the President of Afghanistan, as highlighted in US Secretary of Defense Gates's memoir. When he was asked if Afghanistan would be better served if it became a parliamentary system, he always rejected it, advising the US government that Afghanistan always needs a strong central government in order to be able to control the country. After all, if there was a parliamentary system, then how could Khalilzad become the President?

Both these instances show that there was a distinct lack of leadership among Afghan leaders and sadly on the part of the American government as well. The United States could have left a lasting legacy if it had been able to implement a parliamentary system in Afghanistan, giving people in the remotest of places the power to elect their state and government officials. This dream of real representation never came to pass because of greed and a total lack of leadership. The USA was depending on Khalilzad to give them good advice, not knowing that he had his own interests in mind.

We all knew America would not stay in Afghanistan for ever but one of the last points that really drove home the idea of a failure of leadership had to do with the untimely withdrawal of the US forces and the victory of the Taliban. It all started with President Trump wanting to make an effort to win the US election, so he set a deadline that was too soon. No one was prepared for it; not the Americans and not the Afghans. The Taliban were the only ones that were happy. Then President Biden won the election and instead of reversing the withdrawal or delaying it, he decided to make an even earlier exit. The US military and intelligence predicted that the Afghan government would fall within nine months of the American withdrawal. Well, if they knew this, then doesn't it indicate a complete lack of leadership to decide to leave anyway? The Taliban knew it had won the war.

And, finally, let us look at the massive Afghan National Army which was swept aside by the small Taliban force in a matter of two weeks. The Taliban do not number more than 30,000 or 40,000, but they scared the Afghan National Army so much that the Taliban barely had to fight to take over the whole country. The Afghan army – comprising around 250,000 soldiers – didn't even fight. When the Taliban entered the capital, there was no resistance against them. One of the main reasons for this was that the army had lost faith in their leadership. For years the Presidents told them to stand down and not fight the Taliban. As I mentioned earlier, those Presidents were playing with ethnic politics and wanted to be on the good side of the Taliban and the rest of the country. They thought that if they supported all Pashtuns, even if they were terrorist Taliban, they would seem like a strong Pashtun leader. When America left and the Taliban started its offensive to fill the power vacuum, the military understood that the government was not going to help them or give them support. So, they ran and left the country to burn. There was a lack of leadership even when it came to national security.

In no way am I anti-American, anti-Western or anti-Afghan. I think that if we are to look forward to a future without the Taliban, then we should understand what brought us to this situation in the first place. Everyone that was involved in Afghanistan over the past twenty years, who had any sort of power or influence, is to blame. As I have shown over the past few pages, blame does not lie only with the Afghans, Afghanistan's neighbours or the world – the blame is spread wide and far, starting with the Afghan so-called leadership.

The Afghan people do not want the Taliban, but they also do not want to go back to the ultra-corrupt system of governance that we had before the Taliban. Afghans are different now.

Young women know their rights, they are educated and have a lot of experience in different fields. They no longer will be satisfied with the status quo. Young men have changed too and so have the elderly. Free press, television, radio and social media have given everyone over the past fifteen years a voice and access to different kinds of information and helped them to see how other people around the world think and live. Even children have seen a change in their lives. That is why it came as such a shock to most of the population when the Taliban took over for a second time.

We need a renewed leadership. All those that had their chance and decided to only fill their bank accounts and squabble over which ministry they should have should no longer be given a place at the big boys' table. Younger Afghans should be given a chance to lead, a new generation that is sick of the war, the corruption and the fighting for power. I know they are there.

You can see it in the young women who are filling up the world of social media with their words of resistance, in the journalists who are attacked by the Taliban for reporting the truth about the killing and beating of innocent people, in the human rights activists who beg for justice, in the women's rights activists who stand in the face of terror, in the singers who sing the songs of freedom, in the cricket players who shed a tear while playing international games – it is in all the people who stand to protest the Taliban because they do not believe in its fundamentalist ideology.

Afghanistan is not lost because the Taliban took over. It lives in all the people that stand for truth, justice and an open-minded society. Most Afghans are real Muslims but would never think of themselves as fundamentalists. I know that one day, we will realise the dream of a free, secular and modern Afghanistan. Until then, let's keep the candle of hope alive.

Mahmud Khalili is an Afghan-American writer. He is the author of *Afghanistan Decoded: Perspectives in Domestic and Foreign Affairs.*

CHAPTER 6

A CONVERSATION WITH FORMER MINISTER OF THE INTERIOR MASOUD ANDARABI[1]

MASOUD ANDARABI

HISTORY REPEATS ITSELF

The last time I left Kabul, I felt that history was repeating itself. When my father was my age and I was the age of my kids, we had to flee Kabul at night because the Communist regime had decided to prosecute my father for his allegiance to Ahmad Shah Massoud. At 2 a.m., my brother and I were woken and taken to travel by road to Pakistan. I returned to Afghanistan in 2002 after the interim government of President Karzai had been formed.

When politics overwhelmed my role as Minister of the Interior, my disputes increased with President Ghani. He removed me after I had just returned from the front line of war in Zabul, a southern Afghan province, and I left the country for the US. I returned in late July 2021, for a month to see what was going on. And then four days before the collapse, I was lucky to come through a normal route, not through military airplanes, and got back to the United States, where I remain.

AFGHANISTAN DURING KARZAI'S GOVERNMENT IN 2002

President Karzai had lived in the Pakistani city of Quetta not very far from Kandahar, so he was well engaged with Afghan elders during the Cold War and was familiar with Afghan culture. However, President Karzai did not form a strong governance structure and platforms to better manage the international aid that came to Afghanistan. Corruption became part of his governance and no solid actions were taken to fight the warlords who were playing a major role in the corruption. Even once he himself said, 'I know my ministers are stealing money, but I want to tell them to spend it inside Afghanistan and not outside Afghanistan.' So, he did not take firm actions against the corrupt government officials. President Ghani had similar problems, but we could see that the deepest flaw in the approach of the Ghani government and its Western sponsors was that they were dealing with local problems but trying to fix them with only national solutions. In part, that was because the US and the UK understood how modern states work but did not understand the local nature of the problems, but it was also because Ghani did not know the language of the people. He was a fake in that respect; he was not the right person for Afghanistan. He pretended that he knew the local people and the local problems, that he understood the traditions, but he was just pretending, and that meant that his support was actually wafer-thin outside Kabul.

WEAKNESS OF STATECRAFT

There were leaders who understood what was needed and were effective. The Chief Executive of Afghanistan from 2014 to 2020 and then head of the High Council for National Reconciliation, Abdullah was one such leader, but he was not a Pashtun – he is only half Pashtun on this father's side. The West decided at some point that a Pashtun had to be in charge and not a Tajik. For twenty years, this notion that Pashtuns should have the power was very much dominant. But the irony is that as a mixed Pashtun and Tajik, he was actually acceptable to the Tajiks. Of course, he made mistakes, but he was a charismatic person. His biggest mistake was not to stand against President Ghani in the last six months. As I said in an interview in the *National Interest* in 2021, 'Everyone in Kabul, from the intelligence, from military, from diplomatic … we were all talking about how badly Ghani was running things … the consensus was that whatever he was doing was going to sink us all.' But Abdullah, who might have been able to mount a challenge, seemed to not do much. At the same time, the Afghan Parliament members and some other key leaders who could also stand against Ghani seemed to have their minds already made up that they would go to the mountains to fight against the Taliban. The situation might have been reversed if they had engaged.

THE NEW GENERATION

I was one of a generation of Afghans who grew up in the years after the intervention and we made our careers in this time. I joined a UN Development Programme called the Afghanistan Information Management Services project. Through this experience I became interested in IT systems and decided to do my bachelor's in IT. I quickly rose through the ranks and became a technical manager, leading a software development team providing governance solutions in Afghanistan in 2010.

This is what could happen in these years: a friend asked me to come and help with the National Directorate Security (NDS) on the IT side. They gave me an address. I went there and I became an adviser for three months and then developed a five-year plan. On the back of this I was appointed director for signals intelligence (SIGINT), and my work combined detailed information technology and SIGINT. The UK and the US were only interested in SIGINT because they had their own people and protection, but they were not very interested in developing IT for the management of the NDS. I tried to bring them together so that our own capability could get more support. I was promoted to deputy for operations, a very important position in the NDS. I was there for four years until the director-general resigned and I was acting director for a year. I went to the American University's School of International Service to obtain my master's degree in international service with a focus on security and intelligence. After two years, I was appointed as Acting Minister of the Interior and then politics got involved and it was only really at this point that my career became political – in essence I am a technocrat.

Many of us have been trained during the past twenty years. Many of us have now left the country. This is the first major reflection I want to offer on the prospects for the Taliban government: it is going to lack people with the expertise it needs to run a modern state. Many Afghans will then face the choice of leaving if they have not left or going back if they feel safe to do so.

I have been quite critical of President Ghani on a strategic level, but he did make some positive changes. He worked on economic procedures which changed a lot of processes and improved connectivity. He made those upgrades. And he also allowed the next generation to come to the front of the Afghan government. He retired 2,000 people from the old school. These are things that he did successfully, but in order for there to be results from those changes, he needed to allow that younger generation to actually exercise some executive authority. For those changes to work, we needed a different kind of leader who would have given authority to those new people and widened his trust circle and not narrowed it to two or three people. Ghani was a micromanager; he wanted to know everything you did. At the Ministry of the Interior, President Ghani would read every single report and document he received from the ministry and then write an instruction for each and every one, sometimes instructions that were already part of our standard procedure, but still he would write something. I had an office of ten guys sitting there to make him happy because if he was not getting the report, he would be annoyed with you. Sometimes I would not even read his instruction because it was already part of our normal method. I was just making him happy by sending back his action reports.

Ghani's government collapsed when he fled claiming that there was a threat to his life. It was perhaps the most decisive thing he did. On the last day, the President escaped. At noon, he supposedly informed his chief of staff that he was going to take a nap. The chief of staff was in the dining room eating when he heard the helicopter. 'What's going on?' someone asked. 'The President's gone.' He didn't tell his chief of staff who was there in his office. Forget about the minister of defence or interior or intelligence or anyone. I mean, he grabbed the bags and left.

The Taliban is now in power, but it doesn't mean the mentality of this new generation has changed – there is a new generation of Afghans and they pose a direct threat to the Taliban.

WESTERN ATTITUDES TO PASHTUNS

Abdullah won the first round of the last presidential election and then the second round was contested. If the US had backed his election, things would have been different. There would have been a President acceptable to Tajiks – remember it was the Tajiks who dominated the army. It was the Tajiks who were sacrificed in the fight in Helmand, not the Pashtuns. Abdullah should have been tested once as President, which I think the international community blocked. I believe they made a mistake in giving the election to Ghani; they legitimised him. He would have never been the President. The second time, the last time, if the US had not shown up to Ghani's inauguration day, if they had showed up to Abdullah's inauguration, Ghani would have been gone, the army and the police would have stood with Abdullah.

But by that time the US had left the stage. The Americans were very silent in the last six months, as if they were just watching this happen, and the UK appeared to have no foreign policy of its own. It just gave up and left it all up to the Americans. President Ghani did not seem to know what was going on. Amrullah Saleh, Ghani's first Vice-President who was previously part of the Mujahideen and head of the NDS, only listened to Ghani and distanced himself from the people. Throughout his time as Ghani's deputy, he served as loyal puppet for Ghani and nothing else. That was the main reason I left the government.

This was a political defeat and not a military defeat. The Taliban came back because of the Ghani administration's mismanagement. Afghanistan had a trained and well-equipped army, trained not only by the US but also by NATO and the UK, and it was a capable force that was brutally mismanaged. Ghani did not understand the depth of the issues and relied on a trusted few Pashtuns who formed an inner circle – they may have misled him about the real situation. If Ghani had worked otherwise when he realised the US was leaving, then things could have turned out differently. That was the difference I had with him before my removal. He did not understand what was actually going on with the US, with the peace talks and with the Taliban. In March, I warned that the US retreat from Afghanistan would give an opportunity to the Taliban to rise and it was also obvious that the Taliban's ties to the terrorist group al-Qaeda were intact. I was sacked for questioning the government about the security situation in Afghanistan. It was impossible for me not to raise these questions because intelligence is where I came from. The Taliban and other terrorist groups' relationship is as one – there is no difference. They are the tactical arm for the Taliban's fighting capability. Al-Qaeda, anyone, you name it, the twenty groups that are there, are very much with the Taliban. The foreign fighters have become part of the Afghan landscape; they have been there for twenty years for the Taliban forces, giving them money and support and making ammunition, IEDs, mines, everything. The one exception is ISIS-K. In some areas, there was fighting between the Taliban and Daesh but elsewhere they made coalitions.

There is a tactical relationship between the Taliban and Daesh in Kabul, as well as with the notorious Haqqani network, which provides the Taliban with internal security. I doubt that the attack on the Americans at Kabul airport would have happened without the involvement of lower-level groups.

There will be continued focus on these terrorist links when Western governments come to a greater understanding of these connections. The drugs trade is an area that even in this era of isolationism the West should want to talk about. Or is there just nothing we can do except to put what pressure we can on the Pakistani government and other governments that the Taliban is talking to? In the early days of the peace discussion, a key point raised was on counter-narcotics. But in the final talks in Doha and in the Trump deal, it did not feature.

PAKISTAN AND CHINA

The UK could have played more of a role, especially with Pakistan and perhaps even in the peace talks. All the UK seemed to do, like me, is complain about the US. But it was equally a partner with a lot of influence – and not just on Pakistan, on the Taliban as well. Overall, we have all been very soft on the Pakistanis because of our own interests. I understand that you had to be careful how you managed the Pakistanis, but we could have done more, even from the beginning, pushing back on them while they were actively running those camps in Pakistan.

Pakistan should also take note that when the Taliban was in government last time, they were not friendly neighbours. Their chatrooms are full of Pashtun nationalism. There was a video that went viral on social media when a Pakistani truck came across the border with the Pakistani flag flying. And the Taliban told them to remove the flag and asked them, 'Why have you brought a Pakistani flag to our side of the border? Take it off or we will tear it down.' It is indicative of the complexity of the Taliban–Pakistan relationship. At this stage, the Pakistanis have the upper hand in terms of influence. The Haqqani are their baby and they are now the biggest players in Kabul because the Taliban who were in Doha and others are seen to have been close to the West in the past two years. For now, Pakistan through the Haqqani is empowered. Pakistan will try to use that influence.

The Taliban also has to reassure the Chinese. It is already doing what it can to support the country and it will get recognition. The Taliban can manage both of these key relationships. Some members of the Taliban will object to the influence of Pakistan but on just an emotional level, not in a practical way – they will defend the idea that this is their country. It will be a point of pride for some Pashtuns: 'We should be a country that has a proper border.' We don't want to fight on those legacies, you know, so this type of mentality will develop. In the coming five years, Afghanistan under the Taliban is not going to be a country open to open relationships. There are going to be back-channel relationships, there's going to be manoeuvring, but little out in the open, and the West has got very limited leverage left.

One thing the West does have is the $9 billion of Afghanistan's currency reserve sitting in vaults in Washington, and withholding it is going to be the cause of a humanitarian crisis. It's pretty obvious. Any observer would say that it's going to be a very difficult winter, particularly with Covid, and the pressure on the West to let some of that money go will be enormous. It's very tempting to see

if there's some sort of leverage and it's difficult to leverage humanitarian assistance, but there's got to be some opportunity there to
gain concessions in exchange for funds. I would be disappointed if
we simply bankrolled this Taliban government. I think Joe Biden
might see that as a pragmatic way forward because it gets Afghanistan off the front pages and with no more American casualties.

As should be clear by now, I believe we should have seen another Afghan President who would not have trusted these Yanks
to run the country. But from the reports that I've seen, we've now
got the absolute opposite, which is a government that isn't running,
departments where ministers aren't able to be reached, they're not
turning up, and the people who have been put in charge of departments have no real interest in running them. The buildings and
the physical infrastructure are there but I am questioning whether
the structure can survive for very long without the people who can
actually make the system run. Lots of the people who were trained
to run that structure are gone, and if not gone, then they don't feel
safe to go back into a government role or are trying to get out of
the country. Democracies perish very fast. My worry is that we haven't got much of a window, but whatever happens next, we will
not be starting from scratch again – we've got twenty years' worth
of structural work – but we will be dealing with a West which is
dominated by isolationism.

The other question is what happens to the collective knowledge
of this generation of Afghans who are now scattered across the
world – and will they want to come back. If the cycle is five to ten
years, then yes, I believe some will come back, but if it is longer, I
am not so sure. We have been educated in Afghanistan over the
past twenty years and it will take us years to build new lives in the

West. I think it will be harder for this generation to return. There should be some kind of effort to keep us together, to keep us connected, to share the knowledge that we have with those who are trying to keep things going in Afghanistan.

Overall, I am feeling optimistic. I think perhaps we just have to be a bit patient and there's a small chance that this government will morph into something more inclusive over the next number of years. It's possible. On the other hand, we might see it collapse into a terrible mess. Either way, it's going to be a very tough time for the Afghan people and we're very conscious of those that we made promises to. There are lots of people still desperately keen to leave Afghanistan and get to the West and we have a responsibility to help them if we can.

Masoud Andarabi was Minister of the Interior of Afghanistan from 2019 to 2021.

CHAPTER 7

DISPATCHES: EXTRACTS FROM THE JOURNALISM OF HOLLIE MCKAY[1] IN AFGHANISTAN

HOLLIE MCKAY

INTERVIEW WITH THE *WASHINGTON EXAMINER*, 27 AUGUST 2021

McKay and [her photographer] Simkin made their way to the border of Uzbekistan, about 65 miles from Mazar, but not before meeting with Taliban elders to secure permission to leave the country. The Uzbek Consulate helped secure a Taliban escort to bring them through the group's various checkpoints between Mazar and the border. 'The elders were trying to spin a bit of PR to me that they weren't the same Taliban anymore, and they respected human rights and all this kind of stuff,' said McKay, who interviewed Taliban members along the way. 'But I think it was fairly clear, as I was probing him, that what they wanted was a very stringent version of Sharia, and that definitely meant a woman was relegated to the home and covered in a burqa if she ever stepped out … I wouldn't say that I was fearing for my life at all. I think that I'd spoken to enough people and collected enough information that made me feel confident that the Taliban was not interested in harming a woman or a foreigner … I think I was more curious than anything, curious in the sense that I wanted to understand how they act and how they behaved,' she said. 'If I was that fearful, I probably wouldn't have felt comfortable going down that route.'[2]

Hollie McKay returned to Afghanistan at the beginning of September 2021. She has been filing stories from there since. These are selected extracts of Afghan voices from those dispatches.

…More than twelve hours later and in the dead of night, we reached Kabul: a city that exists in a way that is a shell of its former self. I rose early Sunday morning, the beginning of the working week, the sights drawing up remnants of 'old' Afghanistan: fruit stands opening on street corners, men huddling in small groups peering over a video on a smartphone, and women emerging without male chaperons from their homes – around half without a burqa. Only the streets are a muted shadow of their former selves; the vibrancy and laughter have given way to a sense of laying low and constant anxiety. 'Have you had problems? Aren't you afraid?' whispers one watermelon seller, his hazel brown eyes wide with worry.[3]

The Taliban patrol the streets – always armed to the teeth – on foot and in armoured trucks and police vehicles, easy to spot with their more coloured clothes and aggressive walk … 'Kabul has become a jail for me,' one young professor whispers, his face ashen with an agony that is hard to fully comprehend … 'There is no guarantee of life for us,' one well-dressed young journalist tells me, his eyes wet with tears. 'I can't feel safe myself, and I may be threatened in the coming days. I need to go somewhere safer, and I am asking you for help on humanitarian grounds.' ... 'It is going to be okay,' I respond, silently wishing that I was not telling a lie.[4]

•   •   •

'We are worried about the girls. We need them in school. I need to work, but I am not going until I get paid,' [Nisreen, a teacher and local women's rights advocate,] explains. 'Girls are going to be left behind, the coronavirus pandemic started this in leaving girls behind, and we need them to catch up. And people are starting to become hungry.'

'Amendments will be made based on our new laws. Islamic scholars will make the decisions,' says Abdul Hakeim, chief of staff for the Minister of Education. 'We want an Islamic perspective, and this means separate classes and transport. Once this is sorted out, girls can continue education for a lifetime.' ... 'We cannot teach our kids music and other things which are not part of our society,' Hakeim continues, adding that the Taliban of 2021 will be far more open-minded than the rule that started in the 1990s. 'Now, we have advanced policies and strategies to catch up with the world. Back then, we did not have access to the resources and no capacity for new buildings or schools. Now we have much more power to make the changes.' Yet Hakeim stresses that the country's dire financial situation means that they urgently need support, not from other governments but non-governmental organisations. 'Other governments want to implement their own mythologies and thinking on the local people,' he says. 'We want [schools] to run on our terms.'[5]

• • •

'I admit that, at first, I was not that supportive [of Nilab's love of taek-
wondo]. It was just not part of our culture,' Nilab's long-term fiancé,
Baktash, confesses. 'But now I am so proud of Nilab; I know that
taekwondo is so good for her and her future. It gave her a dream.' For
each athlete who has escaped, there are many more stranded.[6]

'I joined taekwondo because a woman in Afghanistan should be
a fighter for herself; that is why I started. But then I fell in love with
it,' Nilab recalls. 'Most of the time, I was going out of the house and
seeing other ladies being teased. I did not want them to come to me
and be teased; that is why I should be ready and fight them back.' An-
zoorat, seven years her junior, with porcelain skin and a soft-spoken
poise, says she wanted nothing more than to follow in her sister's
footsteps to prove she could stand up for herself and for others. 'I
started in gymnastics, and after that, I saw my sister doing taekwondo. The fighting and the demonstrations were so interesting to me,'
she confides, in almost a whisper, as if to shield her voice from the
Taliban lurking in the streets outside. 'So that is how I started.'[7] An-
zoorat, who was in her final year of high school, has been unable to
complete her studies since the Taliban came to power. The outfit has
also prohibited the thing she loves most in the world – taekwondo.
'There is nothing left here. Under the government of the Taliban, we
cannot do anything for ourselves or our country,' she says softly. 'All
we can do is stay at home.'[8] 'Every girl's life has changed, especially
for athletes. We cannot play again,' Aryane Shamim, the 23-year-old
Women's Tennis Coach in Kabul, tells me with melancholy. 'Our
hope is gone. It is very hard – we don't have a future.'[9]

• • •

'Life was good when Americans were here,' one elder Mohammad tells me, undeterred by the Taliban fighters glaring over his shoulder. 'Economically, it was good; people were busy. But after they left, the economy got weak.' … 'If we stood with the Taliban, Americans would kill us. And if you stood with Americans, the Taliban would kill us,' noted another elder Mohammed Ali, who is around seventy. 'We couldn't do anything at that time.'[10]

'Here, if the father was a Talib, then the son was a soldier in the ANA [Afghan National Army]. Then the brother and uncle would be Daesh. But somehow, everyone is a splinter group of the Taliban,' explains one 33-year-old Korengal local who asked to be identified only as Safi. 'That is how it is here.' … And for sixteen-year-old Irfan, who lives at the foot of the valley and meets me secretly in an abandoned workshop – where we sit on broken car seats and sip tea until a prying Taliban comes to investigate what is happening – his family has been pulled apart by the conflict that has claimed his entire childhood. 'My dad was Taliban, but he died fighting years ago. So then my brother became ANA, and my other brother belonged to no one,' the rail-thin, timid teen boy says. 'But he died a few months ago. A howitzer (field artillery) was fired and landed in front of the house, just as my brother was coming out.'

'I want to be a doctor; I want to make something of myself,' he continues. 'But I can only go to school sometimes; mostly, I have to work and do daily chores.'[11]

• • •

Last week, the Pentagon declared it had concluded its probe into the 29 August Kabul drone strike. A release pegged the blast as an 'honest mistake' ... the Air Force blamed 'confirmation bias', 'communication breakdowns' and 'execution errors'. 'I heard that the USA says it does its work honestly, but this is not honesty,' Aimal [a relative of the ten innocent Afghans killed in the US drone strike] says of the report. 'We are all civilians. My brother [Zmaray] did not have contact with any military. Yet they targeted this area.' The ten victims all lived together with fifteen other extended family members, including Zmaray's three brothers. Zmaray, whose name has been spelled in previous reports as 'Zemari', was killed along with three of his children: Farzad, eleven, Faisal, sixteen, and his oldest, Zamir, twenty, a student. In addition to Aimal's daughter Malika, a great-niece, Sumaya, just two years old, was also killed, along with Zmaray's nephew Naser, thirty – who had worked closely with US special forces in Kandahar and was less than a week away from getting married. Zmaray's youngest brother, Romal, who was sitting in the living room when the drone struck, lost all three of his children: daughter Ayat, two, and sons Bin Yamin, six, and Arwin, seven. 'No one has contacted us at all,' fellow brother Ajmal Ahmadi, thirty-three, affirms. 'Last time we came, someone lost consciousness. So we cannot come here; the mothers are not in good condition,' Ajmal continues. 'The family is still in shock. We haven't recovered.'[12]

...[Athlete] Sabihah, twenty-four, points out her painstakingly long days are punctured with reading books, helping with household chores, and watching television. Yet, most of all, she fantasises about an organisation assisting them to evacuate. 'When you want to kill a society, you kill the youth first,' she says solemnly. 'And then everything is dead.'[13]

•   •   •

On a quiet late fall afternoon, groups of women huddle over overflowing rice plates and tea in the 'family garden section' of a popular Kabul café. Since the sudden Taliban takeover on 15 August, it has remained a safe space for all walks of life to venture from their homes. Until now. 'You are a journalist? I don't think so,' one lanky Afghan man sneers at me, interrupting lunch and claiming to be Taliban intelligence. 'Where is your identification?' It marks the first time since the dramatic government change that such an intrusion in a private place has unfurled. It left me with an unsettling sensation of what is to come as the Islamic Emirate of Afghanistan consolidates controlling powers across the struggling nation of 38 million.[14]

'Mothers can't feed their children,' laments Muhibullah Ahmadzai, medical director of the Germany-sponsored Irene Salimi Children's Hospital in Kabul. 'That causes all sorts of congenital disabilities. And family violence is rising.' The unspoken reality on the ground is also the drastic rise in mental illness. After decades of endless conflict and combat, along with their lives being yanked from beneath them in an instant, girls and women are hardest hit by bouts of extreme depression and anxiety.[15]

'We rely purely on Allah,' Ghaws-u-deen, thirty-five, who sells Afghan fried food on the street, tells me with a brave smile. Almost every retailer I speak to on the dusty streets tells me that business has dropped from anywhere between 50 to 90 per cent since the

Taliban takeover. On top of it, the price of staple goods from bread to petrol to meat to cooking oil is ascending. The latter, one street burger vendor named Amir Mohammad explains, has more than doubled in recent months from the equivalent of $9.80 a container to $22. Some streets are stuffed with the starving and scared, selling their household items to fill their growling stomachs. At the same time, other areas that once bristled with vibrancy are boarded-up skeletons – their owners having fled and left their livelihoods behind. Sadly, the financial meltdown – driven in large part by Washington immediately freezing $9.5 billion in aid marked for Afghanistan followed by the World Bank and International Monetary Fund (IMF) suspension on funds – has meant much of the budding young generation have had to stop their studies. 'It costs too much money to keep studying,' one Afghan, Waheed – who took a job two weeks ago as a travel agent instead – tells me.[16]

It is hard to believe that it has been more than three months since the Taliban took the Presidential Palace. Afghans are resilient people, and life goes on – even without the buzz of music and foreign cash flow. Cafés and restaurants are still open (and many can be spotted smoking cigarettes or the popular waterpipe known as Hookah), commercial aeroplanes have resumed transits across the country and to some international destinations such as Islamabad and Abu Dhabi, hotels lure tourists, and cars continue to clog the narrow and ancient Kabul streets.

Yet the doom and gloom of a humanitarian catastrophe cling as the winter winds roll in and snow glazes the serrated mountains of the beautiful, bleeding country. It is a dilemma that the United States and much of the international community will be forced to painfully reconcile with – either recognise the new Taliban regime and release the funds that could stop innocent Afghans from starving to death or pariah the country and hold out for a longer game in the hopes the regime eliminates terrorism and values human rights.[17]

Hollie McKay is a foreign policy expert and war crimes investigator based in Afghanistan. She focuses on warfare, terrorism and crimes against humanity. She is the author of *Only Cry for the Living: Memos from Inside the ISIS Battlefield.*

GHULAM:[1] A YOUNG MAN TRIES TO ESCAPE BEING RECRUITED BY THE TALIBAN

———

'The Taliban said to me,
"We'll take you by force if we have to … Where is your son?"'

There are many rumours and reports of the Taliban forcibly recruiting across Afghanistan, but few are prepared to talk openly about it for fear of retribution. Ghulam (not his real name) and his family have been pressured by the Taliban to join them and train as a fighter in a large military camp across the border in Pakistan. This is his testimony.

Ghulam knew that he couldn't resist if he was forced, so he had to find ways to delay:

I've worked in a fuel pump station for years and live at home. One day, I was with my family when they [the Taliban] sent us a letter saying they are recruiting in all thirty-four provinces and that we must 'stand with them'.

They took some of the neighbours by force and they threatened to take us too. I said I was thinking of joining anyway and it would be much better to let me do it in my own time. But as I delayed, life became very difficult for us. It was very threatening because we knew they had already taken other people.

Three people were said to have joined them from our village, but the Taliban took them by force because they had worked with the previous government.

The Taliban said to me, 'We'll take you by force if we have to.' I said, 'Please give us a bit more time to decide who should join you so we join you by choice.' This worked for a while, but in the end I had to just tell them that I could not join. My family was afraid the Taliban would take me by force. So then I had to flee my own home and go to live elsewhere, in secret, where I couldn't be found. When I checked in with my family, my father said, 'They come every day and ask for you and knock on the door. "Where is your son? It is compulsory to join us!"' My parents told them that I went to Iran. I feel like I no longer exist in my own country.

Ghulam has younger brothers. He worries about the older ones getting recruited, but also for the younger ones who would be left behind.

'After a while they left with the new recruits to cross the border to Pakistan. That is where they do the brainwashing and the basic training. All of that is organised in Pakistan. Three to four of the neighbours disappeared that way and no one had updates for weeks.'

However, one of Ghulam's neighbours did recently manage to contact his family. He was calling from outside Afghanistan. He said the Taliban had taken them in a big convoy of vehicles, first to Paktia, then to Khost and Waziristan and finally to Pakistan. He was at a large Taliban military camp where he'd been told all the fighters received their training before being posted off to different destinations.

Ghulam feels fortunate to have escaped the Taliban's attempts to recruit him so far, but he is angry that he must live with the constant fear of another recruitment letter arriving, or another knock on the door of his family's home.

NEIGHBOURS

———

CHAPTER 8

ISLAM-INSPIRED WAYS OF AVOIDING THE RESOURCE CURSE IN AFGHANISTAN

OMAR AL-UBAYDLI

INTRODUCTION

A basic principle of economics is that the larger the volume of inputs one has, the greater one's capacity to produce, and hence the more one can consume. According to this straightforward logic, development economists writing during the first half of the twentieth century emphasised the positive role that natural resources can play in the growth of an economy.

Towards the end of the twentieth century, economists began to note the poor performance of certain economies in spite of their large endowments of natural resources, such as the Netherlands and the Democratic Republic of the Congo.[1]

This observation, which was formalised with statistical analyses of the growth of these economies, spawned a large sub-literature in the field of development economics known as the 'resource curse' literature: rather than benefiting the economy, natural resources might actually impede its growth, due to a variety of economic and political factors.[2] Scholars analysing the mechanisms linking resource income to poor economic performance also surmised that the same principles applied to foreign aid.[3]

While resource-rich countries such as the US and Australia seem to have avoided the resource curse, in 2021, the same cannot be said of Afghanistan, which continues to have one of the lowest standards of living in the world. In fact, it is arguably facing a three-dimensional version of the resource curse. The income associated with mineral exports, illegal drugs exports and foreign aid has arguably contributed to the poor performance of the Afghan economy by inducing corruption and armed conflict.[4]

As the Taliban-led government begins to formulate an economic strategy for Afghanistan, all is not lost. The voluminous resource curse literature has gone beyond mere description to include prescription, too, as understanding the mechanisms by which natural resources adversely affect an economy allows scholars to propose countermeasures.

This essay explains the main mechanisms of the resource curse and argues that they have indeed been operating in Afghanistan. The essay also provides constructive suggestions on overcoming the resource curse tailored to Afghanistan's unique circumstances. In light of the Taliban's declaration of an Islamic republic, the essay's suggestions are grounded in Islam, with the hope that this will make the government more receptive to the proposals.

AN OVERVIEW OF THE AFGHAN ECONOMY

In 2002, in the wake of the US-led invasion of Afghanistan, the country's level of per capita income (at purchasing power parity, meaning adjusted for differences in cost of living across the world) was approximately $1,200. During the ensuing twenty years, the economy grew robustly, albeit unevenly, resulting in the per capita income level almost doubling to $2,000.[5] However, in 2019, it remained 213th in the world of out 228, indicating a persistent problem of low living standards. Over half of the population is below the poverty line.[6]

According to several indicators, Afghanistan remains in an early stage of economic development: almost half of the labour force are employed in agriculture, which itself accounts for almost one-quarter of GDP when excluding opium. Precious stones (primarily gold) account for almost half of its exports, with vegetable products accounting for most of the remainder, again excluding opium.[7]

Though Afghanistan's current income from minerals is presently quite small, geological surveys conducted by the USSR and the US during their respective occupations of the country suggest the existence of mineral reserves with a value of over $1 trillion, which include iron, copper, lithium, rare earth elements, cobalt, bauxite, mercury, uranium and chromium.[8] While concessions for extracting some of these minerals have been granted to Chinese companies, these projects remain at an early stage.[9]

In contrast, opium production is a mature and stable industry in Afghanistan. Due to the commodity's illicit nature, data on opium is less reliable, but Afghanistan allegedly accounts for over 80 per cent of the world's opium production, and opium production contributes up to 11 per cent of the Afghan economy.[10]

Following the US-led invasion, foreign aid has played a central role in the Afghan economy: it has exceeded $1 billion annually since 2002, and averaged almost $5 billion per year in the period

2006–19, compared with a GDP of approximately $20 billion.[11] However, while the new millennium witnessed a sharp increase in foreign aid, the Afghan government has received significant volumes of external assistance for two centuries, with the list of donors including the British, the Americans, the Soviets and, more recently, the Pakistanis.[12]

Finally, Afghanistan's fiscal situation is perennially dire. It does not even have a credit rating and has failed to register a budget surplus during the past twenty years, while registering numerous large deficits.[13] Its currency reserves are also dwindling, leaving the government with extremely limited options for exercising economic policy.

WHAT IS THE RESOURCE CURSE?

Through the lens of the resource curse, an economy is described as being 'resource rich' when it has a valuable natural resource – usually petroleum but also certain precious minerals – that is extracted and exported with minimal value added via a local production process.[14] The income generated by the natural resource should be large internationally speaking, either on a per capita basis or in terms of its contribution to GDP or exports. The literature posits that being resource rich can adversely affect the economy in one of three primary channels.

This first is via its impact on exchange rates and hence non-resource exports, known as 'Dutch disease' following the Netherlands' experience with this channel during its own oil boom in the latter half of the twentieth century. Exporting the natural resource leads to an increase in the value of the currency, making its non-resource exports more expensive and thus less competitive. Since the natural resource sector tends to be more capital intensive and less technologically dynamic than other sectors, the resulting contraction of the non-resource sector usually leads to sluggish growth and rising unemployment.

Moreover, this theory has been expanded to include the fact that resource booms tend to siphon capital and labour away from sectors that are more productive in the long run, such as manufacturing and services, in the pursuit of the short-term gains associated with the natural resource.

The second channel is via the impact of resources on the quality of governance. In general, scholars have argued that resource wealth induces corruption. Senior politicians dismantle well-functioning institutions to gain access to resource income, and lower-quality, kleptocratic political candidates exert higher effort at securing office. Moreover, by undermining the need to levy traditional taxes, natural resource income subverts the development of state capacity, and of the civil oversight that can limit government malfeasance. Notably, this impact also runs in parallel with the tendency of resource wealth to fortify authoritarian regimes, thereby decreasing the likelihood of transiting to a stable democracy.

The third channel is that resource wealth can increase the likelihood of violent civil conflict as factions vie for control of the associated income. The adverse economic consequences are manifold: people fight instead of producing and investing, the fighting causes a lot of damage, foreign investors are dissuaded from investing in the economy and so on.

Before applying this theory to Afghanistan, it is worth noting that foreign aid income has potentially isomorphic effects on the economy because it is almost an extreme version of a natural resource: the income generated has minimal dependence on any productive effort on the ground, and so it engenders conflict over its control, sometimes breeding corruption and violence.[15]

A final remark is that resource curse scholars have synthesised their initial findings and developed theories that explain the differential impact of natural resources and foreign aid on income, i.e. the observation that some countries benefit from natural resources and foreign aid, while others seem to suffer. Put concisely, the key factor is the quality of state bureaucracy and political institutions when the resource income materialises. Mature democracies with effective bureaucracies, such as Norway and Australia, are able to realise the benefits of the natural resource at the level of the economy, with all groups sharing in the benefits. In contrast, authoritarian regimes with weak bureaucracies squander many of the benefits via negative-sum competition, and those that are realised are concentrated in the hands of a small minority.

THE RESOURCE CURSE
IN AFGHANISTAN

Unfortunately for Afghanistan, it satisfies many of the criteria that are typically associated with the resource curse. While the authoritarianism of its political system decreased in the years following the US-led invasion, according to the Polity 5 dataset,[16] it continued to show weak levels of democratisation, as well as having a weak bureaucracy and endemic corruption.

Coupled with this institutional proclivity to exhibit the resource curse is a sizeable contribution of foreign aid to the economy, along with a large potential contribution from natural resources. In fact, several analysts have attributed the geopolitical attention that Afghanistan attracts from great powers like the US, Russia and China to its large reserves of these valuable minerals.

Agricultural exports are not usually classified as a potential source of the resource curse, primarily due to the fact that they are produced, sometimes using labour-intensive methods, rather than being extracted in a manner similar to oil or natural gas.[17] However-er, in the case of the opium sector in Afghanistan, the illicit nature of the output leads to inflated prices which can potentially result in the aforementioned mechanisms associated with the resource curse being active. That includes violent conflict over control of the resource, with all the damage it entails, and poor governance and high corruption resulting from the large, covert revenues.

Regrettably, in addition to satisfying many of the criteria asso-ciated with the resource curse, Afghanistan exhibits many of the expected outcomes, too. Its perennially low levels of state capacity are often attributed to the government's historic failure to build a tax base, stemming from its preference for foreign aid.[18] The readily available aid-associated revenues have meant that the government never attempted to build the structures required to manipulate the country.

Corruption is an acute problem stemming from the state's klep-tocratic tendencies, with Afghanistan ranking 165th out of 179 in the 2020 Corruption Perceptions Index.[19] Moreover, violent con-flict between factions vying for control of foreign aid and opium income has massively curtailed the country's ability to attract for-eign investment due to the low levels of security. Further, consist-ent with the Dutch disease version of the resource curse, the opium sector, which is technologically stagnant and disconnected from the remainder of the economy, siphons away human capital due to its labour-intensive methods, meaning less time for education, and less labour for more productive sectors.

While there are many reasons for the persistently low living standards in Afghanistan, there can be little doubt that resource curse factors have historically played – and continue to play – an important role. Can Afghanistan overcome this poisoned chalice, and can Islam play a positive role?

HOW ISLAM CAN HELP AFGHANISTAN TO BEAT THE RESOURCE CURSE

The Taliban's return to government offers an immediate and fundamental change to the resource curse calculus, because many (if not all) donors have responded by suspending financial aid. Given the Taliban's ideological proclivities, and the actions that it has taken during the first few months following the US's departure, foreign aid is likely to remain at only a fraction of the levels achieved during the US occupation.[20] Therefore, in principle, this could lead to a diminution of the adverse consequences of the foreign aid version of the resource curse.

However, any optimism associated with this channel should be tempered by the fact that foreign powers will continue to use financial aid as a tool to pursue their own agendas, which frequently contradict the interests of regular Afghans.

Moreover, given the relatively warm relations between the Taliban and China (China's foreign minister openly received Taliban representatives in Beijing during July 2021), and in light of Chinese companies' success in securing extraction rights for Afghanistan's mineral deposits, there is a risk that the Taliban will compensate for foreign aid shortfalls with rising natural resource income over the long run, keeping the economy firmly in the resource curse's grips.[21]

Nevertheless, the Taliban has shown that it is capable of patience and strategic foresight, and so all is not lost. In particular, Islam can be a source of inspiration for policies that can help Afghanistan to overcome the resource curse in a manner consistent with the government's ideology.[22]

The first step is to stop opium production. Recreational narcotics are unambiguously forbidden under Islam,[23] especially if they are known to cause severe physical and psychological problems, and if they contribute to social problems, all of which apply to heroin. That consumers are predominantly non-Muslims is irrelevant, since it is the responsibility of Muslims to try to set an example to non-Muslims in case they might convert, rather than causing their society to disintegrate via an opioid epidemic.

While the Taliban might have invoked the clause that a state of war allows for extraordinary measures, regardless of the jurisprudential validity of such a claim, the war is now over, and there are no de facto challengers to the Taliban. Therefore, working towards the elimination of opium's contribution to the Afghan economy is a move that would both be righteous from an Islamic perspective and contribute to alleviating the resource curse suffered by Afghanistan. If enforced with the appropriate security apparatus, the move would also help the economy by decreasing the incidence of violent conflict that previously reflected factional competition over control of opium production.

The second step is for natural resource income to be distributed directly to Afghan citizens, as opposed to accruing to the central government.[24] This can be justified on Islamic grounds by noting its likely effectiveness as a countercorruption measure, since corruption is strictly prohibited under Islam, especially among the ranks of society's guardians (the government). The system used by the US state of Alaska, wherein residents receive periodic bank transfers reflecting their share of resource rents, would be a suitable model for the Taliban to consider.

Given the administrative difficulty of implementing such a system in Afghanistan, a feasible alternative that yields comparable results is for the natural resource sector to be privatised, and for the shares to be distributed to Afghan citizens in a non-transferrable manner. Afghans can then collect their share of the resource income via their dividends.

A third step is for the Taliban to draw inspiration from economically successful Muslim-majority nations, such as Indonesia, Malaysia and the UAE, as they draft a coherent economic strategy. As mentioned above, the illicit opium trade is a critical source of income for many Afghan citizens, and so banning opium production requires a new income source. Helping their people to earn dignified and productive livelihoods is a primary responsibility of an Islamically minded government, and the success of other Muslim nations should be leveraged for the development of a homegrown Afghan strategy.

The UAE, which is by far Afghanistan's most important trading partner,[25] owes much of its success to establishing a capable bureaucracy and developing sound governance for key state institutions, all in a manner consistent with Islamic principles. While the UAE has not completely averted the clutches of the resource curse, its recent past contains many examples of sound management of natural resource income.[26] The Taliban has much to gain from studying the Emirati experience, and should seize the opportunity to do so.

THE PROBLEM OF
VESTED INTERESTS

Effective techniques for escaping the resource curse have been known for years, yet many countries actively shun them because of a fundamental conflict of interest: while the economy as a whole suffers as a result of the resource curse, certain smaller groups – often including kleptocratic elites in government – can benefit handsomely, making them extremely reluctant to adopt the requisite reforms.[27]

This is clearly a concern with the Taliban, which likely uses illicitly gained opium, natural resource and foreign aid income to advance its interests. This is why it is critical to emphasise the consistency of the proposals with Islamic principles, as ideology is a central component of the Taliban's legitimacy and hence power.

In fact, in 2000, prior to the US-led invasion, the Taliban banned opium production, ostensibly due to it contravening Islamic principles.[28] While the ban was effective, it was short-lived, as the invasion led to its lifting and to the resumption of large-scale opium production. However, in 2022, the Taliban looks like it is here to stay for a long time, and so demonstrating the consistency between Islamic principles and resource curse countermeasures is potentially crucial to its success.

CONCLUSION

Like many countries that suffer from the resource curse, Afghanistan has huge economic potential that remains unrealised, to the detriment of its people. The direct economic benefits of opium, minerals and foreign aid have been swamped by their negative consequences, including poor governance, rampant corruption, endemic insecurity and violent conflict. The result is that the country has one of the lowest living standards in the world, along with a weak and ineffective government.

As the Taliban asserts its power, appealing to Islam offers a plausible – albeit still unlikely – way for Afghanistan to address its problems with the resource curse. While 21st-century Muslims might disagree with some of the policies pursued by the Taliban in the Islamic republic of Afghanistan, all Muslims should be able to agree on the need to stop exporting opium, and on the need to eliminate corruption. In this regard, positive engagement with the rest of the Islamic world might hold the most promise in rehabilitating Afghanistan's economy and transforming its natural resource wealth from a curse to a blessing.

Dr Omar Al-Ubaydli is the director of research at the Bahrain Center for Strategic, International and Energy Studies (DERASAT), and an affiliated associate professor of economics at George Mason University.

CHAPTER 9

THE VIEW FROM IRAQ

HAIDER AL-ABADI

'**S**addam Hussein will be gone within a year,' said the man in the dark suit sitting across the large mahogany table from me, as nonchalantly as if he were reporting on the weather outside. His eyes were dark and serious and his grey hair was beginning to show traces of an invasion of white, starting at the edges and working its way towards the top of his head. His flawless suit and commanding presence seemed fitting of the opulent conference room where we sat in the Dorchester Hotel in London's glitzy Mayfair district on a grey autumn day in 2002.

The man's name was Zalmay Khalilzad, an Afghan-American diplomat and senior adviser to the Bush administration on Afghanistan and the War on Terror. His latest appointment had been to the position of 'Ambassador at Large for Free Iraqis', responsible for coordinating preparations for the post-Saddam Hussein era. That was why he had come to see me.

In 1976, I left my home in Baghdad to undertake my master's degree in engineering in the United Kingdom. While I was gone, three of my brothers were jailed, tortured, and two of them murdered by the Ba'ath regime in Iraq for being members of the political opposition. In 1980, my passport was confiscated by the regime as a result of my own political activity within the student opposition movement and I became stateless. Spurred on by the vicious attacks against my family, I continued to organise in opposition to Saddam Hussein's brutality. By the time of Khalilzad's visit in 2002, I had been in exile in London for twenty-six years and was leading the Iraqi Dawa Party in the UK.

Khalilzad was searching for allies. He had requested meetings with various Iraqi opposition figures, hoping to drum up support for a US invasion that would topple Saddam Hussein. My colleagues and I within the party discussed his invitation at length, unsure of how to respond. The drums of war had grown louder and more intense throughout the year since 9/11 and it was clear some kind of military intervention in our country was on the cards. But the Americans had already had an opportunity to remove Saddam during the first Gulf War and they had stopped short, leaving tens of thousands of hopeful Iraqis to be massacred in silence when they stood up to the regime in the wake of Saddam's defeat in Kuwait. This time we were cautious, all too aware of the game-like nature of US policy in the Middle East and reluctant to become pawns in their strategy. Still, it couldn't hurt to hear what he had to say.

And so there I sat in the lavish hotel conference room alongside one of my colleagues from the party, listening as Khalilzad regaled the Bush administration's vision for a free Iraq. 'You have a window of opportunity,' he told us, 'but that window will not be open for long.' He proposed that we join an opposition movement under the umbrella of the US to topple Saddam in exchange for a stake in ruling the new, free Iraq. After the meeting, we discussed his pitch at length within the party, ultimately agreeing to politely decline his offer. Although we were eager to see the end of Saddam and the Ba'ath Party, the Americans were heading for war. Without a clear understanding of what such a war would look like, what destruction it might cause to our country and our people and what America's ultimate goals in Iraq were, we could not agree to be part of it.

The war in Afghanistan had given us hope, proving that the US was serious about getting rid of its enemies. But we remained on our guard. Iraq was not Afghanistan – although the American policy community seemed to have lost sight of that fact entirely at the time. The US invasion of Afghanistan had gone ahead with the full support of the international community. Afghanistan, after all, was a direct enemy of the US that had shocked the international community with its brutal attack on the World Trade Center. In the eyes of many around the world – and particularly those walking the corridors of power – America was within its rights to retaliate.

But Iraq was a different story. The links between al-Qaeda and Saddam were tenuous and the accusations of weapons of mass destruction shaky at best. When Khalilzad came to see us, I had no doubt the US would invade. America had demonstrated its audacity and its commitment to destroying its enemies, whatever the cost, time and again. What that invasion would look like, however, and the extent to which it would be driven by the interests of the Iraqi people as opposed to the private interests and political whims of suits in Washington, remained to be seen.

The story of what happened next has been told a thousand times, and I'm not here to repeat it. The endless cycles of violence, the pervasive corruption, the trillions of dollars wasted – all in the name of fighting terrorism. Zalmay Khalilzad himself went on to become one of the key drivers of US policy on Iraq and Afghanistan, known for his cosy relationships with controversial political figures like Ahmed Chalabi and Hamid Karzai. And almost twenty years after our meeting, he would negotiate the stunning US withdrawal from Afghanistan, leaving the country in the hands of America's sworn enemy.

Eight years ago, Iraq was heading in a similar direction. In the years since 2001, the War on Terror created more terrorists than it neutralised and recruits had flocked to Iraq to join the ranks of radical Islamist groups like al-Qaeda. The US withdrew in 2011, leaving behind a security vacuum that was exploited by terrorist groups seeking to capitalise on the chaos left behind by the occupation. After decades of dictatorship, attempted genocide, sanctions, occupation and sectarian civil war, Iraqis were about to witness yet another period of brutal violence. One that would horrify the world, bring the country to the edge of collapse and threaten to destabilise the entire region.

By the end of 2012, a group called the Islamic State in Iraq (ISI) was gaining notoriety in Iraq after launching a series of prison breaks and deadly bombings. By the middle of 2013, it had occupied many areas of the north-western Anbar and Nineveh governorates and changed its name to the Islamic State in Iraq and al-Sham (ISIS), or Daesh, to use its derogatory Arabic acronym. At the end of 2013, Fallujah fell into Daesh's hands, creating a sense of déjà vu for the Americans who had recaptured the city from insurgents less than ten years earlier. Daesh continued its rampage across the northern and western parts of Iraq throughout the following year until it controlled around 40 per cent of Iraqi territory. It was also expanding virtually unchallenged in neighbouring Syria, taking advantage of the turmoil created by the civil war.

The organisation finally captured the attention of the international community over the summer of 2014 with its brutal and well-publicised executions of foreign prisoners and so-called infidels, and the attempted genocide of the minority Yezidi community. By this point, international pundits and policymakers appeared convinced that Iraq would not survive. Some were talking about the division of the country into three parts – Sunnistan, Shiastan and Kurdistan. All were frantically trying to work out how to stop the spread of this brutal and shockingly successful terrorist organisation, which was on the verge of penetrating neighbouring countries including Jordan and Saudi Arabia, threatening the security of the entire Middle East and consequently the global order.

It was against this backdrop that I became Prime Minister of Iraq in September 2014, with the world's toughest fight on my hands. But somehow, over the course of the next three years, Iraq prevailed. The country came together to defeat this most bloodthirsty and destructive of enemies, uniting across ethnic and sectarian lines to bring our country back from the edge. Somehow Iraq, although still plagued with the problems created by decades of war, corruption and sanctions, became whole again.

As I watched the scenes unfolding in Afghanistan over the summer of 2021 – the bearded, black-clad, AK-47-wielding men rolling into cities on the back of pickup trucks; the devastated women crying into TV cameras, terrified for their lives; the desperate young men dropping from the wings of American planes in the sky like tears falling into a sea of blood – I asked myself why. The

US and its allies left a similar mess behind in Iraq. The flawed and misguided attempts to install democracy and security, the cycles of hatred and violence created by years of humiliating occupation, the spectacular political and military miscalculations, both tactical and strategic – all of these factors have existed in spades in both Iraq and Afghanistan. Why, then, has Afghanistan failed where Iraq succeeded? Why was Iraq able to be its own antidote to the poison of Daesh, while Afghanistan has never been able to rid itself of the Taliban?

Of course, many would cite the contextual differences between our two countries and between Daesh and the Taliban. But the answers to these questions do not lie entirely in these differences, nor in the specific actions – or lack thereof – of Western occupiers. These factors have played their part, but this is not the whole story. Reflecting on a term as Commander in Chief of a military that achieved a victory the world thought was impossible, I can see clearly what went wrong in Afghanistan. While Iraq, at every turn, strengthened its domestic capability and united its people in the fight against Daesh, the Afghan government has remained entirely reliant on its foreign allies. Like a child building a house of cards outdoors on a breezy day, protected from the looming winds only by the towering figure of his Uncle Sam. As soon as Uncle Sam moves, the house falls down.

• • •

One of the main thorns in the side of the so-called War on Terror, and something that remains to this day, is the failure of the West to see Iraq and Afghanistan as unique contexts. In Western media and policy discussions of the War on Terror, the words Iraq and Afghanistan are used almost interchangeably as if they were part of the same problem, two sides of the same coin. There are some similarities between us, of course, although those similarities mean more to the West than they do to Iraqis and Afghans: the majority of the population are Muslim, both countries share a border with Iran and both are home to lucrative natural resources. But we are more different than we are similar.

I could write an essay about the historical, cultural and political differences between our two countries, but that would likely take up the remainder of this chapter. The similarities between Iraq and Afghanistan are not rooted in a shared history, culture, religion or language. Even the tribal dynamics of the two countries – often cited as a legitimate reason for comparison – are not as similar as they appear. Although tribes are still present in Iraq and exert limited authority in some, mostly rural, areas, a central government has existed for a long time, even before the foundation of the modern Iraqi state a century ago, when the Ottoman Empire had a greater impact on the lives of most Iraqis than any tribal authority. In Afghanistan, this is not the case. The tribal system remains dominant, with tribal councils governing the everyday lives of Afghans in a way that has not been reflected on a large scale in Iraq for centuries.

The similarities between us come less from ourselves and more from what the West has projected onto us through their imagination of the global order and their catastrophic attempts to colonise us: recent histories of occupation; a leading role in the disastrous spectacle that was the War on Terror; the existence of extremists hell-bent on violence and willing to kill and terrorise their own people to defeat their enemies. This is the first mistake: the assumption that what works in one terrorist safe haven will work in another.

Even the Taliban and Daesh, although they share an extreme interpretation of the Sharia and equally horrific capacities for violence, are two very different beasts. Daesh by its very nature is an international, ideologically driven organisation. Its leaders, supported by its team of psychologists and technologically astute recruiters, succeeded in bringing together people from a diverse array of cultural and socio-economic backgrounds to fight under their umbrella. Under the banner of the so-called caliphate, marginalised former Iraqi Ba'athists and poor and illiterate young men from struggling North African countries like Tunisia and Egypt lived and fought alongside wealthy Emiratis and educated Europeans.

The Taliban, meanwhile, although reliant on its religious dogma for legitimacy, was and remains to this day localised by nature, hailing from a specific ethnic and tribal – namely Afghan Pashtun – background. Unlike Daesh, its ranks are not filled with soldiers from diverse backgrounds and cultures. In fact, Taliban fighters have largely failed to unite even their own fellow Afghans behind their cause, even though they share a common history and speak the same language. While Daesh focused on a global ideology that sought to establish an Islamic caliphate across the entire Middle East and remake the world order, the Taliban has focused its efforts locally, seeking instead to rewrite the history of Afghanistan in its image and avoiding confrontation with other extremist groups outside the country's borders.

This focus on a local agenda has arguably been one of its greatest strengths. Once the initial hot-blooded excitement of the War on Terror subsided and Western countries were left with blood on their hands and the immense burden of rebuilding from scratch the countries they destroyed, their interest in fighting the Taliban subsided. Why continue to pour billions of dollars into fighting an enemy that has no ambition outside of one nation? Unlike Daesh, the Taliban can be tolerated as long as it stays in its Afghan box. Afghanistan's regional neighbours have seemingly agreed for some years now. As long as the Taliban's ambitions are local and not international in nature, it is not an immediate danger to regional security and can be dealt with, pragmatically if not diplomatically. Major powers in the region like China, Pakistan and Iran all appear perfectly happy for the Taliban to rule in Afghanistan, provided it toes the line and keeps its political vision strictly focused within Afghanistan's borders.

The West's failure to understand the complex differences between Iraq and Afghanistan, along with the differences in vision between Daesh and the Taliban, go some way towards explaining why the Taliban has succeeded where Daesh failed. But this is just one piece of the puzzle. Another key reason is the failure of the US and its allies to appreciate the importance of winning the war of ideas, morals and values, as well as achieving a military victory. This is a mistake I have watched the US repeat time and again throughout my life.

As a young teenager aspiring to a career in engineering yet fascinated with politics, I used to listen to reports of the US war in Vietnam on BBC Arabic Radio from my home in Baghdad. The US seemed to be winning every military battle, yet it could not win the war. I came to realise then that all the military might in the world cannot convince a people to support you. Tanks and guns cannot persuade a population that you have their best interests at heart and that you will rule them justly and compassionately – or even that you should rule them at all. Military capabilities will never convince people that foreign powers belong in their country, choosing their politicians, profiting from their resources and shaping their futures.

From 2001 onwards I saw America make the same mistakes in Afghanistan and Iraq, throwing all the resources in the world behind a campaign that only served to radicalise and alienate local people, every day creating new iterations of the very threat it was supposed to be eliminating. The torture of prisoners by the US army has been well documented – black sites, stress positions, sleep deprivation, dehumanisation. Shock and awe were perpetrated not just against Saddam Hussein and the Taliban but against ordinary families, woken from their sleep in the middle of the night by soldiers pointing guns at their heads, turning their houses upside down and forcing them from their beds into the streets in their nightclothes. Soldiers were ordered to make their presence known, to keep people afraid and compliant. Looking back, it's easy to see how their actions perpetuated the problem, feeding the cycles of violence that would breed terror and inflict unimaginable suffering on the very people they were supposed to be liberating. This kind of behaviour will never win you a country.

Even throughout its retreat from Afghanistan, after twenty years of learning and relearning this lesson, the US seemingly remained oblivious to the importance of controlling the narrative behind its actions. It calculated its achievements in Afghanistan in purely military terms – how many troops had been trained, how many arms the Afghan army had to defend themselves against the Taliban.

Yet the US failed to realise that the very act of negotiating with the Taliban, along with its determination to stick to a strict timeline for withdrawal, sent a powerful message to the Afghan people that they were on their own. If even America was talking to the Taliban now, meeting its deadlines and respecting its legitimacy, what could the Afghan government do to protect them?

The Taliban, of course, made the most of this in its propaganda campaigns, trying to convince the Afghan people that there would be no point in resisting the regime, that its victory was inevitable. With little effort being made on the part of the US to counter this message, the country believed it, fearing the repercussions if they tried to resist. Meanwhile, the Taliban used its vast financial resources to buy over warlords and communities who saw little alternative than to accept. The number of soldiers trained, the number of weapons in the hands of the government – none of this mattered when the people already believed that their country was lost.

The US and its allies may not have learned from their own mistakes, but we in Iraq certainly did. When Daesh rolled into northern and western Iraq and established its so-called caliphate, our military crumbled in the face of the threat. Was it because Daesh was militarily more capable and better resourced? No. It was because fighters shrouded themselves in an ideologically woven façade of terror, laced with skilfully manipulated traces of Islam designed to provide religious legitimacy. Through their shocking use of violence, amplified through their savvy exploitation of internet algorithms and the media's thirst for drama, they carefully constructed the narrative that they were undefeatable.

I knew this wasn't true when I became Prime Minister in 2014. And so I set about constructing a different narrative, one based on nationalism, unity, compassion and self-reliance. I pushed back against claims made by some of my own commanders that the people living under Daesh control were terrorist sympathisers, if not terrorists themselves. I urged them to care for the people in the areas they liberated, to show them that the country had not given up on them, that we still cared and saw them as Iraqis first. Slowly, we started to see results.

It started with the sharing of meals between our soldiers and the local people in the areas they liberated from Daesh. Eventually, they were sharing not just meals but intelligence and information on Daesh tactics and locations. By bringing the people with us, by uniting them behind an idea of a country that they were a part of, we began to chip away at Daesh's claims that it was us that people needed protecting from. What had at first seemed like a tough, militarily enforced exterior turned out to be nothing more than a delicate, brittle eggshell, formed not from battle-hardened fighters and high-tech weaponry but from a brittle ideology that we had now shattered.

The idea of an Iraq that could defeat Daesh was based on unity and the idea of a shared future. But that idea had to be Iraqi at its core. We could not claim to be fighting for Iraq if we were not Iraqis fighting – of this I was sure. And so I made self-reliance a pillar of our campaign. If we relied on our allies too much, what would happen when they eventually got fed up with fighting our battles and left? Western nations' appetite for war is unreliable. It only takes one mistake, one election, one cleverly fought media battle to turn the tide. We had seen it before, most recently when the Americans left Iraq in 2011 and left behind a vacuum that was exploited by Daesh. I was not about to let it happen again.

We likely could have defeated Daesh more quickly had we relied on the superior equipment and fighting capabilities of our allies' militaries, but the victory would not have been truly Iraqi and we would have lost the narrative I was trying so hard to build, along with the hearts and minds of our people. I never asked our allies for advanced support or requested those infamous 'boots on the ground' – in fact I rejected such offers on multiple occasions. We needed to build our own capability if we wanted to achieve a victory that was truly sustainable. If we relied too heavily on the Americans or any other country, we would set ourselves up to fail.

Our allies were essential for Iraq's victory, I do not dispute that fact. They supported us from the skies, providing air cover and psychological support for our own soldiers on the ground. Instead of accepting foreign troops to do the fighting for us, we gratefully accepted training from our allies, building the capacity and experience of our own troops so that they could fight their own battles. We gladly worked alongside our regional and Western allies in the process of planning our campaign but stopped short of inviting them to fight alongside us, wary of depending too heavily on them and diminishing the 'Iraqi-ness' of our victory.

Of course, there were some areas where we could not build our capability in time. For example, there were certain intelligence capabilities that would have taken many years to develop indigenously, and certain heavy weaponry we had no means of securing. In such cases, we gladly accepted support. Our British allies conducted invaluable intelligence missions from their base in Cyprus, scanning areas such as Anbar and Nineveh from the skies and feeding back information about Daesh's activity and capabilities, which the Iraqi army could then act upon. The US, meanwhile, generously provided us with AT4 anti-tank weapons to fight back against Humvees that Daesh had fortified with tonnes of explosives to make them almost impenetrable. Examples such as these were important not only militarily but also psychologically, because they gave our troops the sense that they had what they needed to win and that the world was behind them. But I always told our commanders, if we can do it ourselves, then we should.

This, I argue, is the most important factor differentiating Iraq's victory over Daesh from Afghanistan's fall to the Taliban: in our darkest hour, Iraq stood on its own two feet. Afghanistan, meanwhile, failed to detach itself from the legacy of twenty years of reliance on the US and its allies. And so, for now at least, it seems that any hope for a free Afghanistan and a truly Afghan victory over the tyranny and extremism of the Taliban has been lost. The Afghan people are no longer reliant on the West to guarantee their futures but are instead waiting to see whether the Taliban leopard has changed its spots.

Of this, I am not so sure. Although Taliban members have learned to speak English and certainly seem more adept at using the media to get their messages across, we will have to wait and see whether their practices have truly changed. Whether we are really witnessing a Taliban 2.0 or just a carefully crafted PR campaign concealing the same beast that wreaked havoc on a nation and terrorised its people in the 1990s.

Regardless of whether their ideology and violent practices have evolved, the leadership certainly seems to have grown up somewhat. The original Taliban of the 1990s were religious students, young men filled with ideological zeal and bloodlust, searching for power to feed their hungry egos. They didn't think they needed money or international support to succeed and were genuinely surprised when large segments of the Afghan population welcomed the American intervention against them. The Taliban we are seeing today have at the very least learned from that mistake. They may not relish the idea of forming diplomatic relations with other nations and integrating themselves into the global order they so despise, but they know they cannot afford to make enemies – domestic or foreign – who might one day pose a threat to their authority.

So far, the Taliban's strategic and PR blunders have been limited. Its campaign to seize control of the country was well planned and well organised, starting by securing the borders and major roads before moving into populated towns and cities. It has allowed foreign journalists to continue to operate in Kabul, keenly aware of the importance of projecting a reformed image to the outside world. And, so far, it has mostly violent clashes and large-scale crackdowns against local populations. Even as brave groups of Afghan women have risen up to protest its rule, the Taliban has, thus far, allowed it to happen. I imagine that this in particular must have been quite conflicting for the regime. On the one hand, it goes against everything the Taliban supposedly stands for. But women's rights have become a token issue used by Western governments to justify aggression and criticise their enemies. At this early stage in the game, it seems, the Taliban leadership is being careful not to give them that opportunity.

But whether this will continue remains to be seen, and what kind of a future lies ahead for the people of the 'Islamic Emirate of Afghanistan' is unknown. Will the strategically adept and media-savvy Taliban leadership be able to control the rank and file in the less educated and heavily armed conservative, rural areas where opportunities are few and the competition for power intense? And will the women who have been allowed to protest thus far be targeted later, quietly, to frighten into submission others who might defy the Taliban?

During the days of Saddam Hussein, the Ba'ath Party would rarely crack down on protesters and regime opponents in public, refraining from spraying bullets on crowds of people and thus making it difficult for the international community to criticise their actions. If you protested against them, they would come for you later, torturing you until you broke in one of their many secret prisons and strategically leaking the excruciating details to maintain a shroud of terror and mystery that would deter others. Thousands of men and women, my brothers included, disappeared into the night, never to be seen alive again. If the Taliban decides to implement similarly clandestine counter-attacks against its opponents and critics, there will be little hope for freedom and prosperity for the Afghan people. As Iraq under Saddam clearly demonstrates, you do not have to attack Western infrastructure to pursue policies of terrorism and depravity.

If it is able to turn the page on its history of violence and oppression, however, there are arguably opportunities for the Taliban to create a more positive future for the population under its control. For example, if it is able to rein in corruption from the outset and show the people that it is pushing back against the corrupt systems and practices that have prospered in Afghanistan over the past twenty years, its hopes of building trust and support will become more tangible. It ought to turn its religious conviction away from exclusionary policies and violent inter-sect competition, and towards tackling injustice and corruption if it hopes to prove to Afghans that it can be trusted to rule.

The Taliban also has the benefit of operating a quick and efficient judicial process – which, of course, in the past has been manipulated and used as a vehicle for violence and terror. But if it harnesses these efficiencies and implements justice on a local level, it may be able to build trust among communities that have been fighting for years against the tide of bureaucracy and red tape.

If Taliban members themselves partake in corruption, however, the people will see through their fragile veil of religious legitimacy immediately, which could make things very difficult for them going forward. The leadership must make a choice to fight corruption and bureaucratic red tape from the outset and work hard to ensure this stand is being replicated by its representatives across the country.

The greatest risk for Afghanistan and the wider region going forward is the threat of terrorism – not necessarily emanating from the Taliban itself, but from other groups and organisations which will likely now feel emboldened by its victory against the global policeman that was the United States. On the one hand, the Taliban could choose to offer safe haven to such groups, which could cause problems for Afghanistan and its neighbours. On the other hand, if the Taliban refuses to align itself with other groups such as Daesh going forward, this could sow the seeds of a rift between extremists that may threaten to destabilise the entire region. A prime example is the Islamic State in Khorasan Province – also known as Daesh-K or ISKP. The Taliban and Daesh-K have been embroiled in a bloody battle that has mostly taken place behind the scenes but has at times spilled onto the streets of cities like Jalalabad. With the US gone and the Taliban in control of the country, such clashes risk sparking a greater ideological conflict between extremists. The Afghan people will inevitably suffer the consequences, and the security of the Middle East and western Asia will hang in the balance.

This in particular worries me, having witnessed first-hand in Iraq Daesh's potential for ruthless destruction. The terror inflicted by non-Arabic-speaking extremists – as Daesh's foreign cadre clearly showed – can be much worse than that inflicted by Arabic speakers. I don't wish to diminish the horrors perpetrated by Arab terrorists in the name of Islam, merely to point out the heightened potential for misunderstanding and manipulation of the words of the Quran when you don't understand the nuances of the language it was written in. A battle of non-Arabic ideologies in Afghanistan could lead to a humanitarian catastrophe and inflict terror worse than even Daesh in Iraq was willing and able to inflict.

The people of Afghanistan – and indeed Iraq, in the event of a regional spillover – have witnessed enough terror and bloodshed to last many lifetimes. When I think back to that autumn day in London, sitting with Khalilzad in the Dorchester, I feel foolish when I remember the sense of cautious optimism I felt when he talked about removing Saddam Hussein. That image seems somewhat of a cliché now – the sharply dressed American politician speaking confidently (some would say arrogantly) about bringing freedom and democracy to the Middle East from the comfort of his five-star hotel. Such encounters likely became routine for Khalilzad, an expert negotiator and famous pragmatist. I imagine the

Khalilzad of 2022 repeating this performance in not too dissimilar five-star hotel conference rooms, these days in Doha, sitting across from Taliban leaders instead of Iraqi opposition figures. I wonder whether he ever gets déjà vu.

Dr Haider al-Abadi was Prime Minister of Iraq from 2014 until 2018. He led the country's successful military campaign against Daesh as Commander-in-Chief.

CHAPTER 10

HOSTILE TAKEOVER OF AFGHANISTAN – REGIONAL APPROACH AND INDIA'S CONCERNS

ARUN SAHGAL AND SHREYAS DESHMUKH

INTRODUCTION

In over two decades of Afghanistan's democratic experiment, India has been an integral part of the country's steady progress in institutionalising peace, pluralism and prosperity. Ties between Afghanistan and India go beyond the government-to-government interactions; people of both countries have interacted with each other through trade and commerce over centuries. Both share cultural values, which laid the foundation of deep mutual trust.

From the Indian perspective, the Taliban military victory, without any terms of power, has created a political and administrative vacuum. This is exacerbated by inter-factional rivalries, a deteriorating economic situation and a huge sense of despondency.

From the Indian geopolitical context, the emergence of the Taliban-dominated state of Afghanistan on India's western continental arc – which is already dominated by two hostile neighbours acting in collusion – poses a major strategic challenge. This is exacerbated by a Pakistan-sponsored proxy war. Statements coming from the present Haqqani-dominated pro-Pakistan Taliban regime are a source of concern and provide a warning about the regional appropriation by radical forces which will have a negative impact on India's external and internal security. There is no doubt that, for India, the Taliban's military victory and creation of an Islamic emirate is an adverse and inimical development.

BACKDROP

In a span of over a hundred years, Afghanistan has experienced multiple governance models. These models have invariably sparked new ideological conflicts in the country and stirred geopolitical competition among its neighbours. Today, Afghanistan continues to bear the weight of its geographical position.

In the first Great Game, Afghanistan was seen as a buffer state by both Tsarist Russia and the British Empire. The second time, Afghanistan's strategic space was contested during the Cold War through the proxies of the United States and the Soviet Union. As a consequence, Afghanistan became a sanctuary for militancy and global jihad resulting in 9/11 and the global War on Terror. The US withdrawal from Afghanistan for the first time in decades has resulted in the removal of the footprint of foreign forces leading to a strategic vacuum culminating in the creation of the Islamic Emirate of Afghanistan.

The United States has done a complete circle in the two decades of war in Afghanistan. It started by defeating global jihad and its support base (including the Taliban) that provided them sanctuary. In February 2020, under duress and fatigue of the long war, it negotiated a patently one-sided settlement with the Taliban. The Doha Agreement provided legitimacy to the Taliban, despite being a banned organisation, and assured the release of thousands of incarcerated fighters when the war was at a critical juncture. The Taliban made few concessions, the most important being ceasing hostilities against the US and the coalition forces. The Taliban never really stopped operations against Afghan security forces, which were largely carried out through proxies such as ISIS and IS-K. Even its joining of the intra-Afghan dialogue was largely notional and demand-driven, aimed at stalling the process.[1] This led to the collapse of Ashraf Ghani's democratically elected regime, a meltdown of the Afghan National Defense and Security Forces and eventually the country falling into the Taliban's lap.

The Taliban offensive of August 2021, which was comparable to that of conventional military operations, demonstrates the rebel group's extensive planning and preparation for the campaign. In its fight against the Taliban, the Afghan government and the NATO coalition forces strongly relied on Special Forces and air support throughout. This was contrary to the lessons learned from most counter-intelligence and counter-terrorism operations, which suggest the centrality of ground holding, creating a counter-insurgency grid and seeking out insurgents through cordon and search operations. The criticality of this strategy was area domination and winning the hearts and minds of the local population through effective local governance. This not only deters insurgents but boosts the confidence of people in the government's capabilities to provide succour and security. These are important lessons that India has learned in its decades of counter-insurgency and low-intensity operations.

In the case of Afghanistan, the actual fighting strength of the Afghan National Army (ANA) was much lesser than the numbers projected.[2] To add to its woes, there was institutional corruption in the higher echelons of the Afghan security system, which was repeatedly highlighted in the reports from the Special Inspector General for Afghanistan Reconstruction. The structural weaknesses and lack of experienced leadership in the Afghan National Security Forces also contributed to the rapid fall.

The Taliban took over Afghanistan without ceding any of its extremist characteristics, implying that its curated geopolitical journey would not have been possible without covert support from other states. The hasty withdrawal of coalition forces, whose timelines were dictated by the Taliban, has been a great blow to US prestige. Consequently, the US has no footprint in the Eurasian heartland, and it is two contending coalitions – China with Pakistan, and Russia with the central Asian republics (Tajikistan and Uzbekistan) and Iran – which are shaping the narrative not only in Afghanistan but throughout continental Asia. These developments have serious geopolitical ramifications not only for the Afghanistan–Pakistan region but globally.

REGIONAL PERSPECTIVE

Countries in the region are worried about whether the withdrawal of foreign troops will lead to another cycle of violent extremism from the Taliban. Developments in Afghanistan are also affecting regional security strategies. Some of these include strengthening the Sino–Pak nexus, firming up Russian influence in the central Asian republics through the Collective Security Treaty Organization (CSTO), increasing Iranian salience and boosting the importance of west Asian countries as honest brokers in conflict resolution. These realignments are being driven by the common threat of terrorism and the possible rise of radical Islamist forces in the area. Despite recognition of the challenge, there still appears to be no coordinated approach or attempt to shape a common regional strategy.

The distinctiveness of India's policy towards Afghanistan, which goes beyond geopolitical considerations, has been a major stability factor for its north-west neighbour. Indian leadership has always promoted political stability in Afghanistan and consistently used soft power, diplomacy and economic assistance to achieve this purpose. During the Cold War era, both the Soviets and the Americans appreciated India's efforts in supporting Afghanistan's stability, wherein India played the role of the honest broker to end the Afghan conundrum.[3]

Later, post-9/11, India continued the same policy in Afghanistan and invested in infrastructure, social development and people-to-people contact, providing much-needed reconstruction and development assistance, including medical facilities. In an important difference from other international aid and humanitarian agencies, India routed all its assistance through the official channels of the Afghan government. In the present context, while the Taliban take-over remains a political impediment, it is equally proof that India did not invest in the regional geopolitical competition, but rather stayed away. Only time will tell the effectiveness of India's stance on Afghanistan.

PAKISTAN

Historically, Pakistan invested in a weak Afghanistan for multiple reasons: a colonial legacy of the disputed nature of the Durand Line,[4] ethnic Pashtun nationalism transcending borders[5] and an obsession with 'strategic depth'.[6] Pakistan's strategy in Afghanistan – such as supporting the Mujahideen during the Cold War, backing the Taliban during the Civil War and providing a safe haven and logistical support for the past two decades – was all aimed at turning Afghanistan into an ideological 'client' state that serves its strategic interest. The dubious role of Pakistan was always recognised but seldom countered. Instead, it was drafted as a firm base for operations against the Taliban and subsequently the main conduit for political negotiations. With the United States' adversarial relations with Iran, and central Asian states like Uzbekistan and Tajikistan being landlocked, Pakistan, with its seaports and a logistic corridor, became the country of choice for supporting US and NATO forces' operations in Afghanistan. A there-is-no-alternative (TINA) factor operated which Pakistan exploited to the hilt, resulting in the US providing over $34 billion in aid, assistance and equipment for counter-terrorism operations.[7]

After the Osama bin Laden episode, there is no doubt that the US administration started to become aware and critical of Pakistan's intentions with regard to its counter-terrorism policies. Nonetheless, the US endured Pakistan's political engagement to bring the Taliban to the negotiating table for a conciliatory ending to the long-drawn-out war in Afghanistan. A process which was initiated during President Obama's administration in 2013–14 culminated in the Doha Agreement of 2020. Subsequently, the Taliban, with the support of the Pakistani military and its intelligence agency (ISI), crossed the threshold from being a disparate insurgent group to a credible military and political force, driving the US to sign a practically one-sided peace deal. The result was that, given the US's core dependency on Pakistan, the country once again emerged from the margins and became the centrepiece of the US's exit strategy.

The piling sovereign debt, poor economic performance, rising domestic extremism, international criticism and political pressure from the West over Afghanistan had pushed Pakistan to a place where it could not have sustained the international pressure much longer. The Taliban's swift victory in August 2021 was a lifeline that brought Pakistan to the centre stage, making it a primary arbitrator in the political resolution of the Afghanistan imbroglio. This is apparent in how Pakistan has become the focal point of the evolving multinational strategy comprising China, Russia and the US in shaping the regional consensus on Afghanistan, including intelligence coordination. Despite this, developments in Afghanistan are not particularly comfortable for Pakistan.

A major Pakistani concern relates to a Pashtun-dominated Taliban and the possibility of Pashtun nationalism extending across the Durand Line and further up the Indus River. It is for this reason the ISI supported the Pashtun Haqqani network, and Hizb-e-Wilayat, to restrain the fires of nationalism west of the Durand Line and its eventual fencing. Further, by installing the Haqqani network as the dominant group in the interim Taliban government, Pakistan has de facto extended its influence into Afghanistan.

Moreover, to stop the spread of Pashtun nationalism internally, Pakistan has adopted a hard line towards the Tehrik-i-Taliban

Pakistan (TTP), while supporting Pashtun nationalist forces in Afghanistan. The aim is to ensure that the TTP is subjugated to accepting Punjabi hegemony and curtailing its anti-national activities.

It is surprising that, despite Pakistan's apparent duplicity in shaping the regional narrative, Washington continues to harp on about Pakistan as the TINA factor with no option other than doing business with the Pakistani establishment, including attempts to secure bases for over-the-horizon interventions.

CHINA

Amid the hostility between Pakistan and the former Afghan leadership, China preferred to deal directly with the latter.[8] Chinese concerns are different and diverse from those of Pakistan and other state actors. They relate to direct threats from radical Islamist and terrorist groups such as the East Turkestan Islamic Movement (ETIM), the Islamic Movement of Uzbekistan and others supported by IS-K, particularly their influence in the Wakhan Corridor, a narrow strip of Afghan land bordering China.

In 2012, during President Hamid Karzai's visit to Beijing, President Hu Jintao proposed a strategic cooperative partnership with Afghanistan. The joint declaration indicated that China was reluctant to invest in the unstable country.[9] In 2014, Foreign Minister Wang Yi travelled to Afghanistan. It was the last such visit of a senior Chinese official to the country. The trip marked a shift in China's Afghan policy as it coincided with the announcement of the US's time-based approach for the withdrawal of its troops. In the following months, China actively established contact with the Taliban and Afghan leadership and started taking interest in the reconciliation process.[10] The first round of the China–Pakistan–Afghanistan Trilateral Strategic Dialogue was held in February 2015.[11] It was clear then that China was channelling its Afghan policy through Pakistan.[12]

With the installation of an interim Taliban government in Afghanistan, China's political overtures have intensified. China's enhanced outreach is intended to secure Xinjiang from the extremist influence of outfits like the ETIM and to enhance regional connectivity. China is keen to leverage the Taliban government in Afghanistan to 'link up' through multifaceted continental connectivity. Afghanistan's extensive mineral deposits, said to be in the region of some $3 trillion, also provide a compelling rationale.

Consequently, China is busy enhancing its somewhat modest profile. To deal with the looming humanitarian crisis, it extended a $31 million emergency aid package to the interim Afghan government the day after its formation.[13] Following the US withdrawal, the Taliban sees China as the only country that can help in Afghanistan with the reconstruction and the mounting humanitarian challenges.[14] It has expressed willingness to receive help under the Belt and Road Initiative, allowing China to undertake strategic connectivity projects.[15] China is also all set to establish an industry platform in Kabul to explore possible investments and reconstruction efforts.[16]

In the international arena, China has been the chief spokesperson of the Islamic Emirate of Afghanistan for lifting sanctions and restoring $9.5 billion in frozen assets belonging to Afghanistan's central bank.[17] The US had frozen these assets and stopped shipments of cash to prevent the Taliban government from accessing the money as the Taliban had already been warned that taking power by force would result in a cut to non-humanitarian aid.[18]

Furthermore, the Chinese have been eyeing the Bagram airbase (formerly the largest US military base in Afghanistan)[19] in a move largely seen as an attempt to set up an intelligence and monitoring facility in Afghanistan, in collaboration with Pakistan.[20] This development has profound security implications for India and other regional actors, including the US.

Besides the above, there are other trends suggesting that a new Great Game is brewing in the region,[21] foremost being China and Pakistan's joint push for influence. Russia, on the other hand, has of late hardened its position on the Taliban and is unwilling to recognise the interim government, while maintaining efforts at forcing the Taliban to a more inclusive agenda, addressing women's and human rights, as well as greater say for ethnic minorities. Russia no longer calls the Taliban 'terrorists', having replaced the term with 'radicals'. Iran, too, is concerned over increasing attacks on Shias and the treatment of Hazaras. It has presented peace overtures by offering to open borders with Afghanistan for trade and negotiations with Pakistan to rein in the Taliban government. Iran is also concerned about the activities of IS-K and developments in the Panjshir valley.[22]

From a broader Chinese strategic perspective, the US withdrawal has created a vacuum in its backyard which is too important to ignore. China is unlikely to invest in Afghanistan in any significant way until it perceives stability, a capacity to govern and, above all, a wider recognition of an all-inclusive government. In addition, China is likely to seek guarantees against the use of Afghan territory as a launchpad by global jihadi forces like IS-K, al-Qaeda and others operating in this area and see the installation of the Taliban as the first step in the eventual creation of a 'caliphate'. How the Taliban manages these dichotomies against the backdrop of its strong Islamist moorings will be an important test of its intentions and capabilities.

Importantly, there are differences in perceptions between China and Pakistan over the future of the Taliban state. China believes a more moderate and inclusive Afghanistan is important for regional stability, while Pakistan's desire is for a Pashtun-dominated governance structure (via the Haqqani network) that keeps ethnic minorities on the margins of the governance.

It is important to underscore that China looks at Afghanistan from the multiple prisms of regional stability, connectivity and dominance. It perceives Afghanistan as a fulcrum connecting south-central Asia, whose dominance is of strategic importance. It also helps in isolating India's continental interests in the West.

RUSSIA, THE CENTRAL ASIAN REPUBLICS AND IRAN

Post-9/11, Russia took the lead on cooperating with the US on Afghanistan. The countries established a joint working group to counter the extremist threats,[23] which was later named the US–Russia Working Group on Counterterrorism.[24]

Even though Russia did not have a cordial relation with the Taliban, Moscow has always called for an inclusive peace dialogue, taking the moderate elements of the Taliban on board. The Russian perspective was driven by the increasing cross-border influence of Islamist forces – in particular, Salafi Islam, which influenced IS-K – forcing the country to reach out to the Taliban. Despite this, Russia also continually blamed the US for the inception of the Taliban but backed a UN-sponsored solution for Afghanistan under a UN Security Council mandate.[25] In an October 2003 interview, the deputy foreign minister of Russia stated, 'Those who used to flirt with the Afghan Taliban have now recognised their links to Al-Qaeda.'[26]

The prolongation of the US operations in Afghanistan, however, did serve as a wake-up call for Russia regarding its own intentions against the backdrop of changing geopolitical situations in eastern Europe, western Asia and northern Africa where both countries have been confronting each other. In 2015, Russia closed access to the northern supply route for NATO's Afghan mission and started demanding the complete withdrawal of troops.[27] These hostilities reached a new level by 2021 where the US blamed Russian agencies for putting bounties on American soldiers in Afghanistan.[28] Russia views the withdrawal of the US and Western coalition forces from Afghanistan as the defeat of its arch enemy, NATO. Post-Taliban takeover, the Russian foreign minister in a press conference chiding NATO said, it 'has to take a more adequate, objective look at the situation with a dose of self-criticism'.[29]

Nonetheless, from the Russian perspective, the US withdrawal in no way mitigated its regional concerns such as narcotic production and distribution and the consolidation of al-Qaeda and others such as IS-K. Further, Russia is not keen on ceding space to China. Therefore, Russia is focused more on a collaborative approach such as strengthening multilateral grouping and extending the troika by the inclusion of India and Iran.[30] The first international consultation after the takeover of Afghanistan that the Taliban attended was the 'Moscow format', during which Russia gave mixed signals.[31] It did not rush to fill the void after the US exit but did not want to leave space for other powers.

Meanwhile, the former Soviet republics of Tajikistan, Uzbekistan and Turkmenistan not only share a border with Afghanistan but are also influential ethnic affinities. All these countries have different levels of engagement with the Taliban. In the past, Turkmenistan engaged with the Taliban on the bilateral level while Uzbekistan actively participated in the multilateral Afghan reconciliation process. Earlier, Tajikistan cooperated closely with the anti-Taliban Northern Alliance, led by an ethnic Tajik-Afghan leader, Ahmad Shah Massoud. As a member of the Russia-led military alliance CSTO, Tajikistan is the only country from the region which has been highly critical of the 2021 Taliban takeover. Further highlighting its stance, Tajikistan awarded posthumously the country's third-highest honour to Ahmad Shah Massoud and Burhanuddin Rabbani in September 2021.[32] Russia has maintained a large military base in Tajikistan, increased the supply of military hardware to the central Asian republics and conducted a series of joint military exercises on the Afghan border after the Taliban takeover. The security interests of these three central Asian countries are aligned with Russia. The situation in Afghanistan is also helping Russia to increase its footprint in the central Asian region to balance China's recent economic expansion in its area of traditional dominance.

In the past decade, Iran and Russia have taken a tactical approach while dealing with the Taliban. Iran's primary interest in Afghanistan is the protection of the Shia Hazara minority from the threat of Sunni extremists. The Fatemiyoun Brigade, formed by Hazara migrants from Afghanistan, has helped Iran to fight against ISIS in Iraq and Syria. Many of these battle-hardened fighters have returned to Afghanistan, and Iran can use them to protect its interests in the future.

Iran also joined the Shanghai Cooperation Organisation (SCO) as a full member during the twenty-first meeting of the Council of Heads of State in Dushanbe in September 2021. The China–Iran strategic agreement of March 2021, no progress on the Joint Comprehensive Plan of Action and reduced US footprint in Eurasia have probably pushed Iran to deepen its engagement with its neighbours. Any instability in Afghanistan could threaten Iran's interests as it tries to evade the cycle of US sanctions. Meanwhile, it may not give up the issue of equal rights for the Hazaras, like Tajikistan continues to fight for the Tajiks of Afghanistan.

INDIAN STAKES IN AFGHANISTAN

Since the fall of the Taliban regime in 2001, India has committed humanitarian and development assistance of over $3 billion, under which more than 500 infrastructure and development projects have been completed in Afghanistan.[33] India always supported the political solution for Afghanistan, but its ideas of a political solution and the Taliban as a political force were different from other regional countries. India has sought inclusivity, rights for women and grass-roots social contact for the development of Afghanistan.

After the opening of the Taliban office in Qatar in June 2013, the Indian foreign ministry's statement read, 'The reconciliation process should not seek to create equivalence between an internationally recognised Government of Afghanistan and insurgent groups.'[34] India's stand was based on the fact that besides the US, which is an external power, regional actors like China, Pakistan and Russia provided legitimacy to the Taliban by directly engaging with it while eroding the credibility and confidence of the democratically elected Afghan government. In his speech at the Ministerial

Conference of the Heart of Asia – Istanbul Process in March 2021, India's foreign minister highlighted that conferring legitimacy or sanctions required a collective approach: 'Collective success may not be easy, but the alternative is only collective failure.'[35]

Axiomatically, the same countries which engaged with the Taliban are now asking for the release of international assistance to Afghanistan as the humanitarian crisis is exacerbated by the failing economy and the heightened risk of terrorism. The reality is that the Taliban-led interim government has little accountability towards the people and continues to rule by fiats.[36]

India's idea of positive peace has a more plurilateral approach as it talks about 'double peace' – that is, peace within Afghanistan and peace around Afghanistan, but not without accountability. Therefore, unlike China and Pakistan, which have already started providing aid to Afghanistan, India has called on a fair distribution of aid to all Afghans, with its foreign minister saying, 'It is therefore essential that humanitarian assistance providers are accorded unimpeded, unrestricted and direct access to Afghanistan.'[37]

In the past two decades, India has invested political and economic capital to operationalise the North-South Transport Corridor, of which the Chabahar port in Iran is a vital connector. However, the Taliban takeover has reignited India's concerns regarding the impact of the change of the guard in Kabul on regional prosperity, which is linked with security. Under the previous Taliban regime, anti-Indian terrorist organisations like Lashkar-e-Taiba used al-Qaeda infrastructure to train their cadres similar to the China-centric ETIM, the Russia-centric Chechen groups and now Daesh's Khorasan chapter, which are threatening the whole region. The refugee issue, the drugs trade, the geopolitical competition to fill the political void left by the US and the smuggling of small arms are some other concerns India shares with regional partners.

Unlike other countries, India maintained its strategic autonomy in Afghanistan. In the past, India worked with Russia, Iran, China and the US. In the new geopolitical realities, the Sino–Pak nexus seems dominant, Russia and Iran are on the defensive and Turkey and Qatar are trying to leverage relations with the Taliban while the US, Europe and Japan still hold economic and political leverage. In these equations, the most suitable approach for India is to work with its Quadrilateral Security Dialogue partners – the US, Japan and Australia – which still have substantial stakes in Afghanistan as major aid-providing nations. As a member of the SCO, India can also keep a check on the extremists' activities in Afghanistan through the Regional Anti-Terrorist Structure in cooperation with Russia and Iran. Russia is also pushing to include India and Iran in the extended troika on Afghanistan. Importantly, India has maintained an airbase in Farkhor, Tajikistan, and jointly operates Ayni Air Force Base with the Tajik Air Force. The operational use of Ayni in emergencies was proved during the evacuations of Indian and other foreign nationals after the fall of Kabul in August 2021.[38] No doubt the recent events in Afghanistan are a setback for India, however, the country is diplomatically and militarily more capable than it was in the '90s to protect its national interests, work with like-minded partners to build regional consensus and support Afghanistan with humanitarian efforts and relief. India has offered to supply 50,000 metric tonnes of wheat to meet the country's immediate requirements.

One of the important challenges that concerns India is the possible leveraging of extremists released from Afghanistan jails to vitiate the situation in Jammu and Kashmir. This is apparent from the sudden spike in attacks and the killing of minorities in the Kashmir valley and infiltration attempts. India cannot allow these forces to destroy its internal security or reverse the development process in the union territory of Jammu and Kashmir. While India is keen to stabilise and normalise its relations with both Afghanistan and Pakistan, it cannot countenance the use of terror or proxy war. Should such a situation come to pass, India will have little option but to take all actions to preserve its national interests. From the Indian perspective, the following two plausible scenarios will drive the Indian regional strategy moving forward:

1. The descent into chaos, resulting in a major humanitarian crisis, the rise of radicalism and the Taliban using punishing and cruel methods. Essentially, rule by the gun. The driver of this scenario will be the Taliban's self-perceived invincibility, having defeated two major powers.
2. A gradual shift to a more inclusive model of governance. The issue here will be dissensions within i.e. between hard-line and moderate factions and the role and leverage of regional players. Societal pressure, humanitarian disaster and the need for international support may also tilt the Taliban towards moderation.

CONCLUSION

The new phase of political developments in Afghanistan comes in the wake of growing intensity and US–China confrontation. Recent interaction between the US and China underscores differing perspectives and the hardening of attitudes. While the US is keen on China stepping in and stabilising the situation in Afghanistan, a euphemism for preventing the rise of extremist forces, China is not interested in piecemeal engagement but a composite deal that addresses Chinese concerns in their entirety.[39]

The fall of Kabul has raised questions over the role of superpowers in the global system. The world witnessed, on the one hand, the US choosing once again its own interest over the so-called ideals of human rights and liberalism, and on the other, Russia and China's unwillingness to impose any moral conditions on the Taliban. The insurgent group too cannot escape from the dilemma of politics vs ideology when governing. For example, the Taliban focused on building close cooperation with China while neglecting the Uyghur issue. It is also seeking international legitimacy promising cooperation with Russia, the US and other Western countries against which it declared jihad for almost three decades. The current Taliban regime is trying to manage in the geopolitically contested world order between China and the US. The group has taken power on a very different turf from when they first took control of Afghanistan in the '90s. Managing this contestation will be the real test for the Taliban in which it might lose some ideological space to other extremist organisations like IS-K, providing a fillip to extremist forces.

After twenty years of sustained insurgency, despite the ideological challenges, the Taliban will not promulgate its win over the superpower but will try to cooperate with the West, China and other regional countries, at least in the short term, to secure its hold on the country. Inclusivity and coercion are the two methods it has in hand. If it adopts inclusivity, then it will end the sole purpose of the implementation of its interpretation of Sharia, and infighting among moderate and hardliners will factionalise and weaken the

Taliban, resulting in the possible collapse of the regime. Alternately, the use of coercion will increase the ethnic divisions within the country and end in another civil war. A stable Afghanistan under the Taliban is the most unlikely scenario. The core issue is: will the chaos be contained within Afghan borders or spill over outside, threatening regional and global security? This is the common concern of all countries, including India. Therefore, more than the Taliban, regional countries require inclusivity in their approach, or they should prepare to face 'collective failure'.

Dr Arun Sahgal is the director of the Forum for Strategic Initiatives, the founding director of the Office of Net Assessment, Indian Integrated Defence Staff, and senior fellow of Delhi Policy Group.

Shreyas Deshmukh is a research associate at Delhi Policy Group. Prior to joining DPG, he worked with MitKat Advisory Services as a geopolitical risk analyst.

CHAPTER 11

'NO END OF A LESSON': THE END OF LIBERAL INTERNATIONALISM AND THE NEW ISOLATIONISM

BRIAN BRIVATI

Sir Anthony Nutting was a minister in Eden's government when it launched and rapidly retreated from its disastrous attack on Nasser's Egypt. When he came to write his account of the crisis, he hit upon one of the most accurate book titles of all time. Suez was indeed 'no end of a lesson'.[1] It seems appropriate to apply that title to the debacle in Afghanistan as the 'forever war' comes to an end. The questions now are what lessons will the West take away from this experience and what does it tell us about the state of geopolitics? The most important issue raised is the welfare and future of the Afghan people, but in addition to that overriding humanitarian concern there are three changing areas of global politics that are reflected in what happened and how it happened. First, the context in which these events have unfolded tells us about the nature of contemporary state sovereignty. Second, these events are going to change the future of peace processes. Third, the end of liberal internationalism and the rise of the new isolationism based on what I call a 'siloed world' have important implications for the future of international law and international organisations.

The Suez crisis proved to be a turning point in post-Second World War British foreign policy and marked the moment at which it was revealed to the British establishment – perhaps the last group of people on the planet to need this reality revealed to them – that Britain could not act with impunity. It is one of the more significant benchmark moments in the decline of the British imperial dream. A dream that had been clung to even after the independence of India and the cost of the world war made the maintenance of empire impossible. It is now joined, for our age, by the fall of Kabul as a moment of reckoning and revelation of a new reality. During the evacuation of Kabul, as at Suez, British armed forces were asked to perform miracles. Kabul showed the UK military at their best, but asked to do the impossible, they naturally failed and thousands were left behind to an uncertain fate at the hands of the Taliban. The complete absence of influence by the post-Brexit UK government on the decision-making that made the evacuation inevitable showed that the UK's influence and status is at its lowest point since the immediate aftermath of the Suez crisis. If, indeed, in geopolitical terms the UK ever really did recover from the humiliation of Suez, it took at least a decade. It will now take decades to come back from what happened in August. Above and beyond the reputation of the UK, what has been destroyed is the possibility of an alternative foreign policy – new ways of managing conflicts, based on the principles that had painfully advanced since the end of the twentieth century, have been undermined. This matters much more than the self-image of the UK establishment because what we have lost is the ability to defend the undefended, protect citizens against their own states and hold perpetrators to account for their actions. For all the flaws of the liberal internationalist moment, these are the things that were being attempted. Instead of a rule-bound international system, what now dominates is a new isolationism which puts at risk the independence of multiple states which might have once hoped for the protection of the international community – for example, Ukraine and the Baltic states in relation to Russia. It also puts at risk minority ethnic groups who face genocide as states act against them with impunity – for example, the unfolding genocidal project against the Uyghurs in China. These states and vulnerable groups within other states now know not to expect help because the fall of Kabul is the latest but not the last instalment of the creation of a new world order based on the 'Trump doctrine'. A doctrine encapsulated in the quote from *The Wizard of Oz* that he used in a 2017 speech: 'There is no place like home.'[2] This means a world order founded on what the philosopher Norman Geras, in the context of the Holocaust, termed the contract of mutual indifference.[3]

We live in a tri-superpower world system and these powers have agreed a contract of mutual indifference with each other – each to do as they like within their own silos of influence. The basis of the Trump doctrine is the acceptance that the world is divided into these silos of impunity in which dominant states determine their own rules in their own spaces and against the enemies that they define. Their actions are defined solely by their interests. The evolution of a universal system of international law through forms of legal globalisation is dead: international law is becoming increasingly redundant and appears ever more outdated. Global institutions are increasingly irrelevant compared with national sovereignty. Russia and China are two of the superpower silos. The declining EU remains an island of law outside the tri-superpowers' silos, but with Merkel gone and Russia pressing on the borders of our near neighbours to get their pipeline, for how long can the EU hold? We are only beginning to understand the extent to which Merkel has managed to keep the lid on the cross-cutting problems of Europe and its near neighbours. It is not a coincidence that at the time of writing Putin is working on manoeuvres threatening the Baltics and Ukraine as Merkel hands over to her successor, with the authority of Germany and therefore of the EU seeping away. The UK has been swimming towards impunity as fast as it can because its recent governments seem to believe that international law is an impediment to foreign trade so they need to override these laws by the assertion of sovereignty. The UK is in danger of drowning in its own irrelevance because there is no one else inside its Brexit-made silo. The US under Donald Trump was fast becoming a third silo outside the norms of international law and practice. Perhaps Biden can change course, but the US President's decision to honour the deal made by his predecessor to end US involvement in Afghanistan and scuttle the NATO intervention does not bode well. The decision by the US President, once known as the leader of the free world, to cut and run from Afghanistan was not a military failure – it was a political, moral and strategic failure that was based on Biden's acceptance of the Trump doctrine where it mattered most in the contested lands between the superpower silos. Letting Kabul fall was one of many decisions derived from that doctrine that are reshaping our world and that have rendered the notion of ethical or norm-based foreign policies redundant. The idealist conception of a foreign policy informed by law and ethics now looks unobtainable. The realists have not only won but they have destroyed the shaky framework for an alternative architecture for managing the relations between states. Trumpian realists have also killed the interventionist principle that states could not act with impunity against their own people or the people of other states. This had been tentatively constructed at the cost of tens of thousands of lives in multiple interventions since the end of the twentieth century. What might have become a global social contract has been replaced by the state of nature in which we now live. A state of nature in which the war of all against all is the only meaningful international norm. The contract of mutual indifference requires the great powers to look the other way when necessary, and that is exactly what Biden did in Kabul in August.

In the manner of its ending, the NATO mission has also undermined decades of work in peace process design and implementation. Peace is famously much more than the absence of war: where once conflict resolution and conflict management focused solely on ending military violence, since the 1990s there have been major shifts in approaches to peacebuilding. Mary Anderson's seminal work *Do No Harm: How Aid Can Support Peace – or War*,[4] in particular, changed the terms of discourse in peace making by stressing the role of external actors in creating the conditions for peace and arguing for social and economic factors to be central to the peacebuilding process. There was none of this in the endgame of Kabul; it was purely the expression of superpower interests and a political negotiation process that was based solely on a deal between the US and one party to the internal conflict in Afghanistan: the Taliban.

This was not an inclusive peace process; it was the opposite – it was an exclusive elite bargain. It was the Trump doctrine in action. In this instance, the US was the dominant external actor that had been instrumental in the defeat of the Taliban twenty years before and had been fighting them intermittently ever since. That external actor simply handed the country back to the defeated enemy. It was reminiscent of a Cold War deal in which the will of the people was irrelevant to the process of the superpower getting what it wanted. Or perhaps the better analogy is that Afghanistan suffered the same fate as the victims of Yalta and Potsdam at the end of the Second World War when millions of people and entire states were shuffled from the free world to the totalitarian world of Stalin's Russia with no reference to their wishes. Afghanistan was shuffled from the US silo to the Chinese silo under the close direction of Pakistan.

The Cold War analogy is, however, problematic. The world of silos of sovereign impunity maintained by contracts of mutual in-difference is different to the bipolar world of the Cold War. There are more actors with more equal or different sources of power in play. Two other global actors can compete with the US for hegem-ony – Russian and China – and other powers are approaching re-gional hegemony in their own often volatile neighbourhoods, for example Turkey. Within the silos, there is a twin track of sovereign-ty. The dominant power has a kind of operational sovereignty. This is not totalitarianism, but it is the power to ensure that nothing of importance, like joining a regional economic association, can take place without permission. This means that the subject states, like Ukraine, Pakistan and much of central Asia, have an increasing-ly diluted sovereignty. Afghanistan now joins those states whose autonomy is heavily restricted and whose sovereignty exists more on paper than in fact.

To understand this new reality, you need to look closely at who is going to benefit from the natural resources of Afghanistan under the regime of the Taliban. The answer will be the Chinese. Here, as in many African and central Asian states, the Chinese will control resources and the Belt and Road Initiative will build and control the infrastructure. China has been preparing for this for a long time. Afghanistan is, of course, landlocked. The dry route to China is through a 47-mile stretch of border which is mountainous. The nearest deep-water port, Gwadar, was built by the Chinese on the coast of Pakistan and the roads connecting this port to China are already constructed. In other words, much of the infrastructure for the Chinese economic control of Afghanistan is in place. This infrastructure will allow the Chinese to control and extract the natural resources of Afghanistan using predominately their own facilities and thereby bypassing making a contribution to the development of the Afghan economy. This was exactly the same way that Gwadar itself was built and it is one of the major sources of the unpopularity of the development in this region of Pakistan. The Taliban leadership will, of course, benefit financially from the relationship, but the direct extraction of the economic wealth of the country will dilute to the point of irrelevance the idea of Afghan sovereignty.

It is not only peace processes and sovereignty that have been undermined or perhaps rendered obsolete by this way of deciding the fate of nations and their people. What emerged from the debates raised by Anderson's book was a liberal interventionist approach to conflict: military intervention with the aim of the protection of people and the implementation of UN resolutions. These developments culminated in the Responsibility to Protect Resolution, endorsed by all United Nations member states in 2005, the aim of which was to prevent genocide, war crimes, ethnic cleansing and crimes against humanity. After that resolution, there was, for a time, a marked shift in approaches to conflict transformation, a movement from a peacebuilding-centred model, in which the aim was to stop the killing, towards concepts of prevention by intervention, resilience-building, sustainable peace and inclusive peace processes, in which the aim was to stop the killing and to try to address the reason that the killing was taking place. Alongside the development of responsibility to protect, this liberal internationalist philosophy provided the political will to attempt to make the content of United Nations resolutions more than just the path of good intentions that paves the road to hell. In essence, they need the willingness to intervene to be meaningful.

The political journey of my generation of liberal internationalists began with Tony Blair's Chicago speech, in which he articulated the vision of an end to the appeasement of oppressive regimes when it was in the national interest, and ended with Joe Biden's address, in which he told us that this had never been about nation-building.[5] The extent and persistence of conflict across the globe had substantiated the need for better and more sustainable peacebuilding initiatives and also interventions. These kinds of initiatives and interventions need decades-long commitments and immense strategic patience. If these interventions were not about nation-building, then what was it about: defending narrow national security? Making the space to cover our retreat to isolationism?

A new form of resource-based imperialism as the Stop the War movement has always argued?

If, as I did, you carried the banner of Tony Blair's Chicago speech into countless debates with those Stop the War advocates, you have to ask yourself, now, and for ever after, what was it all for? The hope of the responsibility to protect and the expression of liberal internationalism as liberal interventionism is not just dead, it is deeply buried beneath multiple political weights that will not see it emerge in my or I suspect my children's lifetimes. There are reasons to think it will be back one day, but these are mainly reasons derived from an innate optimism that the world we now see cannot continue on this road indefinitely. That one day there will again be a plausible attempt to base the relations between states and their peoples on the responsibility to protect and on the establishment of government by consent. There might also be a return to trying to make the relations between states be based on international universally recognised and enforced norms derived from international law. If, as many will argue, this is never going to happen, those who have said all along, like Conor Foley – in his brilliant but ultimately futile book, *The Thin Blue Line: How Humanitarianism Went to War*[6] – that there was never any hope of achieving the objectives of these interventions, will be proved right. But what is laid more deeply to rest in the fact and in the manner of the scuttling of the NATO mission to Afghanistan is that, again as many argued at the time and have argued since, there never was a unity of mission between the advocates of interventions like Afghanistan. There were those liberal internationalists whose holy scripture was the Chicago speech, the new American century neo-liberals whose business was nation-building to create global capitalism and the realists whose text was revenge for 9/11 and US national security. President Joe Biden spelled it out when he stated what he always seems to have privately thought: 'Our mission in Afghanistan was never supposed to have been nation-building'. But as we will now discover quickly, and I suspect at terrible cost, it is impossible to have one without the other. Unless we help to build national and sustainable structures in countries like Afghanistan, then we will never have security. Where writers like Foley are right, and I was wrong, is that the projects of nation-building must come from within – it cannot, unless the country is reduced by utter devastation to a year zero like Germany and Japan after the Second World War, be imposed from the outside by force.

Or rather, it can be imposed but then it must be maintained, built and rebuilt, funded and refunded, for generations like South Korea has been.

Instead, the withdrawal from Afghanistan is the expression of the extent to which we live in a world divided into silos. Not multipolar because what has been constructed by China and Russia are not separate poles that exist in a balance of power with other poles, nor an ideologically divided world in a Cold War sense with the balance of power resting on a balance of terror based on mutually assured destruction. It is not even a sphere-of-influence world in which multiple great powers protect the interests of what they define as their own backyards. What we see now are silos which actually seek to expand the geographical trade routes and physical control of resources within these defined areas – this is not just influence, but it achieves a dominant operational sovereignty within these silos and destroys, in any meaningful sense, the sovereignty of the subject states. These are then silos in which new rules and laws are applied based on sovereign impunity of the states that are dominant – Russia, China, Turkey, the US, the EU. Between these super-silos are contested spaces.

What we are also seeing is the ceding of the contested spaces, like Afghanistan, by the US to China, and to a lesser extent Russia. What we will now see is the physical absorption of the Afghan economy by China and the geopolitical influence of Russia, though this is more complex because of the history of the two states. What we are also seeing by extension is a massive increase of Chinese influence in Pakistan by the proxy absorption of Afghanistan into China's silo.

The air of international law and human rights is sucked out of the Chinese silo as economic interests take over from all other interests. The real victims, therefore, of the end of liberal internationalism and the new silo-based isolationism are those whose human rights intervention was designed to protect.

It was not as though the West lacked the opportunity to make the idea of nation-building a reality in Afghanistan. They had been there for twenty years, deploying immense resources and an elaborate apparatus of expertise in capacity building. In fact, there has developed a generation of capable Afghan administrators, and the physical infrastructure for the governance of a modern nation state was built. These people and these buildings were largely unable to operate because of systemic corruption and perhaps also a failure of the capacity-building project itself. After all, all nations are built and all interventions are about nation-building – they have to be.

The UN report 'Threats, Challenges and Change, A More Secure World: Our Shared Responsibility'[7] argued that we lived in a different world in 2004 from the world we lived in when the UN was founded in 1945. In discussing sovereignty, the report argued:

C. Sovereignty and responsibility

29. In signing the Charter of the United Nations, States not only benefit from the privileges of sovereignty but also accept its responsibilities. Whatever perceptions may have prevailed when the Westphalian system first gave rise to the notion of State sovereignty, today it clearly carries with it the obligation of a State to protect the welfare of its own peoples and meet its obligations to the wider international community. But history teaches us all too clearly that it cannot be assumed that every State will always be able, or willing, to meet its responsibilities to protect its own people and avoid harming its neighbours. And in those circumstances, the principles of collective security mean that some portion of those responsibilities should be taken up by the international community, acting in accordance with the Charter of the United Nations and the Universal Declaration of Human Rights, to help build the necessary capacity or supply the necessary protection, as the case may be.[8]

The same report also outlined the criteria for legitimate intervention:

207. In considering whether to authorize or endorse the use of military force, the Security Council should always address – whatever other considerations it may take into account – at least the following five basic criteria of legitimacy:

(a) Seriousness of threat. Is the threatened harm to State or human security of a kind, and sufficiently clear and serious, to justify prima facie the use of military force? In the case of internal threats, does it involve genocide and other large-scale killing, ethnic cleansing or serious violations of international humanitarian law, actual or imminently apprehended?

(b) Proper purpose. Is it clear that the primary purpose of the proposed military action is to halt or avert the threat in question, whatever other purposes or motives may be involved?

(c) Last resort. Has every non-military option for meeting the threat in question been explored, with reasonable grounds for believing that other measures will not succeed?

(d) Proportional means. Are the scale, duration and intensity of the proposed military action the minimum necessary to meet the threat in question?

(e) Balance of consequences. Is there a reasonable chance of the military action being successful in meeting the threat in question, with the consequences of action not likely to be worse than the consequences of inaction?[9]

If this notion of sovereignty and these criteria for legitimate intervention are ever to be returned to, and if the international community is ever to recover its will to fulfil the responsibility to protect, then perhaps there also needs to be criteria for withdrawal after an intervention has been completed. These might render it even more unlikely that we will see interventions attempted in the future, but if they are, these might also determine the terms and the circumstances for withdrawing after an intervention:

1. Is the political situation in terms of internal and external threats to the rule of law stable and sustainable?
2. Is the economy viable without the continued provision of transitional funding necessitated by the intervention?
3. Is the security situation predictable and containable with the state's own resources?
4. Does the government have sufficient legitimacy to govern and sufficient respect for the political process to give up executive office if defeated in free and fair elections?

The lessons of the withdrawal from Afghanistan should be a re-examination as outlined above of the terms on which we intervene and the terms on which the international community withdraws after an intervention. They should also be about what the international community does during the intervention and the process by which the intervention ends and 'peace' is established. These lessons might one day indeed be applied. For now, however, the real lessons that are being learned concern the nature of this moment in international relations. If the international system now comprises silos of sovereign impunity dominated by superpowers or regional powers and if relations between these silos are based on contracts of mutual indifference, then there are two kinds of safe spaces left. The first safe space is inside one of these silos, accepting a restricted sovereignty in exchange for the protection of high walls. The other safe space is to have no natural resources and to be located on no strategically important land or sea routes. There are very few countries that can take this safe haven position. The most dangerous place is to be in a contested land between these silos in which the operation of indifference has not yet been defined. Afghanistan was, until the Trump deal, one such contested land. It is no longer. It is now securely in the Chinese silo.

Dr Brian Brivati is a visiting professor at Kingston University and director of the Stabilisation and Recovery Network.

SAKHI:[1] LOSING MY CULTURE OVERNIGHT

———

For Sakhi, music, libraries, cultural centres and cafés give meaning to life; if they remain closed, he no longer feels like life in Afghanistan is worth living.

Sakhi (not his real name) used to dream of being a member of Parliament. That may seem a lifetime ago now. He's a civil rights activist and entrepreneur who, before the Taliban's takeover, fulfilled one of his other dreams of opening and running a bustling café. More than a café, it was a cultural hub, a place for events and performances, political talks, poetry readings and other exciting happenings.

Sakhi loved to bring people together, connect them and build community based on shared ideas. Alongside running the café, Sakhi was still politically active and never gave up on his political ambitions. In 2021, he had even decided to start producing his own content to help push certain conversations forward that he believed in. He bought some decent camera equipment and prepared to launch his first show.

However, everything changed in less than twenty-four hours on 15 August 2021, when the Taliban entered Kabul. Sakhi immediately knew what was at stake. He would have to close the café immediately. It was suddenly very important to keep a low profile or inevitably face being made into a target.

Despite growing rumours of the Taliban's imminent arrival, Sakhi went to his office as usual the next day at 8 a.m. At 10 a.m., he got a call from his sister in a state of distress. She had just been called by her daughter's kindergarten and told to come in and pick her daughter up. The schools and kindergartens had been ordered to close. Things suddenly seemed very real. She needed Sakhi to go get her daughter. Sakhi put the phone down and left the office straight away to go and fetch his niece from school and take her home.

On the way back to the office, he says he noticed the city suddenly felt totally different. Everyday scenes had been infused with a sense of hidden urgency. There was confusion and chaos just below the surface. People were on the edge of panic, but surely this is just temporary, he thought, the government will have expected this, they must have a plan.

And that's when the phone started ringing. First it was his close family. Soon it seemed like relatives he hadn't heard from for years were suddenly calling him, to talk, to worry, to plan. Strangely, no one already had a plan. It wasn't that they hadn't seen it coming. It's just that they hadn't wanted it to be real.

Once at his office, he rushed inside to get his laptop and some crucial documents. He locked up as quickly as possible and made his way home on foot.

It wasn't much later that he found out Ashraf Ghani, the former

President himself, had fled the country and that the Taliban had entered Kabul.

Since the Taliban's takeover of Afghanistan, Sakhi says he has no income and lives in fear of persecution inside his house in Kabul. Because he had dared to speak out against the corruption of the former government of Afghanistan and the atrocities committed by the Taliban, he has been living in fear for his safety ever since they took control. He says he sees no future if the situation continues like this.

According to the general amnesty announced by the Taliban when they took Kabul, no one from the opposition would be persecuted. However, Sakhi does not believe they will be true to their word and says some of the activists – people like him – have already disappeared. He suspects they've been kidnapped by the Taliban. In any case, no one knows what has become of them and he thinks that he may find himself in the same position soon.

Sakhi says he feels like Afghanistan has gone back half a century overnight. It's the change in freedoms for women and technology that will have the most effect. 'Women will be imprisoned by the Taliban inside their houses, and the educated population will be deprived of technology.' For Sakhi personally, it's the music, libraries, cafés and cultural centres that have always brought meaning and meaningful experience to his life in Kabul; if they remain closed, he no longer sees a life for himself in Afghanistan.

FOREVER WAR

CHAPTER 12

'THE ENEMY IS
IN KABUL'[1]

———

ALIA BRAHIMI

There is a maxim attributed to Napoleon, that one should never interrupt the enemy while he is making a mistake. In that spirit, during the chaotic final days of the US-led withdrawal from Afghanistan, Taliban fighters helped the effort along. They agreed not to attack departing forces[2] and to provide security for the airlift of foreigners and their allies from the Kabul international airport. According to the Commander of US Central Command Kenneth F. McKenzie Jr, the Taliban were 'actually providing the outer security cordon … around the airfield … and we will continue to coordinate with them as they go forward'.[3] Taliban leaders also agreed to open secret corridors through the city so that convoys of buses could carry evacuees to the airport.[4] This dizzying turn of events seemed to vindicate one of the central ideas shaping the Taliban's strategy during twenty years of insurgency: that, to win, all it had to do was to not lose – and to outlast coalition forces.

Alongside this firm commitment to the doctrine of strategic

patience, the Taliban was empowered by a clear strategic narrative grounded in the concept of national self-defence. After 2002, the Taliban successfully transformed from a failed Islamist government with no manifesto[5] to a nationalist insurgency. Its spokesmen began to describe the so-called International Emirate of Afghanistan as a liberation movement opposing Western colonialism.[6] The jihad against occupation by the Soviet 40th Red Army in the 1980s had demonstrated the power of channelling nationalist sentiments within an Islamic framework, and its unifying effects.

The Taliban also benefited from a clear strategic centre of gravity which 'lay in Afghanistan's 40,000-odd villages'.[7] In its rebirth as an independence movement, defending Afghan people, property and honour from foreign invaders, the Taliban twinned nationalist and Islamic values and sought to mobilise a distinctly rural constituency. It 'play[ed] on rural people's distrust for cities, which are seen as corrupted and corrupting'.[8] This focus on a specifically Afghan authenticity, in opposition to a predatory and impure foreign agenda, was also driven to a significant degree by tribal specificity, as Pashtun communities became the beating heart of the insurgency. Unlike Iraq, where the violence was powered by a fearful Sunni minority, the Pashtuns are the country's largest ethnic group accounting for roughly 40 per cent of the population, and after 2002 there was described in rural Pashtun areas 'a reservoir of dedicated talibs fueled by resentment at the US-backed reversal they experienced'.[9] The Taliban therefore transmitted clear strategic intent, which was to consolidate control over Afghanistan and to re-establish an Islamic government.

By contrast, the means and ends of the NATO mission were opaque, disconnected and in a state of flux. For years, opinion surveys reported that many Afghan respondents could not understand why coalition forces were in Afghanistan.[10] At the same time, Western soldiers 'were taking risks and making sacrifices without understanding how those risks and sacrifices contributed to a worthy outcome'.[11] Indeed, the coalition's mandate oscillated between narratives centred on reconstruction, stabilisation, counter-terrorism, counter-insurgency and nation-building. It was therefore unclear what winning would look like and whether it meant an outright military victory or a negotiated settlement; whether it meant the containment of jihadist groups like al-Qaeda or their eradication; and whether it meant that foreign troops would leave Afghanistan or stay behind.

In defending the departure from Afghanistan, US President Joe Biden attempted to impose a strategic framework *ex post facto*, focused narrowly on counter-terrorism. He argued that the US went in to ensure Afghanistan would never again be used as a base from which to attack US interests and that 'our mission in Afghanistan was never supposed to have been nation-building. It was never supposed to be creating a unified, centralized democracy'.[12] Yet as early as December 2002, the US Congress authorised funding 'to help achieve a broad-based, multi-ethnic, gender-sensitive, and fully representative government in Afghanistan that is freely chosen ... and that respects the human rights of all Afghans'[13] – which had strong bipartisan support on Capitol Hill.[14] Indeed, the US remained in Afghanistan two decades after deposing the Taliban and dispersing al-Qaeda, and for ten years after the death of Osama bin Laden, with 2,461 troops killed in action and $145 billion spent. A version of nation-building was taking place. That this reality did not form part of the terms of reference for the withdrawal capped off the strategic muddle. It also led directly to the abandonment of many Afghan allies, some of whom had worked closely with international forces and aid groups on the basis of security guarantees, as well as a wider segment of Afghan society which had bought into Congress's vision for Afghanistan and had dared to live by its values.

The long-standing ambiguity over what the coalition's mission in Afghanistan was supposed to be was deepened by the decision to invade Iraq in 2003, which for many years demoted Afghanistan to a geopolitical afterthought. As former US policy adviser Jonah Blank put it, the original sin of the war in Afghanistan was going to war in Iraq: 'Failure to provide enough troops, money, and focus on the front end resulted in exponentially more troops, money, and focus down the line.'[15]

The lack of transparency about US objectives was also exacerbated by two key areas of inaction on the part of the NATO coalition. Firstly, the corrupt, ethnically partisan and often parasitic activities of successive allied governments in Kabul and their security forces animated the Taliban's narrative of grievance and energised the insurgency. In particular, the magnitude of corruption, which was 'so pervasive and so destructive in every area of Afghan life',[16] fed a series of conspiracy theories about the coalition's 'real' objectives in Afghanistan. By 2010, Afghans had begun to wonder whether 'the existing mafia economy is what the international community wants to support'.[17]

Secondly, it was an open secret that Pakistan, a major beneficiary of US development and military aid, was undermining the US effort in Afghanistan. Early into the insurgency, Taliban figures enjoyed freedom of movement around Quetta and Peshawar, Pakistani border guards allowed insurgents to freely cross the border in their presence[18] and, by 2008, Afghan authorities were claiming that Pakistan's intelligence service 'provided direct aid to the Taliban in its operations against NATO and Afghan army forces'.[19] Yet for many years the US did not effectively leverage its seniority in the relationship to influence Pakistani behaviour.[20] Furthermore, the unpopularity of Pakistan among Afghans was not exploited on the narrative level, to depict the Taliban as the destabilising creature of a foreign agent.

•   •   •

The denouement of the war in Afghanistan cast a shadow over the 'first great American century',[21] calling into question America's true dominance. One Arabic newspaper described the American pull-out as 'more like an escape'.[22] Moreover, the reconsolidation of repressive Taliban rule surrendered one of the only tangible gains of the post-9/11 wars. The US seemed to signal that it was unwilling to defend its values overseas; and the desperate scenes at Kabul airport suggested that those who were encouraged to live by them risked being forsaken. As a result, the rise of the liberal world order – in which stability was tethered to US hegemony and values such as democracy and human rights, as well as continuity emerging from multilateral institutions – no longer appeared inexorable.[23]

The Biden administration sought to parlay its exit from Afghanistan into a new paradigm of US engagement: a shift from 'relentless war' to 'relentless diplomacy'. Three weeks after the last US soldier left Kabul, Biden used his address before the UN General Assembly to pledge that the US would lead with its values and strength, that it would stand up for its allies and that it would, everywhere, champion the democratic rights of all peoples. But these assertions were undercut by the fact that the US did not depart Afghanistan through a substantive diplomatic settlement;[24] that many of its allies there were discarded; and that it was difficult to envision a graver menace to democracy than the Taliban. At a watershed moment, when power was becoming more dispersed and the post-9/11 wars accelerated the transition to a multipolar world, US global authority was further endangered by the declining credibility of its assurances and the waning myth of its moral exceptionalism.

• • •

The defeat of liberalism in Afghanistan unfolded at a dangerous moment for the wider region. In the Middle East and North Africa, Western-inspired pathways for achieving a better quality of life are closing. Ten years after the wave of pro-democracy protests known as the Arab Spring, the region is less free than before the 2011 uprising. More Arabs are imprisoned, unemployed or living in poverty than a decade previously. The Taliban's triumph in Afghanistan also coincided ominously with regressive events in Tunisia, which had been the only Arab Spring country to achieve meaningful democratic progress: in July 2021, as the Taliban laid siege to several provincial capitals and tightened the noose around Kabul, Tunisia's President suspended Parliament, sacked the Prime Minister and assumed full powers under the executive branch. In addition, within weeks, President Assad of Syria would be brought in from the cold, taking phone calls with King Abdullah of Jordan and the UAE Crown Prince Mohammed bin Zayed, and rejoining

Interpol's communications network, despite having disembowelled the Syrian nation for a decade to sustain his narrow regime. Still, ten years on, socio-economic despair continued to converge, with political dissent sparking fresh rounds of anti-government protests in Iraq, Lebanon, Algeria, Sudan and Yemen. While the drivers for change remained, the direction of possible alternatives to author-itarianism was less clear. The example of the West was less com-pelling, owing to its poor track record of standing by democratic movements abroad and its own crisis of democracy at home.

The evolution of Islamist politics will also be shaped by the Tal-iban's victory after twenty years of insurgency. The US withdrawal vindicated the militant paradigm of seizing power with military tools, rather than through elections or political negotiations. Tra-ditional Islamists who reconciled Islam with democratic processes ended up, ten years after the Arab Spring, back where they began: at best, deposed and excluded from power as in Tunisia; at worst, hunted, imprisoned and forced underground as in Egypt. Mean-while, violent jihadism has become a dominant mode of oppo-sition beyond the Middle East, in parts of Asia and across whole sub-regions of Africa.

The endgame in Afghanistan will also influence jihadism's di-rection of travel. The 'far enemy', Western countries, were targeted by al-Qaeda as a means of weakening the 'near enemy', security states in Muslim countries. Yet the Taliban's success reinvigorates the strategy of direct confrontation in service of a local emirate. These developments can be reconciled by global groups like al-Qaeda: since 9/11, several franchises, for example in Libya, Syria and Yemen, have cultivated a markedly local mission, combining the usual anti-Western tropes with an on-the-ground focus on

governance structures, tribal outreach, service provision and battling with local forces. On the other hand, ISIS, which is at war
with the Taliban in Afghanistan, still fights for supra-national aims,
on behalf of its so-called caliphate. While it may be tempting to
conclude that the Taliban's success will encourage jihad to local-
ise, terrorism focused on the West will remain an important lever
in competition within and between militant Islamist groups. Just
as ISIS will use the ascendancy of its Taliban enemy to rebuild its
external operations capability, so too will it seek to exploit rivalries
within the Taliban as they emerge and harden.[25]

A double vulnerability is now opening for the regimes of the
Arab world. The rapid US departure, and the Biden administration's stark focus on the interests of American citizens in its justi-
fications,[26] may have undermined trust in US security guarantees.
While some Arab states will be central to the US's development of
an 'over the horizon' counter-terrorism strike capability, the abrupt
reversal of its commitment to holding back Islamist insurgents in
Afghanistan makes imaginable a sea change elsewhere. At the very
same time, militant groups across the region may determine that
the Taliban model – of national insurgency in service of an Islamic
government – presents an exemplar to be emulated. This conclusion would put Arab regimes directly in the crosshairs of global
jihadism once more.

President Biden set the symbolic date of 11 September as the
deadline for the US departure from Afghanistan. The aim was to
reassert control and agency over a drifting 'forever war', and to
signify a commitment to confronting the challenges which lay
ahead, rather than behind, including great power competition. But
all signs are polysemous, with a range of possible meanings. What

was intended as an act of strength may be understood by state and non-state adversaries as an act of weakness or hesitation. What is certain is that twenty years after the 9/11 attacks, US global leadership reached a crossroads in Afghanistan. The US may successfully draw a line under its strategic misadventure, contain the fallout from the withdrawal and re-establish its hegemony.[27] Equally, the retreat from Afghanistan may mark the moment when the US-led liberal order manifestly lost confidence in its own capabilities: to defend its values, to stand by its allies, to win wars and to shape the future.

Dr Alia Brahimi is a non-resident senior fellow at the Atlantic Council and a leading specialist in terrorism and political trends in the Middle East and North Africa.

CHAPTER 13

INTELLIGENCE NEEDS UNDERSTANDING: REASONS FOR THE WEST'S FAILURE IN AFGHANISTAN

NICK FISHWICK

W hy did the West fail in Afghanistan? The short answer is that liberal interventionism, in its early 21st-century version, drastically underestimated the challenge of building a post-Taliban Afghanistan.

There are parallels with the way the West misunderstood how the former Soviet Union and its satellites would react to the fall of communism in 1990–91. As the Warsaw Pact collapsed, we tended to assume that the new Eastern European rulers would espouse liberal democratic values, and that that is what their peoples wanted. This assumption was profoundly ignorant and complacent. Of course, liberal ideas had their followers, especially in urban centres. But so did other beliefs and behaviours – nationalism, religious fanaticism, racism, corruption, crime, cronyism and the cynical misuse of state power. So, the landscape east of Vienna looks a lot less comfortably liberal-democratic than most of us would have expected thirty years ago.

When Western troops overthrew the Taliban in 2001, the assumption was (a) that the 'Afghan people' would be sick of the Taliban – their brutality, their technophobia, their misogyny, their bigoted version of Islam and their incompetence as rulers; and therefore (b) that Afghans would welcome the establishment of a government committed to democratic elections, human rights and the rule of law. (a) may have been correct – we don't know; (b) was at best hopelessly naïve.

If the West had taken a more clear-eyed view of Afghanistan before it intervened in the autumn of 2001, then it would have seen formidable odds stacked against it – not against the relatively simple task of booting the Taliban out, but against the prospects of leaving Afghanistan under the control of leaders who would not support al-Qaeda, and who would enable decent lives for the population. 'History' was against the West – as the name of the Gandamak pub in Kabul used to remind us. The geography of the country makes authority uniquely centrifugal. Afghanistan's only non-Talib leader of any real stature or vision, Ahmad Shah Massoud, had just been murdered by al-Qaeda. Opium production, supplying the lucrative international markets in Europe and elsewhere, was at massive levels and local crooks and warlords competed to control the trade while countless local farmers had no other means of livelihood. The economy was trashed. Since 1978, the whole country had been traumatised, and civil society gutted, by successive coups, invasion, insurgency and civil war. Crouched around Afghanistan were big, ugly regional powers with very clear and often conflicting senses of their own interests, which ultimately came before whatever the interests of Afghanistan may have been.

I could go on, and at length. Let's just agree that the challenge was massive. The West would have to get all the major calls right if it was going to have any chance of succeeding. It's more than possible, of course, that we were never going to succeed; we will never know. But what we do know is that we made a number of mistakes and failed to deliver one of the Afghan people's essential requirements: security.

The Western effort in Afghanistan was gravely weakened by the incoherence of its – the West's – leadership. Hamid Karzai and then Ashraf Ghani were the republic's Presidents, but like the pope they had few divisions. Karzai's real authority in his early days as President was such that he was referred to informally as the 'Mayor of Kabul', so little was his power outside the capital; many would add, so little even inside the capital. To get stuff done, the President needed the help of those who controlled the real legitimate power in the country – those who commanded tens of thousands of NATO troops. So, for the President, the key figure was the International Security Assistance Force (ISAF) commander: a general, usually but not always American.

The ISAF commanders were all outstanding military officers, exemplifying all that was best in modern Western military leadership. But their skill set did not include policy or diplomacy. There were lots of other people around town who did specialise in these, or at any rate thought they did. The British ambassador, the EU and UN heads and above all the American ambassador were people who could advise the Afghan President on his statecraft – because he often cried out for advice – and who could send sophisticated analyses to their stakeholders back home of what Afghanistan needed. But even if their assessments had been essentially the same – there is no way of knowing at the moment, but it seems unlikely – they had no divisions either. If Karzai or Ghani needed a show of force to deter the Taliban, the only person who could provide it was not the US ambassador but the ISAF commander. Who was, in the final analysis, just a soldier.

This mattered more because of the divisions within the West over what we were working for. If you'd asked a British official in, say, 2005, why she was there, she might have said that she was working to build a new Afghanistan: one that respected human rights, voted in free elections and didn't depend on the drugs trade. An American might have said something additional. Yes to the above, but the American would have made much of the key mission of destroying any al-Qaeda presence in Afghanistan, and using Afghanistan as a base to destroy Osama bin Laden himself. And there might have been a disagreement between the American and others on the role for the Taliban, and 'ex-Taliban', in the new republic. So, the US and other Western aims and priorities were not the same and this caused tension within their mission.

Mention of the drugs trade brings us to a secondary but still important area of disagreement. For Western law enforcement, which had been fighting a losing battle against the heroin trade for many years, the invasion of Afghanistan seemed to represent a huge opportunity. Ninety-five per cent of the western European heroin market was supplied by Afghanistan; surely now was our chance to wipe out the supply. But the complexity of the Afghan drugs economy, and the fact that many key powerbrokers in the new republic themselves profited from the trade, meant that no serious attempt was made to tackle the roots of the problem. This was ominous: if we couldn't make progress against drugs, which were part of a vicious circle of Afghan lawlessness, violence and corruption, why did we think we could make progress on other fronts?

This sort of incoherence consistently undermined the confidence of Afghans in the Western mission, and would have convinced the Taliban, even in its darkest days, that the West wasn't going to stick this out. There were countless other own goals. I will leave it for others to explain the decision of the British to send thousands of troops into Helmand in 2006. If it was designed to extend governance to the province, it failed and instead was a call to arms for the Taliban, or rather for any young Helmand male persuadable that the foreigners were outstaying their welcome and that their local stooges were brutal and corrupt. The Helmand deployment also undermined confidence between the British and US troops. Having got themselves into a mess, the British agreed an indirect armistice with the Taliban at Musa Qala at the end of 2006 without consulting the US. American faith in their allies may not have been destroyed but it was certainly grievously damaged.

An underlying, fundamental disadvantage for the West was plain ignorance. Take language. If you spoke to any Iranian, Russian, Indian or Pakistani diplomat in Kabul you would probably find them fluent in Dari or Pashto or sometimes both. I served for eighteen months in the British Embassy and could speak neither. I am not aware of any British or American ambassador (apart from Zalmay Khalilzad), or ISAF commander, having either language. Before 2001, British officials had not been posted to Kabul for many years and we simply did not have a reserve of Dari-speaking

Afghan experts to draw on. And we had no time to build one up. The consequent problems are obvious. Linguistically incompetent diplomats such as myself had to use interpreters for one-off discussions with non-Anglophone Afghans, or we just spoke to Anglophones; imagine – I know it's not an exact parallel – if all Turkish diplomats in the UK spoke only to Turkish speakers in the media, Parliament, etc. And a profound cultural ignorance follows, such as would never be acceptable in other overseas postings. Almost no one knew anything about Afghan history; the most dangerous of us were those who thought we did. It would have been an interesting exercise in, say, 2008 to ask the average American or European diplomat in Kabul who King Amanullah was and what he signified. There was also profound ignorance of Afghan clan and tribal structures. A minority of us thought we were being very clever indeed when we had worked out that there were Noorzai, Barakzai, Achakzai etc. in Helmand, but it didn't get much further than hopeless generalisations that x tribe was 'pro-government' and y tribe was 'pro-Taliban' or 'in the drugs business'. Then there was turnover. A British or American diplomat might serve twelve or eighteen months in Afghanistan and then they'd be off, quite likely working on something completely different. Put all this together and the level of foreign military and civilian officials' ignorance of Afghanistan was comprehensive. It meant that when we needed to get everything right, we lacked the basic tools to do so.

Compare this with someone like Zamir Kabulov, Russian ambassador from 2004 to 2009. Five years. Kabulov had done lengthy postings in Kabul in the 1980s and the '90s, was Central Asian, spoke the languages and had worked on little apart from Afghanistan since the late 1970s. He had also personally lived through the disastrous coups of 1978–79, through the success of the Soviet invasion and through the ultimate failure of the Kamal and Najibullah regimes, thanks in part to Western support for the anti-Soviet Mujahideen. He would have known all the Hekmatyars, Dostums, Ismail Khans, Mullah Omars and so on, in many cases personally. Was he prepared to put all this experience and expertise at the disposal of the West? Strangely, no. I suspect all the Western bungling since 2001 will have caused him endless amusement. And unlike, say, Khalilzad, Kabulov was not a one-off, a special case. The Indian, Iranian, Russian and Pakistani foreign services were stuffed full of people who knew the Afghan country, its history, its people, its languages. We should probably now add the Chinese to that list.

A painful variant on this theme was the command of the crucial British Task Force in Helmand, whose original mission was to spread security and good governance across that most challenging of provinces. A series of extremely capable brigadiers took this command. Being British Army officers, they had very different personalities and were only there for six months each. The impression one got was that each of these officers was concerned not to emphasise the continuity of the British military strategy despite this turnover, but to emphasise the difference between himself and his predecessor. These commanders came from very different parts of the British Army with very different approaches – not my area of expertise but it was obvious to a civvy outsider that a Para commander was different from someone with a Special Forces background who was different from a marine. And it would have been obvious to Afghans, too – friends, foes and fence-sitters alike.

The message to Afghans was that while we were serious in our commitment to the country, we didn't really know what we were doing, and we were only prepared to go so far. Western foreign governments did not have people at senior levels with Afghan languages or expertise. They did not have the resources or the culture to keep Kabulov equivalents focused on the same subject for forty years – including the years after the Soviet withdrawal when Afghanistan was no longer a Western foreign policy priority. Spells in Afghanistan for us civilians were difficult even for six, twelve, eighteen months: you just wouldn't get enough people to commit themselves to three, five or more years of tough language training followed by service in a distant war zone separated from family and friends. For the troops, many lost their lives or suffered terrible injuries, and there was no way that Western public opinion was going to tolerate the level of casualties the Soviets had put up with in the '80s. So, while we should not underestimate the level of Western commitment, or the pain and sacrifices endured particularly by the troops on the ground, we should not overestimate it either. There was only so much we were prepared to put up with.

So, if the basics of what a population can expect of a half-credible government are bread and security, we did not supply them. In a democratic country, such as we were trying to help build in Afghanistan, you do not provide security simply by training, equipping and paying the police, army and security services. We did all that, but it did not make Afghanistan a safe place. To provide security you have to have a real understanding of the sources of power, authority and consent. We did not have that. We did not work with the grain of Afghanistan because we did not know what the grain was and did not make the time or space to find out.

This perhaps explains some of the problems the Western intervention in Afghanistan faced. It does not say that we were 'wrong' to invade Afghanistan after 9/11; the shock of that atrocity made a decisive intervention inevitable. The Bonn Agreement, however, committed the West to a level of support for Afghanistan that it was incapable of supplying – incapable because, ultimately, it was unwilling to do so. That is the lesson that Afghans and others will draw from the Western decision to get out of Afghanistan and from the shambolic and humiliating way in which we did so.

Western governments including the UK will now wish to revert to that state of pre-1979, and then 1990s, shrugging of shoulders about Afghanistan; not our problem any more. But actually, there is now more to play for in Afghanistan than at any time since the 1970s. Many people immediately after Bonn in 2001 thought there had to be a role for the Taliban in a post-Taliban Afghanistan. Well, they have their role now. They clearly have no idea how to run a modern state, and Afghanistan and the world are infinitely different now from whatever the Taliban thought it was controlling in the late '90s. The Taliban itself is changing; and at last some of the old generation of Afghan politicians who have dominated the anti-Taliban discourse for forty years are giving way to a younger generation. The sight of women demonstrating after the Taliban takeover in August 2021 was stirring. This was peaceful opposition, not armed resistance. Perhaps the future will be for Afghanistan to develop a civil, non-violent alternative to the Taliban, rather than for the 'resistance' somehow to bash its way into Kabul. And perhaps in the medium term enough of the Taliban may realise that they have to engage with this.

But, as I write, a sickening human tragedy is threatening Afghanistan: mass famine. A debate about what went wrong and what could go right will have no meaning if the international community allows millions of Afghans, after all they have been through, to starve.

Nick Fishwick served in the UK Foreign Office and HM Customs and Excise service for over twenty years and is a national security expert.

CHAPTER 14

BATTLING FOR NARRATIVE ADVANTAGE IN AFGHANISTAN: NATO TV AND A DIGITAL-FIRST STRATEGY

THOMAS DODD

'If it doesn't show, it doesn't sow'

The above statement – a ground truth – was a key part of the twenty-year conflict in Afghanistan, but few observers[1] understand the role of NATO TV or appreciate the very real efforts that took place during the NATO mission to win hearts and minds inside Afghanistan and explain the mission to people outside the country. This chapter explores that effort, evaluates its successes and failures and assesses what happens next in the information war.

NATO broke with the Cold War organisations' staid and very public affairs-based communication[2] activities following comments made by a departing alliance secretary general, and the swift actions set in motion by his successor. Former secretary general

Jaap De Hoop Scheffer warned, 'When it comes to video, we are frankly in the Stone Age. NATO has no ability to gather video from the field, to show people what is happening. We are also barely on the field when it comes to the web.'³ Scheffer, together with his successor, former Danish Prime Minister Anders Fogh Rasmussen, launched NATO TV at the Bucharest Summit on 2 and 4 April 2008.⁴ Rasmussen had already in October 2007 echoed his predecessor's concern when he stated, 'We are losing the information battlefield, we need more resources and cohesion.'

NATO's communications reform was rightly perceived as a strategic need, but quickly proved to be an opportunity. The alliance had for decades relied upon journalists and others interested in its activities to come to it and request information – rather than have updated information available to them on an ongoing basis. The switch to deploy a digital-first approach that would *pull* content and editorial information to end users also inconspicuously imposed business change by introducing new skill sets and younger staff to the overall workflow of NATO. But the real opportunity was the discovery that most citizens in NATO member countries, in fact also many journalists, had only a vague idea about the role and activities of the alliance; dismantling past perceptions was less important than developing narratives for use on a blank canvas.⁵

The digital-first capability was designed and launched quickly following the political decision to reform communications. An early project for NATO TV was to support the first free Afghan presidential election after the ousting of the Taliban, as well as election day itself, held on 20 August 2009.

The idea was to sell democratic elections to the people of Afghanistan. NATO TV marketed and distributed content to more than 200 broadcast media outlets, including redistribution partners APTN (Associated Press Television News, a news agency), EBU (European Broadcasting Union, a news exchange) and Reuters TV (a news agency) and all major news networks worldwide. Hundreds of media outlets received NATO TV content in the run-up to the election – and nearly all Afghan TV channels received and used NATO TV content.

As NATO TV established a newsroom in Kabul and initiated newsgathering from all parts of Afghanistan, using a mixture of Western and Afghan contractors, the advantage of a completely digital workflow gave NATO TV an edge over other news operations in the country. Not only was NATO TV newsgathering quicker than most other media actors on the ground; it was also distributing material faster to media outlets. A US Defense Department official observed that NATO TV content often reached news outlets, indeed his own facility in the USA, before content from news agencies such as Reuters. The NATO TV advantage of reaching news outlets faster and with relevant and meaningful content supported NATO's strategic requirement of engaging with the Afghan population.

As the capability reached full scale and operated efficiently, including using local hiring, NATO TV output was not only marketed to Afghan media outlets but a process of engagement with each main media outlet was initiated. The engagement drive proved to be relatively easy, as the material was high quality and produced from a journalistic perspective, as opposed to public affairs content emanating from ISAF (International Security Assistance Force) and indeed NATO Public Affairs. The most obvious end-user attraction was that NATO TV updates were most often about Afghanistan and Afghans. The same could not be said about public affairs material, and frequently NATO TV content was used more often by Afghan media outlets than information from the many and disparate military and civilian media production entities under the NATO/ISAF umbrella. This was not every month, but often several months in a row.

NATO TV promoted content to media outlets well in advance of election day. Already in April, four months prior to the election, interest for Afghan coverage from NATO TV was significant – 114 unique media outlets in thirty-six countries placed 165 orders for 658 video packages. Requesting outlets included CNN International, the BBC, Al Jazeera English, Bloomberg, Sky News, Nippon TV (Japan), The Independent Online, VOA (Voice of America) and many others, including Afghan media outlets.

In May, 149 media outlets placed 274 orders for 1,041 video packages. Several international newspaper websites began taking NATO TV content, including *The Sun* (UK). Editorially, longer-form content was introduced, most often focusing on human-interest angles.

In June, 105 media outlets placed 238 orders for 701 video packages. Increased interest was seen from major newspaper websites, but equally so from global news channels and Asian media outlets. The inclusion of human-interest content was deemed a successful genre, as this material was disproportionately requested by media outlets, and NATO TV decided to increase this type of output.

In July, resources were diverted to prepare for August election coverage. In July, eighty-eight media outlets placed 191 orders for 444 video packages. On 20 August 2009, election day coverage was distributed to ninety-six media outlets globally. Even with less new

NATO TV content being made available, interest in NATO TV content remained high from media outlets across the world. Fewer and more in-depth feature packages were distributed; for example, on 8 July CNN used NATO TV content five times, Fox News two times and CNN en Español ten times. Usage suggested that in-depth content, setting the scene for election day, was preferred by media outlets. In August, 262 orders for video packages were placed during the first twenty-three days, with many new takers including Arabic channels such as Alhurra, Al Jazeera Arabic, BBC Arabic, Al Iraqiya TV and CNBC Arabiya. This came about due to an adjustment in marketing NATO TV content to countries in other languages than English (i.e. Arabic).

Political leadership in NATO was from the outset in 2008–09 aware of the disruptive effect of NATO TV on alliance communication operations and the need for content 'from the field' – and searched for a switch to communications output that resonated better with both home and foreign (i.e. Afghan) audiences. In April 2013, then NATO assistant secretary general for public diplomacy, and only two years later the first female President of Croatia, Kolinda Grabar-Kitarović forwarded an appreciation letter to me in which she made a poignant observation about the impact of NATO TV: 'Your products have shaped, and in many ways, defined our narrative.'

In 2013, modern communications equipment and expertise allowing large-scale engagement with the people of Afghanistan was provided to the Afghan government, based on concepts, workflows and technology developed by contractors hired by NATO and anchored at NATO HQ in Brussels, as well as in Kabul. A large Government Media Information Centre (GMIC) was inaugurated in Kabul, largely funded by the US State Department but with contributions from several NATO member countries. In August 2021, the GMIC was taken over and is today used by Taliban spokesmen and political leaders to deliver their narrative to Afghan media outlets as well as international ones.[6] On Friday 6 August 2021, Taliban fighters killed the GMIC head Dawa Khan Minapal and immediately took responsibility for the killing, which was widely reported.[7]

Shaping and defining a narrative is strategically important to both nations and international institutions, and especially so if political leaders see the tools for achieving that as being 'in the Stone Age'. The Taliban has quickly seized upon concepts, workflows and technology integrated into a capability that will support its territorial hold over Afghanistan, a priority for its leadership. The Taliban-controlled GMIC will concurrently provide international news outlets with curated and compelling imagery, thus setting up our understanding of the future that the Talib regime envisages for its Afghan 'caliphate'.

It's predictable and was seen before during the 1996–2001 reign of the Islamic Emirate of Afghanistan; while technology has democratised access to information for most Afghans, the 1996 playbook does not appear to have been updated.

Since the August takeover, the Taliban has controlled modern tools, but it has not shown prowess in using them effectively or planning for coordinated outcomes. The Taliban regime will be able to produce and distribute communications campaigns adequately and is in fact doing so already; its target audience is domestic first and international a distant second. To a domestic audience, the Taliban will be able to support its role as guardians of the territorial integrity of Afghanistan.

Predictable behaviour seen since its August takeover suggests that the Taliban has not changed – for example, media outlets are being gently reminded that women should not be seen in television dramas, setting the scene for a more enforced approach later. Less visible is the disappearing music scene; most music venues and music schools are being guarded by Talib fighters preventing access – and in late 2021, regime spokesmen recommended that all artists look for employment outside the entertainment industry.

The Taliban regime certainly recognises the power of influencing and its approach is as simple as it is likely to be effective. The utility of simple and professionally produced imagery for the Taliban should not be underestimated. Quality imagery served effectively to media outlets *without* accompanying and detailed supporting documentation is an effective use of resources in the short term; imagery will make the object or event depicted into something more emotional, and therefore concrete. In a news vacuum, this taps into a cognitive bias among media editorial managers, especially those far removed from Afghanistan and insight about realities on the ground. In the short term, the effect will be to convince the world that Afghanistan is now more peaceful, stable and – potentially – on a path to female emancipation and freedom of expression. These noble and virtuous aims will track well with Western media outlets from the outset.

In the medium to long term, the Taliban regime will have to substantiate and show that this path has been taken, and cease targeted killings of those who oppose them. Projecting influence outside Afghanistan will be challenging for the Taliban in the medium to long term. Neither will it be a major concern for the new regime; as nationalists, the Taliban will focus on consolidating their gains while reducing the risk of foreign intervention.

At the time of writing, the main news and entertainment TV channels remain on-air in Afghanistan, including ones showing overtly Western content. This in both national languages – Dari and Pashto. While regime-critical journalism is not tolerated, discussion of the country's future dominates television talk shows and topical affairs programmes. In late 2021, new regulations were introduced, curbing the freedoms of media outlets. Apart from leveraging the spread of mobile telephones and access to the web, it will be difficult for the West to engage with Afghan audiences today. That said, several important target audiences now present opportunity; women have experienced enormous change in their lives since the ousting of the Taliban twenty years ago, and represent a key demographic, especially those old enough to remember the changeover. The same applies to Pashto speakers in Afghanistan and Pakistan.

Slightly facetiously, one could argue that a prerequisite for engaging with audiences in Afghanistan today – indeed audiences in all countries around the world – is that Western political leaders recognise that a solution to how we tackle our narrative shortcomings in the long term is necessary, and that they must secure a way to effectuate the changes we need. Defining our own Western narratives rather than shaping narratives in play (a point made by a head of state quoted above in 2013) will require that political leaders recruit new capacity and different skill sets that deliver concrete results in terms of 'sowing' and effectively using pre-defined narratives.

In 2007, NATO needed persuasion tools and capacities that understood audiences and could effectively set narratives. This at scale means addressing multiple audience segments concurrently. That need is even more pressing today. Is the current Western situation, in fact, that doing something substantial rapidly (and being seen doing it) is about how it makes us feel rather than how much it will allow us to achieve the changes that we need now and in the future?

Continuing to provide ineffective services and products as an icon for doing something good about, say, our intervention in Afghanistan is practically the same as telling our domestic audiences about what we do, and then redistributing that to audiences far away from home. This has little to do with any people except home audiences and is not about engaging with other consumers or their reality. The intention is good, but it's a very poor incentive for engagement with audiences. Neither is it a coordinated approach.

Western political leaders need to ramp up the ambition to speak clearly, if reaching hearts and minds is to become more about actual tangible results rather than posturing while seeking virtue recognition, i.e. a switch to actually eliciting feelings of empathy for a point of view and influencing minds. As with other major international political themes, grand promises are made each time international political leaders meet. Fantastic promises are made, such as demilitarising and rebuilding a country. The reality is that a stated wish or intent matters little; what matters is what was achieved. Most organisations and states making those promises have not kept their promises. Audiences in faraway countries understand this.

Compelling Western political leaders to switch to something that will work effectively over a longer perspective – decades – is difficult. Further compelling them to oversee and monitor whether the switch and prioritised objectives were attained makes for an uncomfortable conversation.

We could have approached winning hearts and minds differently – and in the future we could invest in standing entities with a new ethos, delivering real journalism, rather than relying on short-term contractors. This means those involved are employees devoted to their careers, and no longer short-term contractors having to scam their way through each year. As employees, they would have work security and could recruit the best of the best locals in the countries in which they operate. There would be a multi-generational effect, benefiting reporters and, of course, in turn, listeners and viewers. In sum, improved oversight and long-term employees.

PEOPLE

We have lulled ourselves into a high-resolution central focus on ourselves that increasingly fades into low-resolution surroundings, until it completely disappears. Once out of sight, hearts and minds are impossible to reach. An alternative would be a standing entity run as a real journalistic enterprise, with oversight that was autonomous from government – and the oversight entity consisting of politically appointed senior leaders. To avoid political swings or lurches as government are elected and ejected, members of the oversight entity could serve staggered terms. Consider the Cold War success of Radio Free Europe/Radio Liberty; its content was sought out and listened to by Soviet leaders, at very critical junctures in world history, and when their nations faced upheaval. The station worked to get news out of those countries, even when the regimes did not want it out; and it used that news access in a return path to deliver perception change, versioning their content to engage with populations in totalitarian states. Back then, that was the approach when working against totalitarian governments and totalitarian forces. It worked more than adequately.

CAN THE NATO TV EXPERIENCE
BE LEVERAGED AGAIN?

We could envisage innovating much earlier with direct influence engagement, springing interaction from a standby status. It's how we respond with humanitarian aid, except faster and very much cheaper. We could be mandated to respond to every potential trouble spot, be prepped to do so. This would fix a very large part of the problem.

We would need to do more, but do it differently, and we would need to look at the structure of NATO TV as a model. A considerable part of my time was spent living and working in Brussels, securing that NATO leadership and dealing with organisational drag. New entities equipped with new ethos should not be based in and operating from large state institutions; the need to be separate and go to audiences rather than stay at the office is a prerequisite for achieving the changes we need. The conceptual development was to transform a tired and statist public affairs capability into a state-of-the-art and flexible communications capability.

Already back then, that decision recognises the importance of a multi-year, decades-long approach. A permanent fixture. The reality, as we look towards what will happen in the next intervention, if there is one, and the next NATO operation, is that we have a clear strategic need in search of enlightened political support and funding. The risk of organisational drag is the most important constraint of the communication campaign needed not just by NATO but by the West more generally in the war of ideas against fundamentalists like the Taliban, but also against much larger strategic foes likes Russia and China. If governments are not going to deliver these communications strategies, then NGOs or the private sector or a mix of the two must. They have the agility and the openness to new fronts on social media and they can attract experts and specialists with the intellect and the digital execution understanding that are needed. Governments have to commit. The West needs a strategic effort separate from government, protected and able to deliver for ten years. The 'separateness' is a protection from a clearly dysfunctional output. We have had more than twenty years' focus on tools and technology. Today those are available to all. It is about something else; it is about the message. If I were to design a strategy to reach into Taliban-controlled Afghanistan now, it would need to be based on Afghan editors with the personal connections and the experience to cut through to jaded audiences who are media literate and social media citizens. We would need to measure what we are reaching and what impact it is having using real metrics, not fake metrics or even obfuscation.

The game has changed since NATO TV was launched. Today end users, readers across the world, instantly recognise quality and credibility – and if effort has been dispensed in creating, curating and polishing a news piece or other media content, it will hit home. If the reader senses someone sincerely wishes to inform them about something, they will click on that content and read. We could already before 2009 see behavioural metrics, and not only determine who opened and who used our content, and when they did it, but also quickly see if their interest was in hard news, certain geographical areas or in specific topical issues. Viewers right across the world want good content and can sense when they are presented with quality – in some ways they are better at sorting the wheat from the chaff than even seasoned content editors at our end.

Fighting the information war is fantastically expensive and will not achieve anything like the benefits we are being promised. At the start of an international crisis or war, we often hear politicians say, 'We have to do everything we can now.' Do we really want to do everything at the same time, and how do we achieve that? We have to ask ourselves do we want to spend it all now – if you think a theatre of war and an intervention is important, then you are going to spend it all on that intervention. But if it's one of many problems, you're going to spend part of your budget on certain projects and then a lot on other projects too.

The world's most powerful defence and security alliance fell behind in communication, abdicating influence and recklessly throwing away advantages and Western progress within public diplomacy. Being effective in shaping perceptions, i.e. delivering tangible results when doing something about perception, has an immensely long-term impact. Nothing we will do in Afghanistan will have a measurable impact over the next five years on the target audiences, but it probably could initiate a change in how influence work is carried out at our end.

Remember: technology has made broadcast efforts just one piece of distribution. There are more platforms than ever before, and we have to address them all. The statement about communication by NATO being in the Stone Age was right. We now need to recognise it is about how we tackle this problem in the long term. Not about what we do and want to be seen doing in one year, i.e. measures of performance, but about how we effectuate the changes we need. The bottom line is that if there is any question about what the role of NATO should be in the future, and what the Western alliance needs to be in the future, then the answer is it needs to be fighting and winning the information war.

Thomas Dodd is a former special adviser to NATO, where he led the development and launch of NATO TV, and has co-founded several successful digital businesses. He continues to advise governments and corporations globally.

CHAPTER 15

THE INTELLIGENCE FAILURE AND THE CULTURAL FAILURE OF THE WEST TO THINK IN GENERATIONS

PHILIP INGRAM

As a former senior military planner and intelligence officer, I have studied and briefed Afghanistan in detail, lost soldiers under command as well as friends and colleagues in a campaign to achieve what in the end? These pages are very much my thoughts about how and why the situation in Afghanistan failed in such a spectacular way and what the implications for the UK are going forward. They are based on my significant global operational experience over twenty-six years' service, deployment on countless operations and many years as a military planner.

This immediate situation was caused by President Trump's agreement to leave Afghanistan.[1] President Biden could have reversed the order but instead just chose to delay it. Once the Taliban and the people of Afghanistan knew that the coalition were leaving, they knew what the future would hold. Just as the Taliban had been reminding those in the countryside for twenty years, it was coming back.

On 31 December 2014, coalition combat operations, including the US Operation Enduring Freedom, ended. The Afghan National Security Forces (ANSF) assumed responsibility for security in Afghanistan from 1 January 2015 and NATO transitioned to a new, non-combat mission called Resolute Support. The core aim of Resolute Support was to support the ANSF. The message to the Taliban in waiting was clear: the international community was leaving, not all at once, but the time frame, in Taliban thinking terms, would be short.

From an intelligence perspective, the cessation of combat operations would have resulted in a huge reduction in ground troops and their supporting tactical and operational intelligence collection capabilities: in essence, a partial blinding of the UK and the coalitions' ability to monitor what was happening. There would be a much greater reliance on higher-level collection platforms and capabilities, the Special Forces, airborne assets and human intelligence from MI6, the CIA and some military capabilities that were still around, as well as on space-based assets and the Afghans themselves.

There would be a much larger reliance on the intelligence capabilities in the Permanent Joint Headquarters at Northwood and the Defence Intelligence Staff in the Ministry of Defence, to keep the Joint Intelligence Committee (JIC), and therefore the cross-departmental machinery of government, informed.

However, the die was cast in the UK's own prediction.[2] As Brigadier Rupert Jones, former commander of Task Force Helmand, argued in an MoD policy paper, 'I would say that the ANSF have flourished in their own independence. I think it's been our stepping back that has allowed them to graduate onto the next level. The reality is the Afghans don't need our assistance day to day.' And how dare any subsequent commander say anything different, especially when the newly promoted Major General Rupert Jones became the deputy commander of the Combined Joint Task Force – Operation Inherent Resolve in Iraq before becoming assistant chief of the general staff? It would take a brave commander to brief against what the high-flying General Jones had assessed, and the MoD had published.

However, only two years before that policy paper, the secretary general of the UN said in his regular report, 'Little has changed in the underlying dynamics to mitigate a deep-seated cycle of conflict. Furthermore, a diminished international presence will have a significant financial impact in many areas that, at least in the short term, may even exacerbate predatory behaviour, with a reduced flow of money encouraging criminality.'[3]

So, what changed in those two years to make such a significant difference? The answer is nothing. The UK had published its policy paper, effectively setting the foundation to underpin all activities post the end of combat operations and set the conditions for final withdrawal. Therefore, the political pressure and the military strategic pressure to comply will have been huge.

UK military commanders believed in their own successes, they ignored warning signs and developed a self-misinforming groupthink that enabled them to spin positivity to more senior military commanders and politicians. The cynic in me would say they did so to get promotions, knighthoods and peerages. But how can I justify such a brazen statement? Let me offer one example. In 2007, a senior officer's intelligence briefing noted, 'We have indications that the Taliban have received training from Lebanese Hezbollah regarding Improvised Explosive Devices (IEDs) and have acquired the capability to manufacture and deploy them. Taliban tactics will likely change over the coming months to be more IED centric than conventional fighting.' This was, in fact, my own assessment from secret intelligence at the time which I presented to the senior officers of a formation that had just returned from almost a year in Afghanistan. The response to my brief sums up what went wrong throughout the whole campaign when the most senior officer in the briefing, the chief of staff, stood up and shouted, 'I will not have any more defeatist intelligence briefs from you or any of your team, that will never happen,' and stormed out of the briefing. That was 2007. There have been 27,539 civilian casualties from explosive violence in Afghanistan in the past ten years. Of these, 77 per cent (21,637) were caused by IEDs.[4] In total, 828 troops died from IEDs in Afghanistan. This means that 48.2 per cent of total military deaths between 9 September 2011 and 9 October 2020 were attributed to IEDs in Afghanistan.[5] So, how and why did that particular chief of staff get it so wrong? Simply put, my intelligence didn't fit the narrative he had been briefing for almost a year in country, and it didn't fit the groupthink, so it was ignored. I have heard many similar examples.

Having lost our tactical intelligence collection capabilities – patrols out around the villages, among the people, our trusted eyes and ears, our own soldiers on the ground – other intelligence capabilities would be critical to maintain situational awareness. This can only be partially replaced by debriefing local security personnel as they can always say what they want you to hear.

However, NGOs and the like continued to operate on the ground and report what they saw. Traditionally, I have experienced NGO reporting in other theatres to be unreliable as their motivation is to stimulate donations and to maintain the mission need. These aims may have coloured the acceptance of their reporting. The point is intelligence is a very human activity and relies on personal relationships to ensure trust.

Trusting local Afghan intelligence capabilities, no matter how well they have been trained, is a potential recipe for disaster given the amount of corruption that existed endemically in the structures of the Afghan government. As Deborah Lyons, the UN secretary-general's special representative for Afghanistan, noted in her fourth annual anti-corruption report, titled 'Afghanistan's Fight against Corruption: Crucial for Peace and Prosperity',[6] the Afghan government needed to recognise 'that its previous anti-corruption efforts had yet to positively impact the lives of most Afghans'. This issue had been long known.

Vanda Felbab-Brown, a senior fellow in the Center for Security, Strategy and Technology in the foreign policy programme at the Brookings Institute, was very clear in her evidence to the US House Armed Services Committee's Subcommittee on Oversight and Investigations looking at the critical issues surrounding the development of the ANSF and corruption in Afghanistan in 2012. She said, 'Few Afghans believe that a better future is on the horizon after 2014. Although NATO and US officials remain optimistic about the success of the counterinsurgency and stabilization campaign, many fear there will be a renewed outbreak of civil war after 2014 when the NATO presence is much reduced.[7]

Felbab-Brown added, 'The standing up of the ANSF has been one of the brightest spots of the transition process of improving Afghan capabilities to provide for their own security and governance. But it is also a big unknown.' She then commented that in her research most Afghans 'were deeply skeptical that the Afghan National Security Forces (ANSF) would be able to fill the security void created by the drawing down of ISAF forces and their far smaller and circumscribed presence after 2014.'

One of Felbab-Brown's more profound observations was that

> when ISAF forces are thinning out they will become more and more dependent on ANSF for ground-level intelligence, particularly for developing and maintaining a good understanding of the broader dynamics in Afghanistan, such as the nature and quality of governance in particular locales, and possibly even for narrow counterterrorism missions.

All of this advice should have stimulated a need for further intelligence analysis to inform cross-government decision-making. There should have been increased effort in bringing together reporting from international organisations such as the UN and many NGOs with greater levels of secret intelligence from all the allied agencies operating across the region. There should have been greater effort working with other regional intelligence agencies such as Pakistan's ISI to maintain a clear understanding of the truth on the ground and Taliban and Afghan intent. Those latter relationships would be the remit of the national agencies – MI6, CIA, GCHQ and NSA

– but Defence Intelligence would have had a key role in analysis, fusion and assessment for many of the JIC meetings.

In reality, Defence Intelligence Staff had cut its three teams of analysts looking at Afghanistan down progressively from 2014 when combat operations for British forces stopped, and by March 2021 there was only one team of four analysts monitoring Afghanistan. What wasn't reported was that the team leader had been redeployed, so in reality there were only three analysts.[8]

Interestingly, the UK House of Lords Select Committee on International Relations and Defence kept a clear watch on what was happening after Trump's withdrawal agreement. In its 2nd Report of Session 2019–21 titled 'The UK and Afghanistan', published 13 January 2021, it said, 'Afghanistan's relative prioritisation as a UK national security issue has slipped since 2010, but the scale of the challenges facing the country, and their potential impact on UK interests, have not diminished.'[9]

Its report added:

The Afghan state remains very fragile, with limited control of territory. The Taliban's insurgency continues, and terrorist groups, including al-Qaeda and Islamic State Khorasan Province, operate in the country … The Afghan government's accountability to its citizens is limited by its reliance on international military spending and aid. Government appointments are regarded as a source of spoils, and warlords and militia leaders retain roles inside the state … The UK has had limited opportunities, and shown little inclination, to exert an independent voice on policy on Afghanistan.

One must question if its observation that the UK had 'shown little inclination' was reflected in the reduction in Defence Intelligence analytical capability during such a potentially critical time from 2014 to 2021?

Given that an evacuation of some description would be inevitable and by its very nature cross-departmental – requiring coordination for the Foreign and Commonwealth Office, the Home Office and the Ministry of Defence at the very least – Defence Intelligence working closely with the national agencies would be critical to monitoring what was happening and any potential deterioration. Increased Defence Intelligence analytical engagement should, in my experience, have been essential.

All through this period the Taliban will have been influencing the tribal leaders and families of all those in the Afghan army and police not to fight. It had been running an alternative social structure for years, while waiting for an eventual withdrawal, making use of its ultimate planning tool. The Taliban operate in multiple generation time frames while we operate in anticipation of the next parliamentary or presidential election or, more accurately, tomorrow's headline or the next social media post time frames.

Felbab-Brown was quite clear in her evidence:

The ANA [Afghan National Army] appears to be increasingly weakened by corruption … The ANP [Afghan National Police] has of course been notorious both for such intense ethnic factionalization, as well as for corruption … In highly contested communities plagued by ethnic and tribal rifts, there is substantial risk that ALP [Afghan Local Police, i.e. those controlled by local politicians not central government, mainly in the rural areas] and other self-defense forces will begin praying on host or neighboring communities, serious abuses of human rights will take place, and the basic security of such communities will be undermined.

The rot started in 2003 when the very real progress that had been made with the original deployment to remove the safe space for al-Qaeda and defeat the Taliban was halted to put Iraq as a priority. The fault for that lies squarely with the then Prime Minister Tony Blair and his spin team misleading the country to an unnecessary conflict that opened a second unnecessary front. The deaths today and tomorrow in Afghanistan can clearly be put at the feet of the Blair–Bush pact!

One thing you never do in a military campaign is split your main effort. Yet the effort put into destroying the Taliban between 2001 and 2003 was halted before it was completed in order to start a campaign to remove Saddam Hussein from Iraq. A strategic main effort was split.

However, that was not the only issue. I am reminded of a conversation I had in London with a good friend, Aimen Dean, who had been a member of al-Qaeda in Afghanistan but having worked for MI6 for much of his time in the organisation had now resettled. We spoke, over a Diet Coke (he never drank tea or coffee), and he recounted stories unbeknown to me at the time he was collating for his book *Nine Lives*.[10]

He told me of a trek he undertook through Nuristan province in Afghanistan where he struck up a conversation with an old farmer who was tending some young saplings, helped by a teenager he introduced as his son. He asked what trees they were and when they would bear fruit, 'Pistachio, and thirty years, they are for my sons' sons,' was the answer.

Aimen went on to explain that this was a perfect example of the mentality of the people in the region. He said that unless the West could think and plan their campaigns in multiple generations, the people of Afghanistan would always know they would eventually be left alone, so their loyalties had to remain with their families, their villages and their tribes. Those loyalties would be influenced by the likes of the Taliban who also thought in generations and would be happy to sit and wait. Until then, they would see occupiers as a source of cash but not long-term safety and stability. This is especially true in the countryside as, in reality, there are two very different kinds of Afghans: those in the cities and those in the countryside. There is no single Afghan identity – it is a loose collection of family, village and tribal groups all with differing agendas and all influenced by powerful tribal groupings who also live in a generational time frame.

Having read numerous briefings and listened to many military commanders at the influence levels – that is, the military political interface where the heavy decisions are made – I heard very few, if any, brief the reality. The reality of the two Afghanistans and no Afghanistan, the reality of multi-generational thinking, the reality of endemic Taliban influence and the reality of the impact of corruption throughout the 'structured' parts of Afghan society and how that affected their security forces and even the ability of the ANA to operate and fight. There was an endemic failure to be truthful because the truth didn't fit initially the military political narrative and then the wider political narrative of leaving.

The overall failure is of real concern for the standing of defence in the UK. While servicemen and women at the tactical level on the ground were making huge strides, improving the lives of the

Afghan people and paying the price with their own lives, limbs and sanity, their commanders at that critical operational/strategic juncture were misleading themselves and political decision-makers.

In 2012, Felbab-Brown said, 'The faster the international community leaves Afghanistan and the more it reduces its presence, particularly its military presence, the more the negative dynamics in the still very-problematical Afghan security environment will be intensified and the fewer means and lesser leverage the internationals will have to combat them.'

In Taliban time frames, the Trump withdrawal agreement led to a very rapid withdrawal, but the Taliban already had its influence and presence in place in all the towns and cities, all the provincial capitals and in Kabul. The start button had been pushed for the withdrawal by the international community and a non-combatant evacuation operation was inevitable. Situational awareness was critical, yet the UK's Defence Intelligence wasn't providing it – its numbers of analysts engaged on Afghanistan were woeful and nowhere near enough to keep situational awareness, never mind contribute to detailed planning.

The Afghan National Army, devoid of the mentoring, air support, intelligence support, logistic support and medical support it got even after the 2014 cessation of coalition combat operations, was never going to fight a resurgent Taliban which had already influenced the country's tribal leaders, village elders and families. A very rapid cross-regional explosion of Taliban presence with minimal fighting was inevitable and obvious, but only if it was being looked for. The Taliban had planned this for a generation, since members of the coalition went to Iraq – the twenty years in which Afghanistan took a different path. There is no other way to describe the failure to see what was happening in Afghanistan in those twenty years than as the single biggest intelligence failure since the fall of Singapore in 1942.

Philip Ingram MBE served in British military intelligence for twenty-six years and is now a journalist and consultant in intelligence, counter-intelligence and security sectors.

CHAPTER 16

AFGHANISTAN: A STRATEGIC FAILURE OF VISION, RESOURCE AND PATIENCE

PAUL CORNISH

AUGUST 2021: THE ROUT OF KABUL

The evacuation from Kabul in August 2021 was no doubt a harrowing experience for all concerned: Afghan troops and police deployed around the airport; lightly armed NATO troops guarding the inner perimeter; aircrew flying transport aircraft in and out of the airport; civilian officials processing urgent applications for passports and exit visas; and Afghans hoping desperately to make good their escape, at risk of arrest by Taliban militia or under the threat of a suicide bomb attack. In such appalling circumstances, the courage of those most directly involved in the evacuation can only be admired. The same should be said of those who planned the operation and ensured that it continued until the last safe moment.

The evacuation from Kabul was a tactical and operational

achievement. But commentators have also described it in other, less complimentary terms – 'Cowardly, disloyal, humiliating, ignominious, imbecilic, incompetent, shameful, terrifying, tragic. Capitulation. Debacle. Fiasco. Calamity.' In military language, the operation seemed far from being a controlled and orderly withdrawal under pressure, from a position of vulnerability to one of strength. Neither did it seem like a hasty, yet still organised, retreat in the face of overwhelming force and the certainty of defeat. Instead, the evacuation appeared to be more of a rout.[1] Is it fair to describe as an 'achievement' something which, arguably, should not have been conducted as it was, should not have been left to the last minute and should not have been run to such a tight deadline?

A balanced assessment of the evacuation would require an unvarnished account of the operational shortcomings and failings that led to it, not least to inform the planning and execution of any future evacuation operations that might be contemplated. Although a full 'lessons learned' analysis is well beyond the scope of this chapter, I begin with a summary of some of the topics that might feature in such an analysis. But this chapter is more concerned with a larger, albeit not unrelated, question. However, we might balance its human and organisational achievements against its operational shortcomings. Does the evacuation from Kabul have wider and longer-term significance? Was it a strategic failure? I will argue that it could prove to be and that if the strong indicators of strategic failure are not openly acknowledged and addressed, then the outcome will be a further realignment and hardening of the international order in ways that will push to the margin the geopolitical, strategic, economic and moral interests of the West.

OPERATIONAL SHORTCOMINGS

When armed force is operationally deployed, for whatever reason, we should expect a very close correspondence between the various functions of state power, most critically the political, the diplomatic and the military. Among the tangle of misjudgements that culminated in the evacuation, the most striking flaw was that the political and, particularly, the diplomatic functions appear to have become detached from the military. The February 2020 bilateral 'deal' struck between the Trump administration and the Taliban was astonishingly short-sighted and naïve. The Doha Agreement seemed to take little account of the complexity of the US military involvement in Afghanistan and of the Afghan government's and its armed forces' dependence on the US presence. The Trump administration also appeared to be wholly uninterested in the fact that several of the United States' allies, as well as NATO, were militarily committed to Afghanistan, that these troops might be vulnerable should the security situation change suddenly and that the governments concerned might wish to have a say in any rearrangement of the West's involvement in Afghanistan. In the end, the Trump administration's talk of a negotiated peace accord with the Taliban, perhaps with a view to a power-sharing arrangement of some sort, turned out to be delusional. The shortage of mature political and military guidance was compounded by the Biden administration's extraordinarily inept decision to set a firm target date for withdrawal, with the result that Western military forces operating in Afghanistan were to some extent cut adrift.

Then there were the alleged failures in intelligence. For reasons which should be obvious, the intelligence background to the evacuation is not yet in the public domain. Some aspects of the intelligence background might, however, be inferred from a series of public announcements that seem to have been based on intelligence assessments. These announcements do not paint a particularly encouraging picture. On 8 July, for example, President Joe Biden memorably informed the world that the Taliban was 'highly unlikely' to end up 'running everything and owning the whole country'.[2] Days later it was reported that US 'intelligence agencies' (unnamed) believed the government of Ashraf Ghani might collapse within six months[3] – albeit not within six weeks. And on 21 July, General Mark Milley, Chairman of the US Joint Chiefs of Staff, argued that 'a negative outcome, a Taliban automatic military takeover, is not a foregone conclusion'.[4] This is not to make an armchair-borne, retrospective critique of decisions made in the most complex and urgent of circumstances. But it is to suggest, on the basis of admittedly slender evidence, that the overall intelligence picture seemed to be patchy when put to the test. Either the capabilities and resilience of the Afghan army were woefully over-estimated, or the Taliban's ability to fill a strategic vacuum was seriously under-estimated. Or both.

The patchiness of the intelligence coverage resulted, almost inevitably, in shortcomings in the planning of the departure from Afghanistan. There had of course been extensive draw-down planning – much of it completed by mid-June. But these preparations had assumed a more orderly departure and appeared to be overwhelmed by both the rapidity of the US and allied exit and the number of people seeking evacuation. When the evacuation became an emergency, the planning proved to be less than robust, unfortunately. Perhaps the most striking evidence of shortcomings in planning and organisation lies in the failure to destroy all key documents in time, before the Taliban could secure them. In some cases, the contact details of Afghans who had worked with Western missions were left intact and visible.[5] In other cases, the identities of some Afghans were reportedly handed to the Taliban in order, apparently, to elicit Taliban assistance in processing applications for evacuation.[6]

Any review of the evacuation will doubtless take a close interest in the decisions and actions of the military leadership. In broad terms, and with the benefit of hindsight, there appears to have been a loss of engagement with a fast-moving and highly capable adversary, culminating in the surprise experienced when the Taliban arrived at the gates of Kabul airport. Even when intelligence was available, particularly the warning of an IS-K (Islamic State Khorasan Province) suicide bomb attack, there appeared to be very little that US and allied troops could do about it. Part of the explanation might be that troops deployed at the airport were very lightly armed and equipped, much of the US and allied military infrastructure having already been stripped away. Bagram airbase, which many commentators have argued could have been a vital operational asset in the final departure from Afghanistan, had been abandoned by the US in early July, leaving behind some $85 billion worth of military equipment and weaponry. The shortage of key capabilities – including large military transport aircraft – could very well have contributed to a reduction of confidence among troops deployed at the airport and, more significantly, to a loss of initiative. Rather than win its victory, it was as though the Taliban was gifted the capture of Kabul and Afghanistan. US and allied troops then found themselves in a militarily indefensible position for which they were unlikely ever to have been trained: largely surrounded by the Taliban and with no room or depth for tactical manoeuvre; reliant, not on their own capabilities and initiative, but on the consent of their former adversary, the Taliban.

Finally, a review of the causes and conduct of the evacuation might also be concerned with the quality of communication between political and military leaders and between allies, and in the way in which the evacuation was explained to those in need of rescue, to the public and to the media. Once again, the quality appears to have been patchy. For example, US military advice to retain 2,500 troops in Afghanistan was reportedly ignored by Biden, as were requests from NATO allies to move the date of final departure beyond 11 September. Had more strenuous warnings been given earlier to US and allied nationals working in Afghanistan, then perhaps more use could have been made of commercial flights before the airport was closed to civil aviation, reducing the pressure for places on military transport aircraft.[7] In the UK, political and military leaders succumbed to the need to speak authoritatively about a confused and volatile situation when they might have been better advised to keep their own counsel, rather than broadcast confused, contradictory and occasionally ill-considered opinions. Senior UK politicians' claim to have been 'surprised' at the speed at which the crisis developed was awkwardly inconsistent with Prime Minister Boris Johnson's assertion that the evacuation was 'planned and prepared for months'.[8] But what provoked most controversy was a series of remarks made by the UK Chief of Defence Staff, General Sir Nicholas Carter. During television interviews with Sky News and the BBC on 18 August, Carter cautioned against describing the Taliban as 'the enemy' and noted with approval that UK armed forces were 'having decent collaboration with the Taliban'. In terms that came uncomfortably close to Russian diplomats' welcoming the Taliban as 'normal guys', Carter's description of the Taliban as 'country boys' living by 'a code of honour' even earned an angry rebuke from a US general.[9]

In spite of these shortcomings, some preferred to concentrate on the positive aspects of the evacuation, depicting it as a remarkable feat and if not a victory of some sort, then at least not a defeat. On 31 August, following the departure of the last planes, Biden described the evacuation of 120,000 people as an 'extraordinary success'.[10] Dominic Raab, soon to be replaced as UK Foreign Secretary, also congratulated British troops, diplomats and government officials who had 'bravely continued their vital work' and had contributed to 'the largest [evacuation] operation of its kind in living memory'.[11] And as the evacuation wound down, Johnson praised UK armed forces and civilian officials for working 'around the clock to a remorseless deadline in harrowing conditions', adding, 'It's thanks to their colossal exertions that this country has now processed, checked, vetted and airlifted more than 15,000 people to safety in less than two weeks.'[12] The least convincing gloss on the evacuation was that made by Ben Wallace, UK Defence Secretary, in spoken evidence to the House of Commons Defence Select Committee on 26 October. While accepting that Western 'resolve' had failed, Wallace sought solace in the claim that armed forces deployed to Afghanistan had never been subjected to military defeat by the Taliban.[13]

Johnson's rhetoric was reminiscent of an earlier crisis in British history. In early June 1940, Prime Minister Winston Churchill addressed the House of Commons on the matter of the recently completed evacuation of British and Allied troops from the beaches of Dunkirk. Following the German invasion of Belgium, the Netherlands and France in early May, hundreds of thousands of troops had withdrawn to the beaches of Dunkirk where they had become trapped, facing either destruction or, at best, capture. The aim of Operation Dynamo was to rescue as many of these troops as possible. Initial assessments suggested that at most 40,000 troops might be saved, but in the end 340,000 were evacuated. This remarkable achievement, of undoubted strategic significance, was saluted by Churchill as a 'miracle of deliverance' made possible 'by perseverance, by perfect discipline, by faultless service, by resource, by skill, by unconquerable fidelity'. It would be unwise to draw too close a comparison between Dunkirk in 1940 and Kabul in 2021. In terms of context, conduct, scale and scope, Operation Dynamo was probably as different from Operation Allies Refuge (the US component of the evacuation) and Operation Pitting (the UK component) as it could be. Except in one respect. Churchill continued his encomium for Operation Dynamo with words that resonate strongly in the context of the Kabul evacuation, or at least should do: 'We must be very careful not to assign to this deliverance the attributes of a victory. Wars are not won by evacuations.'[14]

The evacuation from Kabul could fairly be applauded as a 'miracle of deliverance'. But since the West is not at war with anyone, it would probably be unwise to push the comparison much further, to present the evacuation as the crux of imminent victory or defeat. Nevertheless, the West is, and will remain, strategically engaged with the rest of the world. The question, then, is whether the 'rout of Kabul' will matter very much in the long term? Whatever the shortcomings outlined in this chapter, was it a strategic failure? Or will the West and the rest of the world get over it and carry on, conducting business as usual?

STRATEGIC FAILURE?

There has been no shortage of discussion as to the broader and longer-term implications for the West of the chaotic evacuation from Kabul. Some have offered a phlegmatic interpretation of events, noting that the countries involved in the evacuation – the United States, the United Kingdom and others, as well as NATO and indeed the West as a whole – have all in the past proven their capacity to recover from setbacks and remain functional. The eminent British scholar of strategy professor Sir Lawrence Freedman cautioned against becoming over-excited: 'It is always tempting but usually unwise to draw large geopolitical conclusions from specific events, however dramatic and distressing.' 'The post-mortems on the withdrawal from Afghanistan,' Freedman suggested, 'will most likely conclude that there is no need to make any fundamental policy changes.'[15] Taking a more forthright approach, professor Stephen Walt, a US political scientist, noted:

> A chorus of overwrought pundits, unrepentant hawks and opportunistic adversaries now proclaim that defeat in Afghanistan has left US credibility in tatters. They are wrong. Ending an unwinnable war says nothing about a great power's willingness to fight for more vital objectives ... extricating NATO from the Afghan quagmire will free up attention and resources for more important tasks, such as balancing China.[16]

But if it is unhelpful to become feverishly overwrought, it is surely just as unhelpful to do the opposite, to adopt a Panglossian view that the debacle in Kabul was but a minor perturbation, from which things will soon recover and tick along nicely, or to see it as a timely opportunity for Western powers to free themselves from 'forever wars' to deal with other, larger problems in international security. To the extent that analysts of strategy and security have any real use, part of their value must lie in their ability (if not their temperamental inclination) to conduct dispassionate and measured worst-case analysis. On what basis might it then be argued that the consequences of the evacuation from Kabul – a 'miracle of deliverance' with shortcomings – could prove to have been far from harmless, and least of all advantageous, to the West? How could it be considered a strategic failure?

An important feature of the decision to evacuate Kabul by the end of August was that it was taken unilaterally by the United States. While acknowledging the sovereign right of the United States to decide what to do with its own armed forces, the decision indicated at least the absence, and possibly the complete failure, of the multilateralism so favoured by Western governments wedded to the idea of the 'rules-based international order'. The United Nations, NATO and the European Union were little more than bystanders, and pleas from the G7 and from European governments to depart Afghanistan in a more controlled manner were ignored. US unilateralism caused particular stress for NATO, which had invoked its Article 5 mutual defence clause on behalf of the United States after the 9/11 terrorist attacks. Searching questions were soon being asked about the credibility and coherence of NATO under US leadership, some argued that the Kabul fiasco marked the death knell of NATO's 'expeditionary vocation' and others wondered whether the moment might (at long last) have arrived for the European Union to build a 'military force' to rival NATO. The alliance's secretary general responded by warning that any weakening of the 'transatlantic bond' between the US and its European allies in NATO would divide Europe. Yet the supposedly 'special' bond between the US and the UK came close to breaking point when UK government ministers reportedly questioned Biden's state of mind, suggesting he might have gone 'gaga' or 'doolally'.[17] It can scarcely be argued that the West, and NATO in particular, emerged from the Kabul evacuation looking coherent, dynamic and well led.

Strategy is concerned not only with tangible things such as economic strength and military capability but also with the perceptions formed by others, particularly rivals and adversaries. There can be little doubt that the withdrawal from Afghanistan was an encouragement to authoritarian regimes. The withdrawal was a strategic failure insofar as it created a strategic vacuum that the West's rivals, particularly China and Russia, could move quickly to fill – perhaps in concert.[18] The relationship between Beijing and the Taliban had been deepening for as much as three years before the Taliban coup in August, to the point that the Taliban had taken to describing China as its new 'principal partner'. It seems likely that Afghanistan will be drawn into the Belt and Road Initiative, whereby China provides large infrastructure (such as motorways between Afghan cities[19]) in exchange for rights to extract possibly as much as $1 trillion worth of copper, gas, gold, uranium and rare earth metals. Russia has also expressed interest in investing in Afghanistan, particularly in the extraction of natural resources.[20] It seems inconsistent, to say the least, for Western leaders to have acted in ways that will strengthen those they now insist should be treated as strategic rivals.

Among extremist and terrorist groups, the evacuation from Kabul was seen as conclusive proof of the West's inability to defeat Islamist terrorism. What was perceived to be the humiliation of the West seems likely to encourage jihadist and other extremist organisations around the world to redouble their efforts against the West.[21] In the view of one terrorism expert, IS-K might now take the opportunity to either establish a 'mini-caliphate' in some part of Afghanistan or escalate its use of violence in an effort 'to rebuild its tarnished global brand'.[22] Ambassador Maleeha Lodhi warns of 'regional contagion' as extremist groups use Taliban-led Afghanistan as a safe haven from which to launch 'cross-border terrorist activities'. China, India, Iran, Pakistan, Tajikistan, Turkmenistan and Uzbekistan all have reason to be concerned about threats to the stability of their region.[23] Three of the countries appearing on this shortlist are, of course, declared nuclear weapon states. Threats to the stability of the region might also come from the various 'rogue regimes', including Syria, that joined in celebration of the Taliban's 'thunderous defeat' of the United States and its allies.[24] Whatever their source, threats to the stability of the Middle East and south-west Asia cannot be said to be a strategic success for the West, not least after a twenty-year campaign rationalised as an attempt to eradicate anti-Western Islamist terrorism in Afghanistan.

For as long as morality matters in the West's strategic outlook, and in the rest of the world's perception of the West, then for a number of reasons the evacuation from Kabul can only be described as a moral failure, a visible stain on the image the West hopes that others have of it. The West was perceived to have been disloyal not only to individuals on whom Western civil and military organisations had depended (e.g. embassy staff, drivers and interpreters) but also to Afghanistan itself. As the *Economist* newspaper put it in July 2021, 'America is abandoning an entire country of almost 40m people to a grisly fate.'[25] There was also the unsavoury spectacle of Afghan armed forces and police being blamed for the catastrophe that engulfed them, even though their dependence on US leadership, equipment and support was well known. Biden's casual dismissal of the Afghan armed forces as being 'unwilling to fight for themselves' can only have distressed the families of the 60,000 or so Afghan troops and police who had died between 2001 and 2020, and was described simply as 'dishonourable' by one British veteran of the conflict.[26] There was a perceptible absence of moral judgement in the rampant idiocy of using an aircraft to evacuate abandoned cats and dogs while people waited for a place. And it became abundantly clear that the 'strategic patience' the West had been promising Afghanistan for many years could be abandoned if necessary.

These broken assurances were compounded by the sight and sound of Western governments continuing to insist on their moral credentials and resorting to high-minded rhetoric about championing individual human rights around the world and about the merit of the so-called rules-based international order. In the UK, for example, a security, defence, development and foreign policy paper, published in March 2021, projected the 'Global Britain' idea, one component of which would be 'a renewed commitment to the UK as a force for good in the world – defending openness, democracy and human rights'. In terms which can only have sounded hollow and insincere just five months later, the document went on to insist, 'As a force for good in the world, the UK will remain sensitive to the plight of refugees and asylum seekers. We have a proud

track record of protecting those who need it.'[27] And as the evacuation was underway, the hapless Foreign Secretary announced that
the UK would build 'a global coalition' to stop Afghanistan becoming, once again, a haven for terrorists, to 'prevent a humanitarian
disaster and support refugees', to 'preserve regional stability' and,
most preposterously of all, to 'hold the Taliban and other factions
to account for their actions, including on human rights'.[28]

CONCLUSION

The evacuation from Kabul in August 2021 does not mark the beginning of the end of the West. The evacuation was in important
respects admirable and even a 'miracle of deliverance'. But it was
in many other respects a calamity and will always be seen that way,
whether Western politicians and commentators like it or not. In
the end, the West was seen to have turned and run, showing that
the rhetoric of 'Western values' was disposable and, besides, that
the West could barely defend an airport. There has to be recovery
and reinvention, but strategic 'lessons' will never be 'learned' for
as long as Western governments persist in the delusion that they
were either lucky to have 'got away with it' or in some strange way
victorious, or at least not really defeated. After the evacuation from
Kabul, the only route to strategic wisdom is to undergo urgent
worst-case strategic analysis in order to galvanise some remedial
behaviour.

In the 1952 BBC Reith Lectures, Arnold Toynbee wrote of 'the
encounter between the world and the West'. He argued:

The world, not the West, is the party that, up to now, has had
the significant experience. It has not been the West that has been

hit by the world; it is the world that has been hit – and hit hard – by the West … if any Western inquirer asks [the great non-Western majority of mankind] their opinion of the West, he will hear them all giving the same answer … The West, they will tell him, has been the arch-aggressor of modern times.[29]

After the evacuation from Kabul, there might well be one or two among Toynbee's 'great non-Western majority of mankind' who will come to conclusions that the West's strategic leaders should find deeply discomfiting: the West has been found wanting and the enduring strategic legacy of the 'rout of Kabul' could be that the West is seen as not much different from other large strategic actors in the world, only weaker and much less consistent. Without honest reflection on what took place, and how it appears outside the West, then strategic failure might become unavoidable and perhaps it will be the turn of the West to be 'hit by the world'.

Professor Paul Cornish is a visiting professor at LSE IDEAS, London School of Economics, and an independent analyst, consultant and author specialising in international security, geostrategy, cybersecurity and national defence policy.

CHAPTER 17

THE ROLE OF THE ABSENCE OF RISK-MANAGEMENT THINKING IN THE COLLAPSE OF AFGHANISTAN

SAFA MAHDI

In August 2021, the Afghan government and the Afghan National Defense and Security Forces (ANDSF) collapsed with stunning speed. This speed shocked international observers who, despite not being optimistic about the post-US forces withdrawal era, did not predict that Afghanistan would collapse in this way. The fall has clearly been driven by the fact that both President Trump and President Biden not only set and clearly announced the deadlines for the withdrawal of US forces but then immediately cut the support level to those forces, which left the Afghan troops traumatised. The ANDSF was then unable to stand in the face of the Taliban, even though the Taliban fighters, in many places, did not make an effort in their attacks. They did not need to. This trauma led to the failure of the defence and it pushed many Afghan politicians and government figures to flee or surrender. The argument I want to make in this short essay is a simple one: these events could and should have been at the very least predicted by either the Afghan government or outside observers using the basic tools of risk assessment.

Predicting the course of events based on risk analysis might not have worked to prevent the collapse of the Afghan government. Despite twenty years of efforts, training, international support and billions of dollars spent to build the capacity and push the country to stand on its feet again, the Afghan state could not preserve itself, or at least prove to be able to withstand by defending itself, even slightly, in the face of the Taliban tide that came as a tsunami.

Within a few days, Taliban fighters overran more than a dozen provincial capitals and went to enter Kabul with no resistance, triggering the fleeing of most government figures and signalling the collapse of the Afghan state. The large number of Afghan security forces simply melted away, threw away their weapons. The pace of the military collapse has stunned many international organisations present in Afghanistan, which also failed to predict the rapid fall and were left scrambling to remove their personnel from the country. The Afghan security forces included several capable and motivated elite units, but they were often dispatched to provide backup and support for less-well-trained army and police divisions that repeatedly folded under Taliban pressure. The point of realising the non-readiness and incapability of the government security forces should have been identified and dealt with many years ago. This issue was a key factor that made the security forces stop fighting and submit without any action by the Taliban. However, these issues are not the central subject of this essay, which is concerned with the inability of either international organisations or the Afghan government to predict this sequence of events.

In reality, there should have been multiple risk-management systems examining these questions in different levels of the state and international organisations. Each of these risk-management systems should have been focused on the risks associated with and pertaining to the potential for the collapse of Afghanistan's security system. That none of these systems identified the risks that would come together to destroy the government meant that there was no time for the Afghan government to even think about a plan B. For around twenty years, under the rule of an elected government, and with the support of the US forces in training, capacity building and logistics, this most basic of risk-management systems was not created. Something went wrong to cause an easy handover to the Taliban fighters who had been waiting for this moment for a long time, and their patience brought a result, but it is also important to look at the internal systemic failings.

In sum, my question is: was there any kind of preparedness or preventive security risk-management strategy in Afghanistan prior to the destructive collapse and fall of the state in this surprising way? If we assume that the US conducted this withdrawal on purpose and it knew what would happen in Afghanistan, then why did it not warn the Afghan government? If the US did not know, then why did it not predict this? On the Afghan side, had the government done the preparation needed to think about the implications of this kind of decision? Had it thought of a time where US forces would leave the country given that it had known for some time that the US would leave? Had the Afghan government not thought of building a defensive line against the existing augmented Taliban threat? Did it see the speed with which things would collapse, and if not, why not?

The government security services did not make any effort to confront the expansion and encroachment of the Taliban and barely fired a shot or had any kind of military resistance in Kabul. What happened in Afghanistan requires us to stop, examine and assess the real reasons behind the collapse and the lessons that can be learned and applied in any future context. We can examine the reasons behind the fall of Afghanistan by looking at the following set of factors and questioning why these factors were not picked up and acted on by the risk-management systems of state and non-state actors.

The announcement of the US forces' withdrawal from Afghanistan was a key factor that led the Taliban to act – a factor which encouraged it to prepare and plan for its next steps. In the run-up to the withdrawal, the growing limits imposed on the US training and assisting efforts supporting Afghan military forces also had an important effect. The Taliban exploited this issue to build psychological momentum for itself and cause a drop in morale for its opponents, meaning that it used the announcement of withdrawal and the declining of support as a soft power ploy to influence the psychology of the public, the Afghan government and the defence forces. Both President Trump and President Biden announced deadlines for complete withdrawal without tying such withdrawals to any progress in a peace plan or even thinking about what might happen after the US forces' departure. This must have been done for a purpose, and the Americans must have known what was going to happen, but it was part of their plan to leave the country as an easy-to-swallow bite in the mouth of the Taliban, and both administrations took actions to free Taliban prisoners and reduce US and allied forces without serious negotiations, without any clear peace plan and without any picture of what kind of Afghan government or political, social and economic structure would emerge from any such peace. This raises questions regarding what the US risk-management strategy was for what might happen after the withdrawal, and also if this was communicated to the Afghans and, separately, did the international organisations and other NATO governments understand it?

The issue of poor leadership at the civil level, from the top of the government down, which began almost immediately after the new Afghan government took over from the Taliban in 2004, did as much to weaken the efforts to create an effective national defence and security force as any military mistakes. In many ways, the politics, corruption and incompetence of both the civil and military sides of the Afghan government were at least as serious enemies to that government as the Taliban, and these factors were common knowledge. It is equally clear that the legal system, policing and local security forces were also a growing source of corruption and extortion, to the extent that they functioned at all. Those institutions were not built on solid ground or bases. Corruption was eating away at the body of the Afghan state and expanding to a point that made the Afghan forces a station for profit, not for development or building capabilities. There was also an issue related to the civil and military aid efforts of the US, other donor states and the United Nations Assistance Mission in Afghanistan. It was never properly coordinated, and efforts to create integrated civil-military plans never became effective. Huge amounts of money were spent, and big efforts were made to build improvements, but the plans were clearly useless and inactive. Effective planning efforts were never done. They may have been written well, but they have never been implemented well. There was a big gap between theory and practice. In theory, they looked like they were well designed, but they were no good in practice, and it was evident that the planning had not helped to form a rigid, strong state. The concept of a strong state was nothing but an illusion that the Afghan government created and made people believe in. All of this was well known and widely reported, and all of this should have suggested that if the US pulled the plug precipitously, then the state would collapse as a house of cards.

From at least 2007 onwards, the US, NATO and Afghan governments increasingly denied the existence of critical problems in the organisation, training, equipment and leadership of the Afghan forces. This denial was implicit in the reported levels of unreal success in both force development and combat. These false claims were part of the Afghan government's policy in that it believed that everything would go well and that it would never experience such a collapse. Governments must realise that the lack of serious and real action will one day lead to a major problem – and could even lead to the collapse of the state. As a result of these false claims, the US, NATO and allied forces never fully realised or even thought that they were dealing with an increasingly successful Taliban insurgency. They could not see that after twenty years, the Taliban could come back in a few days and impose its control on the country again. They might have expected that the Taliban would work to trigger some battles, but never to the extent that it would have a wide control of the whole state. This is also part of the illusion or wrong calculations. The international community didn't pay any attention to the collective impact of all the factors in causing such a serious loss of state. The state seemed to put its hope into the elite Afghan forces that could fight, but these forces were in reality far too small and too limited in mobility and sustainability to defend all the population centres, many of which were controlled by power brokers and lacked police and other forces loyal to the central government. It was never clear how the cities could survive on their own, even if the Taliban did not attack them, or how they could defend themselves without effective paramilitary police and local security forces. The Afghan government made mistakes in the security and military sectors, which are the most important sectors for a state to invest in as they are its safety pin to confront any kind of threat or risk that might jeopardise the overall security of the country. The government's mistakes in these areas were the most serious but they were also well known and widely reported.

There was an element of trust built on the presence of US forces in the country, which began to disappear as soon as the announcement of the withdrawal decision was made, even before implementation. As soon as the US cover disappeared, the Afghan forces felt they were not able to confront any kind of attack. They did not possess a real doctrine that would enable them to withstand the collapse of the government. The transformation of the security and militarisation function into a utilitarian function devoid of any ideological or moral commitment to the concept of the homeland, in addition to corruption, made most of the Afghan forces fragile, with no real strong bases or loyalty to the government of the day. Because the coalition focused on the most insecure areas and rarely provided enduring security after clearing them, Afghans were often too afraid to serve in local government. Civilians had little faith that their districts would remain in government hands when the coalition withdrew. The Taliban's intelligent use of soft power mixed with hard power had a psychological effect on the Afghan forces. After the media intensely focused on the precedent of the withdrawal of US forces from the region, this created a negative psychological atmosphere that led to the destruction of the security services' morale and a push to quickly surrender.

Each of these factors was known and the impact of them could have been predicted – in fact, should have been predicted. Countries should realise that no matter how strong they are and no matter how many military capabilities they possess, without having a correct and accurate risk-management plan, they are vulnerable to severe shocks and are exposed to things that they have not considered. The Afghan model is not unique, but it is illustrative of the international community's failure to build a real and strong state that people believe in and work to defend in the most difficult and ferocious circumstances. Likewise, countries must take into consideration the correct assessment of their structural and institutional reality, and not live in an illusion. The political selfishness that countries may reach in building their faith in their capabilities on false and incorrect beliefs will inevitably lead to a state of partial or complete collapse, not only at the security and military level but also in terms of the economy and society. Leaders need to consider how information is shared. In the case of the withdrawal from Afghanistan, devastating pictures, videos and personal anecdotes whipped around social media in real time. For corporate leaders, the lesson learned is to anticipate the breadth and depth of information that could colour their comments or provoke strong emotional reactions. The collapse that took place in Afghanistan does not pose a threat to Afghanistan alone – it indirectly affects the pattern of international relations and international security. This is because the existence of a radical extremist regime may inspire movements in other nations, thereby enhancing extremists' morale and encouraging them to attack vulnerable countries, destroying state structures and turning places into new extremist states.

A key lesson from Afghanistan for America's allies is that they all need to strengthen their own defence capabilities. They cannot assume that the US will just be over the horizon ready to defend their strategic interests. The US can raise very high barriers to its own involvement in regional security problems. Who wins from the Afghan debacle? Terrorist organisations of all stripes win. Al-Qaeda and the so-called Islamic State will have access to their old training grounds. The Taliban's takeover highlights that countries should not place too much trust in the external support of other nations. Because absolute trust and linking the fate of one state to the presence of support from other nations will lead to collapse or other problems if those countries abandon their support. If countries understand how these issues culminated in the fall of Afghanistan, their government forces should at least be able to resist similar situations because they have diagnosed the danger and prepared for it. However, the new Taliban regime will establish a secure state for extremists and encourage rebels in other countries to do the same, despite the differences between Afghanistan and other countries. If similar factors exist, other countries might face the same destiny.

States must learn that no matter how strong they think they are, the change in surrounding circumstances, internally and externally, might affect them. Countries must adapt to risk-management thinking to be able to identify existing risks and design appropriate plans to deal with various types of risks. They must take into consideration the likelihood of changing factors, both internally and externally, and be well prepared for these. International organisations and companies need to also do the same. Risk management is not a nice-to-have tick-box exercise; it is a vital tool for the survival of people, organisations and states.

Safa Mahdi is a professional and academic specialist in the field of international security, security risk management, intelligence and counter-terrorism.

ESIN:[1] A HUMAN RIGHTS DEFENDER ATTEMPTS TO PROTEST PEACEFULLY

———

'Education. Food. Jobs!'

Esin (not her real name) is a writer and a passionate defender of human rights in Afghanistan. She talked to Afghan Witness about the difficulties she and fellow female protestors have faced while trying to stand up for their rights since the Taliban took over Kabul.

When we spoke, Esin had recently participated in protests on 21 October with around twenty-five to thirty other women:

We started our demonstration under the motto of education, food and jobs. Those are the basics that everybody needs. But especially now, women and girls are the ones who have suffered the most since the Taliban took over. Right from the start, the Taliban were not interested in our rights and at the protests they did not allow journalists. They beat some of them with their guns and scared the rest away.

One was shouting 'I am a journalist, I am a journalist!' but the Talib did not care, and berated and beat him until he ran away. We continued to Fawara Aab Square and planned to go to the former building of the Ministry of Women's Affairs, which the Taliban has turned into the Ministry for the Propagation of Virtue and the Prevention of Vice. But the Talib prevented us, and we were faced with the choice of getting a beating or splitting up and dispersing the protest.

We won't stop, we will continue our demonstrations to break the international community's silence over incidents happening in Afghanistan.

One journalist and photographer who spoke to Afghan Witness observed the demonstration as it moved from the area around the Gulbahar Centre in Kabul to the Isteqlal High School:

When we got to the school, a Talib fighter took my hand and pushed me away from the demonstrators. I saw one beat a journalist with his gun, which caused some other journalists to leave. I moved away and went in front of Serena Hotel and then to Da Afghanistan Bank and took some pictures, but the Taliban were not happy and did not allow us to get more shots.

It is not the first time I've seen them beating journalists. I went to cover the Dehmazang explosion (20 October), and they beat journalists there. They don't allow journalists to cover the issues that aren't in their own interests.

The Taliban did not issue any comment on the demonstration or the treatment of protesters or journalists at the event.

Esin will continue to protest and encourages other women to join her in standing up for their rights.

LIBERAL
INTERVENTIONISM

———

CHAPTER 18

THE FUTURE OF LIBERAL MILITARY INTERVENTIONISM POST-KABUL

———

GRAHAM CUNDY

An incompetent government prone to kleptocracy and unable to deliver the expectations of its people. A series of tactical and localised military successes and an overwhelming sense of the tide of history turning. This was not Kabul of August 2021 but rather Kabul in November 2001.

In mid-October 2001, as a young military officer, I found myself with the Northern Alliance and General Dostum's forces fording a river next to a destroyed bridge to the north of Kabul. There was little ceremony: the exchange of considerable amounts of US dollars and a handshake with Taliban commanders marked the fall of Kabul. As in 2021, the change of power in the capital saw few shots fired. Prisoners were released, and save for a few acts of medieval barbarity, there was little retribution. In 2001, Kabul was almost deserted. Decades of civil war, isolationism and economic decline gave the city a post-apocalyptic feel. These events marked the beginning of my ten-year engagement with Afghanistan and south Asia, which spanned war-fighting, counter-insurgency, counter-narcotics and counter-terrorism. Work that covered all of the provinces and most of the districts in Afghanistan and focused on defeating the Taliban's senior leadership. The backdrop to change in power in 2001 was very different from the despair and ignominious Western withdrawal from Kabul in the summer of 2021 – which this time I watched on the news.

Many commentators suggest that the recent hasty withdrawal from Kabul is a death knell for Western military interventionism. From my experience, it is unwise to draw significant geopolitical conclusions from specific individual recent events. What is required is a thorough understanding of the lessons we can learn from our twenty-year intervention, set against the context, the nature and the assessment of future threats. We then need to take a broader view that can only come with time. What will matter in the short term is the effect on Western political will and our appetite to intervene. I do not doubt that the shadows cast from the Kabul withdrawal will add to the liberal interventionist's gloom brought on from the Trump-led global revival of nationalism.

An examination of intervention into Afghanistan is complex, however. First, there is geography: it feels like a poorly put together country. Through regional ethnic divisions and bad inward communications, each region has more in common and daily interaction with its immediate neighbouring country than with Kabul. Moreover, the harsh geography limits the movement, capacity and growth of the population even within each community. Finally, time and the changing nature of Western, and before that Russian, engagement has further complicated the picture.

THE CONTEXT - EARLY INTERVENTION AND THE ESTABLISHMENT OF A NEW STATE

In the wake of the 9/11 attacks, it seemed axiomatic that the UK government would pursue a policy supporting the US. The decision-making that led to the UK's early intervention in Afghanistan was clear. For those of us on the ground in those early days, the British mission and directives were also clear, as was the legitimacy; to destroy and defeat al-Qaeda and deny it Afghanistan as a safe operating base. How this could be done was less clear. Even at this early point there was some divergence between the UK and the US missions. For some, the methods used – from detention camps and rendition to, I would argue, the later kill or capture mission against Osama bin Laden of May 2011 – had overtones of revenge and retribution.

The UK's early military intervention was marked by small but capable forces working largely unsupported and at a considerable range from base. Unusually, we found ourselves frequently ahead of any US presence. The latent networks of British intelligence agencies were significant during this period and, in comparison with the CIA, had considerable depth and breadth, but most importantly they supplied excellent unbiased analysis. Our position of relative weakness in terms of combat power led us to mount an asymmetric campaign. While our ability to provide US airstrikes enabled the Northern Alliance to gain local tactical success, it was our ability to provide intelligence and verify information on the ground and, building on our fledgling relationships, forge alliances within and between Northern Alliance forces that were of significant value. Looking towards a post-conflict stage, these would have a unique strategic advantage, including enabling the Bonn Conference.

Our ability through our presence on the ground to encourage those Northern Alliance warlords capable enough to disrupt the state-building process to instead attend the conference, set the conditions for an agreement to incorporate, rather than alienate, these non-state actors in a centralised Afghan state. The result was the Afghan Interim Authority with a six-month mandate to be followed by a two-year Transitional Authority, after which elections were to be held. This also set the formal conditions for the International Security Assistance Force (ISAF).

ISAF AND NATO EXPANSION

Under ISAF, the conventional military force numbers from the US and NATO increased, as did the number of contributing nations. Military coalitions create a political dynamic of their own. The early drivers and objectives clearly defined in 2001 and early 2002 became increasingly opaque as time passed. A coalition of two became a force of more than 130,000 strong at ISAF's height with troops from fifty-one NATO and partner countries. NATO, I would argue, is not a political entity driven to achieve objectives but more a meeting house to build on like-minded views. Brussels is a long way from Bamian, both geographically and culturally. Political objectives of the grand strategy gradually gave way to the political ambitions of more junior contributing nations. Military commanders and diplomats saw Afghanistan as a means of 'cutting their teeth' or progressing their careers with energy spent on internal coalition building. For some, it appeared that creating a post-conflict Afghan state became a convenience rather than a strategic driver. The US military's Operation Enduring Freedom ran in parallel to their engagement in ISAF, demonstrating the US's divergence. However, UK forces too would run national operations in support of their own objectives when required.

Through their embassies and diplomatic missions, nation states also wanted to be heard with bilateral arrangements and national aid programmes. It could be hard to identify a unified Western diplomatic voice from an Afghan perspective, especially in Kabul. In contrast, Afghans could see that despite NATO's internal factions and the US's unilateral objectives, the military and the military commanders could provide the single issue of security and with that came influence.

With the increase in the military capability of US and NATO forces and the simultaneous write-down of the Taliban, the strength of coalition forces provoked a changing mindset for the military. The early tasks moved from war-fighting to the more nuanced counter-insurgency. However, this too became obscured by operations focused on counter-terrorism and a fixation on al-Qaeda and its affiliates. Moreover, with the US Treasury focus on al-Qaeda after the 9/11 attacks, the money and resources that counter-terrorism attracted led to an often skewed perception of the fundamental nature of the threat on the ground and with it the analysis and conclusions of the capitals of coalition states and their decision-makers.

NATO's expansion in 2006 saw NATO forces replace the light and agile deployment of US forces in the south and east, centred on Kandahar and notably into the Pashtun heartlands and historic home of the Taliban. The hitherto modest presence of US forces had threatened neither the existing tribal-based power structures nor the Taliban, and their occupation was largely uncontested. As too was the heroin poppy cultivation, the significant form of subsistence farming in the south. This was about to change with the influx of ISAF troops.

The UK MoD's initial intent was to reduce and ultimately remove its deployment of forces in Kabul and take responsibility for the regionally strategically significant Kandahar province. However, the delay in political decision-making in London meant that the Canadians took Kandahar province, and the UK now looked to Helmand as a substitute. Prior to UK troops being deployed to Helmand, our understanding of the nature of the task and threat was limited. I am reminded of an early meeting pre-deployment at the UK Permanent Joint Headquarters in Northwood where there was a genuine concern that the US Special Operations Forces in the province had seen little opposition and that the 'task may be too light'. Asked about what we knew about the threat levels within the province, the senior military intelligence officer stated that information was limited and that as far as he knew, 'unicorns might still roam in Helmand'. The subsequent deployments and hard-fought counter-insurgency campaigns are now well known.

Counter-insurgency for the military is a mix of attrition to write down opposing forces and their capability and 'holding the ring' to provide security that enables the processes of a political settlement to form. Western military forces can deliver many of the functions of the state, to a greater or lesser extent, and as clearly seen in the post-invasion of Iraq (the provision of security, sanitation, power and logistics); however, it is poorly equipped to actually govern a country. The creation of Provincial Reconstruction Teams with their political advisers went some way to creating support for a fledgling Afghan political process. The ambitions of the West and the Afghan government were frequently at odds with the needs of the local population and notably so in the south. A failing of the Bonn Agreement emphasised the dominant voices of the northern political elites and at the expense of the Pashtuns. Increasingly, the commitment of the Kabul government and its backers was of an Afghanistan that did not resonate with many, especially in the south. Promises of schools for girls and access to satellite TV meant little to subsistence poppy farmers for whom schooling for any child was out of reach, and even radio was a luxury. Rather than a counter-culture message, what was missing was a counter-narrative that resonated with the populace. Similarly, the Afghan National Army and the Afghan National Police, newly trained and equipped by the Western coalition, were frequently seen as an army of occupation to the Pashtun south and their level of corruption went beyond the Taliban's. In the absence of justice, rough justice will do, and here the Taliban had the edge.

From a British perspective, the operations in Helmand were hard-fought, but many lessons should be learned. The army's six-month operational deployment cycle saw new brigades, each with a very differing formation, tackle the issues in very different ways. There was seldom coherence between each deployment other than a seemingly constant need to occupy, if not control, more ground than the last, even at the risk of 'hollowing out' the centre's security.

This partly stemmed from the direction given by the staff from the often disjointed multinational ISAF headquarters in Kabul and the nature of the leadership of the British Army's brigades.

Brigade commanders frequently had differing views on the nature of operational success. With one eye on the ticking clock of a six-month deployment and the other on the perception of the brigade's, and their own, success, for those who had a more enduring presence, this sent a poor message to the Afghans. I do not doubt that each believed in the merits of their campaign, but whether this matched the long-term interests of the district and region requires more debate.

Some criticism also comes from grand gestures that played more to a domestic audience than the ISAF wider campaign. In 2008, Operation Eagle's Summit, the aim of which was to provide an additional turbine to the Kajaki dam, was one such example. The scale of the operation was considerable, and the risks that were taken to secure the site and the 180km road move were a significant achievement. The operation was widely played in the British press and hailed by NATO as a significant victory that would win the 'hearts and minds' of the Afghan people. The Task Force Helmand commander described it as 'the end of the beginning' of the fighting in Helmand. Arguably it was, but for very different reasons than intended. On last reports in 2015, the turbine remained unmounted, requiring 700 tonnes of concrete to be delivered through Taliban-controlled roads. Additionally, the Taliban took revenue from the current in-place turbines, and the power generation plant of the coalition forces in Kandahar airfield produced more electricity than the turbine would.

Some criticism should also be made towards the messages and

reporting coming back from the theatre. With the emphasis on the success of each deployment, it set expectations in Northwood and Westminster. The temptation was to underplay or ignore difficult issues, perhaps in the hope that if it could be held off for long enough, because of the six-month rotations, it would be somebody else's problem.

One area of some success was the 'train and equip' programme. Although vast in scale and costly, this created a more capable Afghan police and security force, which was bolstered by the British Army's focus on operational mentoring and liaison teams.

Of even more notable success was the creation of the Afghan special forces. Here the focus was on the strategic level and outcome-driven effects, enabled by Western supporting capabilities and intelligence. Their inception and subsequent success owe much to the enduring work of the British intelligence agencies. As the British government signalled a drawdown of its conventional forces and commitment to Afghanistan, much of the critical work countering the rising Taliban threat was laid at their door. Indeed, the Afghan special forces were undoubtedly instrumental in supporting the final effort of the British withdrawal in August at considerable cost.

I have deliberately not mentioned the counter-narcotics effort with Afghanistan. This is a complex area but especially so for the British forces working in the poppy heartlands of Helmand. There were few, if any, locals for whom poppy and narcotics did not have an impact. To try to conduct a counter-narcotic eradication operation against subsistence farmers is at odds with any counter-insurgency policy driven by 'hearts and minds' – at least without a significant 'alternative livelihoods' or agri-reform implementation.

CONCLUSION

The fall of Kabul and the nature of the West's precipitous withdrawal has few redeeming points. Whatever the long-term outcome, it cannot be a strategic success for the West, not after a twenty-year campaign rationalised as an attempt to eradicate the very same anti-Western forces which now rule the country.

The way in which the US executed its decision damages multilateralism and reinforces the view of many in south Asia that the US is a fickle ally. The success of the early military intervention was in part due to the clearly defined objectives and solid political engagement by the intervening nation states. The initial willingness to support the effort materially, financially and with patience is in contrast to the past ten years of the campaign.

What was less well resourced was the post-conflict nation-building. Our expectations of a democratic Afghanistan at peace with itself and its neighbours was overly idealistic. Military capability in isolation from the political and diplomatic process is transitory.

For those who suggest that Western liberal military intervention is over, I would caution that the alternative is to cede ground and influence to autocratic states, which may have a different view. These states have the patience to intervene in the long term and have fewer scruples in how the aim is achieved. It, too, means turning a blind eye to genocide and atrocities.

Technology, stand-off and over-the-horizon capabilities may provide a solution and kinetic effect but are less enduring than presence – they can also give a warped view of conditions on the ground and are vulnerable to distortion and manipulation. While indirect coercive measures such as economic sanctions and diplomatic pressure have a place, we can see today in Belarus that their impact is at best limited.

The UK's post-Brexit 'Global Britain' agenda needs to be more than just words. If Britain is genuinely to be a 'force for good in the world', we must have a clear strategic-level foreign policy based on well-articulated and practised beliefs on what is right. This requires both the conviction to pursue and well-integrated diplomatic, political and military means to achieve. Nevertheless, strategy is not just about capability and intent but also about the perception of rivals, adversaries and allies alike.

Graham Cundy served twenty-five years in the Royal Marines. As a senior member of the national security community, he contributed to the design and implementation of UK defence and security strategy, and managed relationships with a wide range of international security partners.

CHAPTER 19

QUESTIONS ABOUT THE FUTURE OF LIBERAL INTERVENTIONISM

JEREMY PURVIS

———

O nly sixteen months separated the end of Operation Noble Anvil, the US-termed NATO bombing of Serbia in the summer of 1999, and Operation Enduring Freedom, the invasion of Afghanistan in the autumn of 2001.

The debates over the nobility of the 1999 actions without a UN mandate and those of the present on whether we see freedoms which will endure in Afghanistan force us to question what the future is of intervention within or against regimes by others – bi- or multilaterally.

The well-rehearsed arguments by the British government at the time of the latter stages of the conflicts in the Balkans fell square-ly in the bracket of liberal intervention. Those arguments held broadly that sovereign states maintain their sovereignty by uphold-ing universal rights of all citizens, and should they fail to do so, their sovereignty can be abridged. Statesman William Gladstone's arguments after the Bulgarian horrors had a similar thread a century and a quarter earlier in that region, so while not a new concept, liberal interventionism has taken on a more direct tone in the past three decades.

We have come to believe in this period that the previous prevailing norm of non-interventionism was defeasible on the basis that when horrors were perpetrated by a government and there was no internal check to stop them, an external check was required. With that government denying its people universal rights, which should be enjoyed by any person, at any time, anywhere, other governments of nations had a justification for military action to prevent the further abuse of its people.

The invasion of Afghanistan, after an ultimatum to present Osama bin Laden to the US was ignored by the Taliban regime, was not based on such a moral argument. Instead, this was based on fears for national security. And because many nations were subject to the threat, there was a coalition formed for the intervention. When the military phase of the operation ceased, however, the forces remained. The mission was then to remould the country along universal norms with universal rights and freedoms. The continuing intervention was justified as the invading countries considered the Taliban not fit to protect the interests of the Afghan people. A new Afghanistan should be built, the intervening nations believed – one founded on the rules-based international order and in compliance with a universal set of rights.

So, from the Christian socialist morals of the left to those on the right who at home decried an active state in domestic politics but were happy for an active state abroad, a form of consensus had developed. This consensus to continue intervention up to August

2021 was founded on the evolution of a national security operation to a human development or democracy-building presence.

While some will cite the NATO bombings of Serbia in 1999 as a success, others see the Afghanistan mission as one of limited gains. Indeed, many view Operation Enduring Freedom a failure.

With the change of regime in Kabul, any discussions over the future of how external powers intervene, directly or indirectly, in Afghanistan take a more complex nature. At the time of writing, the UN has rebuffed automatic recognition of the Taliban regime as the legitimate government of the country. Some countries have indicated they will never recognise the Taliban formally, while others have said this will be inevitable. The UK has said it will not (yet) recognise the Taliban, but its special envoy has met with its leadership. There is likely to be a multifaceted set of discussions going forward, making previously easy decisions about intervention or non-intervention less clear. One thing which is clear, however, is that the Taliban feels vindicated and will move ahead on the creation of its emirate.

I recently chaired a meeting in Parliament at which the Afghanistan country director of a charity trying to continue delivering services after the Taliban takeover spoke. She was abroad at the time of the final advance and, so far, has been unable to return. She told me that in the interactions with the Taliban representatives, who are trying to be systematic in taking over the various reins of administration, there is a feeling of high confidence among them. After all, the Taliban and previous forces in Afghanistan had defeated the most powerful empires of the twentieth and twenty-first centuries, and as a bonus it humbled the remnant of the most powerful of the nineteenth. Thus, the various assertions that those nations which fled in semi-managed chaos will maintain pressure and hold the Taliban to Western norms ring hollow. Taliban negotiators knew they had succeeded around the table in Doha as much as their fighters were gaining ground through threat and violence.

Afghanistan will now be governed according to the theological approach of the world's fourth Islamic emirate first and follow more recent global constructs of universal rights second.

In this context and with the cautionary lessons we've learned about liberal interventionism since the conflicts in the Balkans, the Middle East and North Africa, what is its future in Afghanistan and beyond?

If we see the latter intervention operation as a failure, what would be the appetite for a former type of intervention? Has the zeal of 1999 been lost with the failure of the 2001 operation?

It is worth recognising, of course, that the debate on intervention is more nuanced. The obviously valid criticism of the moral argument behind liberal interventionism was that it was partial from the start. An approach founded on the moral authority to set aside sovereignty for the protection of universal rights should logically also be applied universally. There should be parity in application. If the threshold of abuse of rights is met in a large powerful state, then it should apply equally to abuses in a smaller, less powerful one. The persecution of a Muslim minority in the Balkans met with NATO intervention, but the persecution of more than an estimated 1 million Muslims (the majority of them Uyghurs) in internment camps in China has met with none. Critics of liberal intervention as well as those who highlight the hypocrisy of the Western powers find common ground. The rise of China and the activism of Russia in the past two decades have also had an impact on the appetite of the Western powers to assert intervention, as well as the scarring of the intervening experience in Iraq.

The UK has further admitted by its actions in Afghanistan that it does not hold to parity of application, even on national security grounds, on simple grounds of scale. The UK stated that even if it wanted to retain a military intervention to prevent a Taliban takeover of Kabul, it couldn't do so without the US being present. The UK integrated review of defence, development and diplomacy stated explicitly that actors within Afghanistan pose a very significant security risk to our nation. British security services have said the terrorism threat to the UK has now increased since the Taliban takeover. Despite this, the UK did not even consider reconfiguring its global military and security postures, or seek to build a coalition of other nations, based on the protection of its citizens. Instead, it stated that US leadership was the deciding factor. This is likely to remain the case for the foreseeable future.

So, with the balance shifting with China and Russia, a new consensus in the US against external aggression, the UK and others choosing to step back from military leadership for intervention and instead deploying a form of cold war posture, and those who put theology ahead of the universality of temporal and not spiritual standards and rights feeling vindicated, what now? Some have argued we are in a new age of impunity. There is some merit to this, but it is not wholly the case.

The world is – contrary to what the daily news may make us think – more stable, democratic, free and tolerant than in any time in recent history. There may be failed states in the future, of course, such is perhaps inevitable, but fewer of them. Abuse of rights and government oppression is perhaps also inevitable. The point is that by a combination of economic development and education provision, governing systems have become more responsive to the needs of their people, and fewer countries are autocracies which impose their will. And where there are failures of governance or dispute, there are now more effective corrective measures. There are also international bodies such as the International Criminal Court which have gained status (even when the US or China step aside or are actively obstructive) and global efforts on climate change and the Sustainable Development Goals are much more international in nature, and accepted as so, than ever before. The very perception of state sovereignty has been slowly shifting in light of these global efforts.

While countries which would not hold to liberal interventionism are stronger now than they were, the tools of the rest of the international community for non-direct military intervention are now possessed by more nations than they were twenty years ago.

The question arises, then, as to what is the sustainable validity of a concept which has its foundation on universality but won't be applied universally, and which also relies on one strong nation and its prevailing leadership at the time. There are some tools that are more flexible than traditional military activities which can be applied. Drone technology, for instance, or cyber capability, global financial transparency tools, more nimble and active sanctions regimes and more transparent economic levers from economies such as the EU. Some have a questionable foundation in international law, and there is a lack of transparency in the use of others, so this is why debates on their use must be included within the debates on intervention.

For example, NATO has rules of engagement on cyber defence,

but not on cyber proliferation or deployment. Indeed, the extension of international law across all the areas of new technology that should be applied to a sovereign state is ripe for urgent global debate. There is a non-proliferation treaty for weapons of mass destruction, but not weapons of mass disruption.

While some of the actual rules of the rules-based international order are challenged by China and others, they do remain, and if adjusted to take into consideration emerging powers in Asia and Africa, they can be replenished and renewed with greater authority. The Sustainable Development Goals are genuinely global in nature and do not rely on the imposition of a set of Christian or Western morals or values. Instead, they are framed in a much wider and global way than any previous set of development rules, be they the World Bank or the International Monetary Fund. This has meant we have seen changes in approach in the world's other three Islamic emirates in the Gulf too, as well as across the globe. This is seen in shifts in both theological and policy thinking across the world for girls' and women's rights, media freedom and transparency in governance. While claims for our influence over the Taliban may ring hollow, suggestions of influence from the Gulf do not.

The technological and globalisation developments that have been marked since the start of the century are relevant. Intervention has a differing set of tools than those of twenty years ago, and in this period the very concept of nation-state sovereignty on tackling global challenges has also shifted. Pressure can be presented in various ways and possibly with greater success. This can be termed 'alternative interventionism' as it means states can build different coalitions of the willing with the ability of using numerous tools, some more targeted to alleviate specific problems, and some appliable by relatively smaller states to larger ones too. The issue is whether or not there is a global set of norms where the sovereignty of a nation can be set aside for a specific purpose.

Picking just one example within Afghanistan: the oppression of women. This is an issue of genuine global concern, but it should be noted that laws to ensure gender rights and opportunities came from presidential decree, not organic law-making. Arguably, these laws have never had consensus support across most of the male population in the country. But if Afghanistan is to avoid being a failed state, the professional, legal, technical and economic involvement of women will be necessary. The Taliban wants to set the parameters of its own sovereignty, but it also is fully aware it hasn't the capacity to govern well to provide essential and then desirable services. Human development intervention through the direct delivery of services via UN trust funds, setting aside theological restrictions, combined with ongoing dialogue and pressure from near neighbours and the three other Islamic emirates, will need to be tested. This is a form of intervention, more complex perhaps and more opaque than a NATO bomber or a drone strike, but likely to be needed. The moral underpinning still stands to a large degree, and perhaps the moral ambiguities of a more complex intervention may have a positive effect as they reflect the reality of major powers unwilling to be consistent or have parity of military intervention. Can we through global pressure deliver human development in a state bypassing that state's organs? This is just one test of the new realities of intervention.

Technological or other forms of intervention do need moral and global legitimacy, however, even if there are countries or agencies willing to apply them, and this is a complex process. It is why the

UN needs reinvigoration. We have just over a quarter-century before the UN celebrates its centenary. The thinking needs to start now as to what the successor to the Sustainable Development Goals are to be post-2030, with the addition of a global set of standards on governance – not a Western set of norms but global; ones that are not determined by a geopolitical challenge for primacy between the USA and China. Demographic, climate, developmental and global financial balances will already be markedly different in 2050. The standards of governance, and indeed the use of tools that states can use against each other, will also shift.

The debates on the Responsibility to Protect need new life, as well as new sets of discussions to review and put on a genuinely global footing the global sanctions that come with certain areas of government abuse. The obvious position of China is a block to certain areas but not to others. Much more proactive work needs to be done for coalitions of the willing in certain development areas, such as women's economic empowerment or media freedom. China needs global markets and it is not immune to global views on soft power. A convening role to breathe new life into a concept which has been battered by inconsistent use, and when used has in some areas been found wanting, is now desperately needed.

If the UK claims to have more freedom to forge a global presence in a post-Brexit world, to exploit its P5 position and its might as a military and intelligence power, this is a debate we need to lead.

Lord Purvis of Tweed is the Liberal Democrats' foreign affairs, international development and international trade spokesman in the House of Lords.

CHAPTER 20

GENERAL DANNATT, THE FOREVER WARS AND THE MILITARY ELITE'S THREAT TO DEMOCRACY

PAUL DIXON

INTRODUCTION

B ritain is a 'warrior nation' that has fought wars almost continuously since 1707.[1] The 9/11 wars in Iraq and Afghanistan
provided the 'military-industrial complex' with the opportunity
not only to stem the decline in post-Cold War military spending
but also to considerably enhance their power over governments.
The prosecution of permanent 'forever war' has contributed to the
rise of authoritarian populism and concerns about the future of
democracy.

There is evidence that both President Obama (2009–17) and
Prime Minister Gordon Brown (2007–10) privately believed the
Afghanistan war was unwinnable but encountered problems in
withdrawing because of the pressure of the military elite and their

allies.[2] President Biden's determination to withdraw the US from Afghanistan in 2021 was probably reinforced by Obama's and his bruising encounters with the military over the 2009 'surge' in Afghanistan.

This chapter argues that the British military elite empowered themselves by maximising their involvement in both the Iraq (2003) and the Afghanistan (2006) wars. Since they were already overstretched before the invasion of Iraq, they were pursuing 'beyond maximum' military involvement in the wars. In 2006, General Dannatt (Chief of the General Staff 2006–09) exploited the military's crisis by breaking constitutional convention and publicly attacking the Labour government. His successor, General Richards (Chief of the General Staff 2009–10; Chief of the Defence Staff 2010–13), also resisted democratic control. The military elite portrayed themselves as the victims of an incompetent government and an uncaring nation. A 'militarisation offensive' was launched, and the 'military covenant' was invented to demand greater resources, respect and power for the military elite.

Senior British military officers, like their US counterparts, have resented and evaded democratic control. Their growing power represents a threat to democracy, but such is the extent of militarisation – the growing and excessive power of the military – that criticism of the military elite, whether from the left or the right, is considered largely beyond the bounds of legitimate debate.[3]

GENERAL DANNATT AND THE DOMINANT MILITARY NARRATIVE

The dominant narrative among the military elite suggests that since they are the 'strategic experts', governments should defer to their judgement on how best to win wars. The generals argued that what is required to defeat the enemy is a united, national political will to demonstrate to the enemy that they will not prevail.[4] Determination is required not just for the 'front line' but also for the 'home front', so that the enemy will be deprived of hope that they can ever win. National will is projected on the front line by the escalation of force, the refusal to negotiate with the enemy and a commitment to 'strategic patience' to fight the long, or permanent, war.[5] On the home front, there must be national unity behind the military elite's strategy.

From this perspective, the operation of democracy – party, media and popular debate and division – represents a threat to the projection of unity that is necessary to show the enemy that the nation will prevail. A 'strategy of optimism' (or deceptive propaganda) is advocated which, regardless of the reality on the ground, always claims that the military is on the brink of victory if only it is provided with 'sufficient' support and resources. Such optimism was used to commit reluctant British, US and other NATO governments deeper into the quagmire of unwinnable and permanent war. Growing casualties created a 'sacrifice trap' where previous losses were used to justify further sacrifice in the vain search for victory in ever-escalating 'forever wars'.

Scrutiny and criticism are portrayed not only as an insult to those who have served and sacrificed but also as potentially treacherous for undermining the propaganda required to defeat the enemy. Authoritarianism and military control are necessary to win wars, and since these wars are 'generational' or 'permanent', then the restriction of democracy is not just a short-term emergency measure. Furthermore, since the military's authoritarian organisation structure is portrayed as the model of efficiency and the spectacularly popular embodiment of the nation, it raises the question as to why we need democratic politics at all?

General Dannatt was a key exponent of the dominant military narrative. On 12 October 2006, he broke constitutional convention and launched a public attack on the Labour government in the *Daily Mail*. The head of the army was described as 'a very honest general' who 'frightens the life out of politicians'. Dannatt stated, 'Honesty is what it is about. The truth will out. We have got to speak the truth. Leaking and spinning, at the end of the day, are not helpful.'[6] He asserted that the government and nation had broken the 'military covenant' by failing to provide the required respect and resources.

A 'militarisation offensive' was launched which involved the heroification of the military and the militarisation of the government and nation. General Dannatt was involved in establishing Help for Heroes, which has promoted the military across civilian society, including sports and entertainment. The military was also promoted in schools, partly to encourage recruitment, by expanding the Cadet Force, turning troops into teachers and putting military subjects into the curriculum. War commemoration was used to foster patriotism and the military were to become more visible, through initiatives such as Veterans' Day in 2006.[7]

The head of the British Army expressed Conservative views. He warned of the 'predatory Islamist vision', opposed multiculturalism and argued that British society and the army were underpinned by 'Christian values'. Military values were superior to those of civilian society, and military spending should be increased at the expense of social security, which protects the poorest and most vulnerable in British society.[8] Dannatt's 'militarisation offensive' launched a sustained barrage of criticism against the government, suggesting that it was to blame for the deaths of British soldiers. His decision to join the Conservative Party in 2009 after stepping down as Chief of the General Staff raised questions about the politicisation of the military elite.

Since 2006, General (Sir; now Lord) Dannatt has blamed the Labour government for 'strategic miscalculations' over the Iraq and Afghanistan wars. He has, generally, exonerated both the military elite and the Conservative government (2010–) from responsibility for failure despite their support for both wars.[9] He expressed three key criticisms of the Labour governments.

First, he blamed the government for ignoring military advice and overstretching the military by simultaneously fighting two under-strength operations in Iraq and Afghanistan.[10] He claimed that the military was 'surprised' by Prime Minister Blair's decision to go to southern Afghanistan, and he warned against the 'perfect storm' of simultaneously fighting two wars.[11]

Second, in Afghanistan, the government had 'forced an under-strength military presence to change its mission from humanitarian security building through development to defending ground against underestimated opposition forces'. Ministers were responsible for the 'yawning gap' between the peaceful intent of the mission and 'the more violent outcome'.[12]

Third, General Dannatt was frustrated that the Labour government didn't properly fund the Afghanistan war and this in effect cost soldiers' lives. The army was fighting with 'part of one arm' tied behind its back, because of a lack of troops.[13]

VERY HONEST GENERALS?

Militarists, whether consciously or unconsciously, have promoted a powerful, conservative-authoritarian political agenda. This has been concealed behind an 'anti-politics' rhetoric which contrasts honest generals with dishonest politicians. For militarists, the military's authoritarian organisation and its superior moral values represent the best of the British nation since the military pledges its allegiance to the monarch and not to the democratically elected government. General Dannatt has expressed a conditional view of military subordination to democratic control: 'Yes, of course we will do whatever the elected government of the day wants us to do, provided the needs of individuals are looked after and we are in balance.'[14]

General Richards was also highly resistant to democratic control. He boasted that his attitude towards seeking political clearance for military operations was, 'Don't ask, don't tell, just do it.' According to General Richards, in Sierra Leone in 2000, 'I more or less ignored my orders from London and committed my soldiers to leading the fight against the rebels.' Later, he challenged Prime Minister David Cameron's control of the 2011 Libyan war because he did not believe Cameron had the wisdom and capability for commanding the military.[15]

A more democratic Britain, with a broader debate, might have better reflected public scepticism of the Iraq and Afghanistan wars and avoided involvement in two unwinnable wars, or at least limited the UK's military exposure.[16] Between 2006 and 2010, General Richards consistently suggested that the Afghanistan war was being won even though there was, behind the scenes, little evidence that this was the case.[17] General Dannatt wanted to build on Britain's 'success' in Helmand in 2009 even as he later admitted that the US marines 'rescued' the British.[18] Theo Farrell's *Unwinnable* suggests that, in contrast to the military elite's optimism, the reality was that by summer 2009 there was plummeting British troop morale: and while the army 'did not break ... it came back battered'.[19]

There are three key problems with General Dannatt's account. First, the Chilcot report found that it was the military elite who had pressured and manipulated for maximum military involvement not only in the invasion of Iraq but also for the deployment to southern Afghanistan. The executive summary concludes:

The size and composition of a UK military contribution to the US-led invasion of Iraq was largely discretionary. The US wanted some UK capabilities (including Special Forces), to use UK bases, and the involvement of the UK military to avoid the perception of unilateral US military action. The primary impetus to max-imise the size of the UK contribution and the recommendations on its composition came from the Armed Forces, with the agree-ment of Mr Hoon.[20]

General Richards lobbied for maximum army involvement in Iraq but in *Taking Command* he regards the invasion as a 'grand stra-tegic error'.[21] Even after the Chilcot report was published, Dannatt suggested that it concluded that politicians were solely responsible for Iraq.[22]

The available evidence suggests that within about six months of the invasion of Iraq, when violence was escalating, it was the military elite who wanted to lead a dangerous mission to south-ern Afghanistan. They manoeuvred and manipulated the Labour government into the deployment and provided assurances that the military could simultaneously handle both the Iraq and Afghan operations. In a pivotal moment in the Chilcot Inquiry, the former head of the military, General Sir Michael Walker, confirmed that the government was following military advice in deploying to southern Afghanistan.[23]

By 2014, General Dannatt appeared to concede the military elite's responsibility for the decision to deploy to Helmand. He suggested that 'we' and 'maybe I' should have reconsidered committing the military to two operations when it only had the organisation and manpower for one.[24] In 2016, he asserted that the army had not pressurised the government into Afghanistan, which contradicts the evidence of both the Chilcot report and Farrell's semi-official army history of Afghanistan.[25] The military transformed the peace-building mission to warfighting when it shifted, without government approval, to the 'platoon houses' of northern Helmand. Now involved in warfighting in Afghanistan while violence was peaking in Iraq, the 'militarisation offensive' deflected responsibility onto the ever-unpopular 'dishonest' politicians.[26]

The second problem with General Dannatt's account of the wars is its inconsistency and incoherence. He claims that the government had ignored intelligence advice that the Taliban would present a formidable enemy, but in his book he states that the intelligence reported 'a generally benign situation'.[27] General Dannatt suggested that Britain could have reconsidered its deployment to Afghanistan in 2006 because of the deteriorating situation in Iraq.[28] But he also claimed that the shift to Afghanistan came because the British had done so well in Iraq and the Afghanistan war was in the national interest.[29] In 2006, he publicly called for withdrawal from Iraq to fight the war in Afghanistan.[30] In 2016, he was critical of Labour ministers who refused to admit that Iraq was a 'disaster'. He described the Iraq war as 'an error of near biblical proportions'. But he also criticised the government for failing to surge in Iraq alongside the Americans in 2007, even though he had claimed the military was already overstretched and had publicly called for withdrawal from Iraq.[31] In 2019, he supported British involvement in both the Iraq and Afghanistan wars.[32]

Third, in Afghanistan it was the military, rather than the government, which was more interested in warfighting than peacebuilding. The military altered the peacebuilding mission by redeploying to the 'platoon houses' of northern Helmand. Importantly, the government was not asked to approve the redeployment even though this move transformed the whole operation.[33]

Although the military elite bore considerable responsibility for the overstretch and the consequent crisis, they portrayed themselves as the victims of an uncaring government and nation which had broken the ancient 'military covenant'.[34] By contrast, the Ministry of Defence's private polling suggested that the military was already one of the most popular institutions in Britain – it was the wars it was fighting that were (and remained) unpopular.[35] The military covenant was not ancient but invented by the army elite in 2000 to increase the military elite's power and resist government control.[36] According to Dannatt, the 'military crisis' had a positive: 'It was the catalyst for the British public to start showing unprecedented support for their soldiers.'[37]

Since it was the military elite who pressured and manipulated for 'beyond maximum' military involvement in the two wars, it was they who should bear considerable responsibility for overstretch and the breaching of the 'harmony guidelines', which protect the mental health of military personnel. Furthermore, the Chilcot report concludes that there were failings in the MoD and the military on the provision of equipment, but funding was not an issue. Jack Fairweather, the *Daily Telegraph* journalist, argued that the military elite were responsible for the debacle over the failure to provide adequately protected armoured vehicles and sufficient helicopters. By contrast, it was politicians, anxious to avoid politically damaging casualties, who accelerated the provision of armoured vehicles.[38]

The military elite and their allies kept up a sustained attack on the government, blaming it for a lack of resources and support that cost the lives of soldiers. In *Brown at 10*, Anthony Seldon and Guy Lodge conclude on Afghan policy, 'It was a moot point whether Brown was shaping British policy or merely managing pressure from the services, and public opinion whipped up by the media.'[39]

In opposition, David Cameron had exploited the military elite's attacks on the government. But as Prime Minister (2010–16), he claimed to have been alarmed at the way the army chiefs ran rings around Gordon Brown, colluding with *The Sun* to whip up support for the troops 'to gain financial leverage for more equipment and more men'. Cameron was going to assert civilian control of defence policy and complained that the military elite wanted to be in Afghanistan 'almost indefinitely'.[40]

The spectacular growth in the popularity of the military makes it more difficult for governments to exert control. Since 2005, 'favourable' opinions of the armed forces have gone from a 'low' of 54 per cent in 2005 to 88 per cent in 2017. The Hansard Society's 2019 Audit of Political Engagement suggested that 74 per cent of the public had most confidence in the military 'to act in the best interests of the public'. By contrast, just 29 to 34 per cent had confidence in political actors. An October 2015 YouGov poll found one-quarter could imagine supporting the armed forces taking over the powers of government, but this increased to 44 per cent among UKIP supporters, important advocates of authoritarian populism. In 2006, Prime Minister Tony Blair considered sacking Dannatt for breaking constitutional convention, but such was the military's popularity and power that he feared an adverse public reaction, so he publicly declared that he agreed with the general.

CONCLUSION: 'THE BUCK ALWAYS STOPS WITH THE BOSS'? (GENERAL DANNATT)

Since 9/11, a powerful transnational militarist coalition has argued that authoritarianism/militarisation is necessary to win the permanent state of global war. This is not an explicit attack on democracy but expressed as an attack on 'politics', with the implication that there is a more effective, honest, non-political and morally superior military way of organising society. This highly political militarist critique is so powerful that the exhaustive Chilcot report has already been 'forgotten' and criticism of the military elite appears to be largely beyond 'legitimate debate'. While there is some accountability on the front line, there is 'almost zero accountability for the high-level decision-making that led to the prosecution of two deeply troubled campaigns'.[41] In *How Democracy Ends*, David

Runciman argues that in 'firmly established' democracies, a coup will take place incrementally and in the name of democracy – it 'simply requires that a democratically elected government be held to ransom by forces it lacks the power to resist'.[42]

Professor Paul Dixon is an honorary research fellow at Birkbeck College, University of London. His forthcoming books are entitled *The Authoritarian Temptation: The Iraq and Afghan Wars and the Militarisation of British Democracy* (Verso, 2023) and *War and Militarisation: NATO's Invasion of Afghanistan* (Edinburgh University Press, 2023).

CHAPTER 21

THE POST-AFGHAN RESET AND THE CASE FOR REBUILDING EU–UK SECURITY COOPERATION

STEPHEN GETHINS

INTERNATIONAL SOLIDARITY SQUANDERED

In the heat of the summer of 2001 in Tbilisi, Georgia, locals had taken to poking fun at the American diplomats for the wall that was being built in front of their embassy. On visits to the Georgian mountains and over dinner, US officials would be teased about hiding behind the wall in what they considered to be a relatively safe city. Given the existential threat posed to the country, just ten years old at the time, by its neighbour Russia, the US presence was considered reassuring by most locals.

A few weeks later in September of that year, the need for that wall became abundantly clear as Georgians, like people throughout the world, looked on in horror at the terror attacks in New York.

The reaction globally was one of immediate and heartfelt solidarity with the United States.

It was a moment that brought the international community together. Offers of support and assistance were made across the world, including from Premier Jiang Zemin of China and Vladimir Putin, who had been President of Russia for just over a year. Even old adversaries demonstrated support, with Cuba offering medical supplies and respectful silences being held in Iran. It was a rare and precious moment of international unity.

Twenty years on, that sense of international unity has all but disappeared. In a world of competing interests and ideologies, it was always going to be difficult to maintain, but more could have been done to build on that moment of rare entente. Those days seem like an entirely different world from the scenes from Kabul airport in August 2021, when more horror was streamed live to our TVs and mobile devices. Once again, there was a sense of the closing of one chapter of history and the opening of another with unknown repercussions.

Tempting as it is, events in Afghanistan cannot be viewed in isolation. Over the past twenty years, there have been significant developments and changes that must not be overlooked. For example, the steady rise of China as a superpower to be reckoned with, a Russia that under the authoritarian stewardship of Vladimir Putin is an assertive international actor and a USA that, though still militarily and economically dominant, does not appear to be the reliable international partner it was once considered to be. Moreover, the EU has grown and been strengthened by further enlargements but struggles to find a coherent international role.

THE UK'S STRING OF FOREIGN POLICY FAILURES

The United Kingdom has also changed dramatically over the past twenty years, both domestically and internationally, with a series of foreign policy setbacks. The legacy of Tony Blair, Prime Minister in 2001, was fatally undermined by the war in Iraq and its aftermath. The French and UK-led intervention in Libya was disastrously hampered by poor planning by David Cameron's administration.

This string of failed interventions has led to a reluctance among UK policymakers to commit to similar ventures. When asked to approve an extension of air strikes against Daesh targets from Iraq across the border into Syria, MPs were notably nervous. The legacy of Iraq, Libya and Afghanistan featured heavily in the reluctance of MPs to approve action in November 2015. I can remember speaking to Labour and Conservative MPs who were haunted by the failures of Iraq in particular. That was reflected in the August 2013 decision by MPs not to participate in strikes against the Assad regime in response to chemical weapon attacks.

This scepticism over military action is reflected in the wider UK public. The legacy of the conflicts over the past twenty years alongside the scenes from Kabul will mean that gaining public approval for any future military action will be as difficult in the UK as it appears to be in the USA. Domestic pressures are the single biggest driver of foreign policy and there is little appetite for further interventions in the foreseeable future.

The lesson from conflicts is that strategic patience is lost at the political level incredibly quickly due to domestic political pressures. This happened in Afghanistan with very little parliamentary attention and oversight provided over the course of the conflict despite vast diplomatic, economic and military investment. Even now, writing just a few weeks after the evacuation of Kabul airport, the intervention and subsequent fallout seems like a distant memory. During my own time in the House of Commons between May 2015 and December 2019, according to the House of Commons Library, there was one ministerial statement on Afghanistan on 11 July 2018 and one urgent question on 29 January 2018 as well as a debate in the Lords on 4 September 2018. That is a shocking lack of attention to a conflict in which UK troops were actively engaged.[1]

BREXIT – THE ELEPHANT IN THE ROOM

During that period, parliamentarians were of course bogged down in the aftermath of the EU referendum. The UK is at a historic crossroads in terms of its place in the world and internal cohesion. The country finds itself in the most isolated position internationally in the post-war period (at least during Suez the UK was joined by France in its isolation). In considering what is next for the UK, it is difficult to ignore Brexit and the damage done by the ongoing chaos. I cannot think of any democratic partners globally who believe that Brexit was a good idea; quite the reverse, with the UK increasingly seen as untrustworthy.

In a report published with the support of the Konrad Adenauer Foundation, Kirsty Hughes of the Scottish Centre on European Relations found:

Where the UK had previously been commonly seen as a pragmatic, serious and highly influential player in European affairs, it is now seen as unreliable, unpredictable and having lost substantial influence by no longer having a voice and vote within the EU. For many member states, a long-standing ally and partner in EU affairs has been lost and a new relationship both bilaterally and between the EU-UK needs to be built.[2]

This is damaging and requires the UK to set out a clear vision for its role and values. There are questions over what the post-Brexit British foreign policy aspirations of a 'Global Britain' mean in practice. It has variously been described by one former UK UN permanent representative as 'deeply misleading' and by a former Foreign and Commonwealth Office permanent undersecretary as having a 'lack of clarity'.[3]

Brexit was driven by narrow political considerations and there has been a failure to set out a clear vision of a future outside the EU. This has been worsened by Boris Johnson's government's attempts to renegotiate the deal and threatens to breach international law. This is viewed dimly in Washington DC and Brussels, as well as in other European capitals.

The recent Aukus deal between the USA, the UK and Australia was seen as a move to counter the threat posed by China in the Indo-Pacific. However, the move has further angered the UK's European allies, most of all France, drawing criticism across the EU. Whereas Australia and the USA are Pacific states with clear interests in the region, it is unclear what the UK gains from the agreement. University of Glasgow professor Peter Jackson was blunt about the UK's place in the world and refusal to engage meaningfully with European partners: 'Size and geography dictate that the UK is a middle-ranking power with core interests in Europe. The nostalgia-infused ideology of Brexit, on the other hand, insists that Britain must always be a world power.'[4]

Former UK ambassador to France Lord Ricketts said, 'I think that can only be damaging to NATO, because NATO depends on trust. The repair work needs to begin urgently.'[5]

A EUROPEAN REALITY CHECK

There certainly needs to be a reality check in the UK and the rest of the Western world on their priorities and how to deliver them. Joe Biden has made clear that the period of the USA pursuing 'major military operations to remake other countries' is now at an end.[6] The USA will now continue to focus its attention on the Pacific region and the rise of China, which is perceived to be more of a threat than failed states or even the challenges posed by Russia.

The damage has been done to the image of Western powers as reliable partners. The Afghans who served alongside Western forces in their country, many of whom have been left behind, will have cause to distrust promises made that are subsequently broken. Other partners such as the Kurds in Syria tell a similar story of 'betrayal'.[7]

Europe itself must consider the reliability of the USA. In return, US policymakers feel Europe must do more to take care of its own security. Across European capitals, there is a dawning realisation that not only is the USA unlikely to make any more significant military interventions but that the Biden presidency is also, right now, the friendliest they can hope for.

The Trump presidency put a huge strain on trans-Atlantic relations and his policy directly contributed to the chaotic withdrawal from Afghanistan and the resulting damage to Western prestige. Trumpism is still very much a force in US politics – the former President gathered more votes in his re-election bid than in the 2016 election and his politics still dominate the Republican Party.

This poses serious questions for European policymakers who will need to reassess security considerations. The US withdrawal from Kabul was met with a sense of frustration and helplessness among European leaders. During the German election, the Christian Democratic Union's candidate for Chancellor, Armin Laschet, described the situation as 'the biggest debacle that NATO has suffered since its creation'.[8] Former Chancellor Merkel described NATO as being 'fundamentally dependent' on the USA in Afghanistan.[9]

It is quite clear that European leaders are now seriously considering the continent's future security needs. In her annual State of the Union address to the European Parliament in September 2021, European Commission President Ursula von der Leyen spent a large chunk of her speech discussing the merits of further defence and security cooperation between member states, saying, 'It is time for Europe to step up to the next level.' She also looked ahead to 2022 when President Macron of France is due to hold an EU Defence Summit and to another EU–NATO Joint Declaration being drafted by the NATO secretary general.[10]

This will appeal to a number of EU members, especially the Baltic states. Russia has made military incursions into other former Soviet states in recent years and Putin has talked of the 'genuine tragedy' of the fall of the Soviet Union and even a desire to reunite Russian speakers living there. The pressure is not just in regard to the military, with hybrid warfare posing threats by cyber, misinformation and financial means.

Elsewhere, there will be nerves about other parts of the EU's near neighbourhood. Wars such as those in Libya, Syria and of course Afghanistan have created a migration and refugee crisis that member states struggle to handle alone. Greece, Italy and Malta, among others, are mindful of the challenges posed by instability in the Mediterranean. Further north, Poland is facing challenges by an increasingly belligerent regime in Minsk. This will be exacerbated by fresh inequalities and challenges as a consequence of the climate emergency and the Covid-19 pandemic.

The EU was established as a peace project in the aftermath of the horrors of the Second World War. It has pursued its goals and brought peace to the continent by delivering security and prosperity. Member states will need no reminding of the threats on the EU's borders, and some will expect that European solidarity should mean more than the wealthier parts of the EU providing financial assistance to the poorer parts. It remains at its heart a peace project.

Von der Leyen's remarks made clear that the European Union is taking its security seriously, and President Biden has talked of the importance of the European Union to the US's security. The former EU ambassador to the USA commented that the President's political commitment to the bloc is even stronger than Barack Obama's.[11] In a joint statement after the EU–US Summit in June 2021, leaders committed to 'launch a dedicated dialogue on security and defence and pursue closer cooperation in this field'.[12]

RENEWING AN AULD ALLIANCE

During the Brexit negotiations, frustration was expressed over the UK's failure to engage in talks about EU–UK foreign and defence cooperation. David McAllister, the German chair of the European Parliament's Committee on Foreign Affairs, has suggested that existing mechanisms need to be used to build security and a cooperation agreement between the EU and the UK, such as action on terrorism or the alignment of sanctions policy.[13]

While there is a willingness to build 'pragmatic' cooperation with the EU in Brussels and other EU capitals, there is little evidence of that in Westminster. The Integrated Review of Security, Defence, Development and Foreign Policy paper published in March 2021 largely ignored the EU.

This drift will be a concern to all Western allies: no country can afford to ignore its neighbours on foreign and security policy. The UK needs to renew its relationship with the EU and find areas of common ground. It is more than a question of geography; European countries continue to be the UK's most reliable partners in areas of trade, education and culture, as well as security.

The challenges in the aftermath of Afghanistan may then provide an opportunity for a reset in the relationship between the UK and the EU by looking at the areas they both do well in and where complementarity is to be found. This needn't be restricted to military cooperation. In her State of the Union address, President von der Leyen said, 'We can combine military and civilian, along with diplomacy and development – and we have a long history in building and protecting peace.'

So, there is plenty of scope in areas where the EU and the UK excel, with the Afghan crisis providing an opportunity for both to explore areas of common interest. The UK and its European partners bring complementary areas of expertise and soft power that will be crucial in building regional stabilisation.

This does not mean revisiting Brexit. There are a range of areas where cooperation in foreign and security policy could build up trust and deepen partnerships. European partners could work together in helping to reach out to partners in central Asia, neighbouring Afghanistan, where there are strong UK business and NGO links. The EU also has a strong interest in seeing central

Asia develop rules-based cooperation and connectivity rather than competition and rivalry.[14] It is easy to see where greater co-operation could be built, such as economic development, border management and the rule of law. To Afghanistan's south, the UK's strong relationship with Pakistan could complement the EU's soft power clout. Looking ahead, there is a strong case for the EU and the UK to work together on the growing refugee crisis.

International affairs and building a future across Europe's neigh-bourhood and Afghanistan is not simply a task for state actors. When the media focus has moved on from areas affected by con-flict, international NGOs undertake the thankless work that makes the difference between a successful or unsuccessful transition to a more stable society. The work of NGOs such as the HALO Trust continues to be important in countries like Afghanistan and elsewhere. The EU and the UK should work together on longer-term funding provisions for international NGOs and government organisations, such as the UN, that will provide stability for that critical work. Furthermore, organisations such as businesses, ed-ucation institutions and the culture sector have a role in build-ing soft power links, and civil society as well as the government have the capacity and resilience that will be vital to build up co-operation with Afghanistan's neighbours as well as in Europe's neighbourhood.

That means the UK learning lessons about taking a different approach to foreign policy. I have been struck by the comments of those who worked on the ground in Afghanistan who were impressed by the positive role that countries like the Netherlands, Norway and Germany were able to play during the conflict.

CONCLUSION

I'm a strong believer in both the EU and resetting the relationship between the constituent parts of the UK. Regardless of one's personal views, we cannot ignore the deep underlying foreign policy challenges that the UK faces and the need to rebuild its relationships with its closest partners.

If Europe is to work together to build a more secure and prosperous future, then it will need to be capable of meeting common challenges. The issues around the neighbourhood – migration, Russia, China and the fallout from the Afghan debacle – will remain regardless of the UK's relationship with the EU.

Part of the UK's problem is that the winner-takes-all approach to elections means that a Westminster government can implement its agenda with a freer hand than most European governments. As the UK has illustrated in recent years, this can lead to more radical governance disregarding the views of the majority where consensus is rarely sought. Perhaps politicians of all parties need to reassess our foreign policy in light of Afghanistan to recapture that sense of international solidarity. As my colleague professor Phillips O'Brien put it, Kabul was 'a moment exposing a long-term reality, not a moment of change', and that requires a realistic change in long-term thinking.[15]

Stephen Gethins is a professor of practice in international relations at the University of St Andrews. He was formerly a spokesperson on international and European affairs for the SNP and spent two terms as a member of the House of Commons Foreign Affairs Committee.

AFGHAN WITNESS 5

GULNAZ:[1] A MOTHER TURNS TO SEX WORK

———

'I can't see any other way to feed the children besides prostitution'

It was morning. Gulnaz (pseudonym) was having breakfast with her children when the phone rang. It was a friend of her husband with bad news. Her husband had been severely injured, and his two brothers killed in an attack on the checkpoint they manned in Wardak province.

That was 2011, and the start of a difficult time for Gulnaz. Her husband had lost one of his legs in the blast and had shrapnel embedded in his head – possibly in the brain – which the doctors did not want to operate on. After a period in hospital, he returned home but struggled to recover. Six months on, after complaining of a headache one evening, he died. Gulnaz was left living with six children and her surviving brother-in-law, who had taken on responsibility for the three children of his brothers killed in the attack.

She was remarried to a police officer, but he too lost his life in a landmine attack on his vehicle in Zabul province. Not long after, her surviving brother-in-law was also killed while serving with the

Afghan army. Gulnaz was left to look after nine children, living at home with her mother.

For years, she struggled to make ends meet as a house cleaner, while also collecting her late husband's police pension. But since the takeover by the Taliban in August 2021, she no longer receives the pension, and the owner of the houses has fled, leaving her without a job. With no income and nine children to look after, she was desperate.

'I had no option but to sell my body to feed my children. It's not a choice but I feel compelled to do it. If I am arrested by the Taliban, I will be killed, but I don't care, my children need food,' said Gulnaz in a phone call with Afghan Witness.

She finds clients through a man in Kabul, who takes a commission in the process. Each client pays her 500–1,000 Afghani – the equivalent of $5–10.

Gulnaz's story is not uncommon. Samia (also a pseudonym) has four children and was the sole breadwinner for the family after her husband died from illness. She had worked in a cleaning company, but after the Taliban takeover in August, the company stopped working and let all the staff go. She had turned to begging in the streets to feed her children, the youngest only two and a half years old. But she could not make ends meet and felt no choice but to turn to prostitution. She says she makes between 400 Afghani to 1,000 Afghani from each client.

'It makes me wish I was dead, but I can't see any other way to feed the children besides prostitution. When I go to sleep, I cry about the terrible life I am living and think about killing myself, but I can't abandon my children,' Samia told Afghan Witness.

The collapse of the former government, state support and the private sector, and the uncertainty over the jobs women are allowed to do under the Taliban, have left many out of work at a time when food and basic services are increasingly hard to come by.

For Gulnaz, Samia and others like them, they feel they have no choice but to sell their bodies to survive and support their families.

THE TALIB'S LOUD RECITATION

تلاوت طالب

——

MASOOD KHALILI

(TRANSLATED BY ROBERT DARR)

Last night I went to the door of that cradle of fidelity's home,
to drink and carry on conversation from evening until dawn.

He said, 'Forgo drinking and wine, forget the tavern and its barrels!
Look at how our people suffer and from what cruelty they cry out!

'The savage Talib plunderers, those henchmen of the vile,
are none but wild beasts severed from reason's community.

'Every night 'til dawn's light, each base and vicious dog
becomes a hyena that attacks the wealthy and poor alike.

'He'll sever heads, cut into breasts, he'll wound and kill.
Then he'll say, "These acts are what God commands!"

'The religion and rite of this base exemplar of depravity
is founded on killing, imprisoning, viciousness and iniquity!

'At dawn he loudly recites verses from the Qur'an,
but come nightfall he'll again swim in Muslim blood!

'Rise up! Let not this base, ignorant murderer become
the dark power ruling over our desperate people!'

Masood Khalili is an Afghan diplomat, linguist and poet. He is the author of *Whispers of War: An Afghan Freedom Fighter's Account of the Soviet Invasion.*

Robert Darr is a translator and interpreter of classic Islamic mystical texts and the director of the Arques School of Traditional Boatbuilding in Sausalito, California.

CONTRIBUTORS

Dr Haider al-Abadi was Prime Minister of Iraq from 2014 until 2018. He led the country's successful military campaign against Daesh as Commander-in-Chief.

Dr Omar Al-Ubaydli is the director of research at the Bahrain Center for Strategic, International and Energy Studies (DERASAT), and an affiliated associate professor of economics at George Mason University.

Masoud Andarabi was Minister of the Interior of Afghanistan from 2019 to 2021.

Heather Barr is associate director of the Women's Rights Division at Human Rights Watch.

Dr Alia Brahimi is a non-resident senior fellow at the Atlantic Council and a leading specialist in terrorism and political trends in the Middle East and North Africa.

Dr Brian Brivati is a visiting professor at Kingston University and director of the Stabilisation and Recovery Network.

Professor Paul Cornish is a visiting professor at LSE IDEAS, London School of Economics, and an independent analyst, consultant and author specialising in international security, geostrategy, cybersecurity and national defence policy.

Laura Cretney is a PhD candidate at Durham University researching the role of diasporas in homeland conflict. She is also the director of an Isle of Man-based consultancy offering insight and expertise for organisations working in the Middle East and North Africa.

Graham Cundy served twenty-five years in the Royal Marines. As a senior member of the national security community, he contributed to the design and implementation of UK defence and security strategy, and managed relationships with a wide range of international security partners.

Robert Darr is a translator and interpreter of classic Islamic mystical texts and the director of the Arques School of Traditional Boatbuilding in Sausalito, California.

Shreyas Deshmukh is a research associate at Delhi Policy Group. Prior to joining DPG, he worked with MitKat Advisory Services as a geopolitical risk analyst.

Professor Paul Dixon is an honorary research fellow at Birkbeck College, University of London. His forthcoming books are entitled *The Authoritarian Temptation: The Iraq and Afghan Wars and the Militarisation* *of British Democracy* (Verso, 2023) and *War and Militarisation: NATO's Invasion of Afghanistan* (Edinburgh University Press, 2023).

Thomas Dodd is a former special adviser to NATO, where he led the development and launch of NATO TV, and has co-founded several successful digital businesses. He continues to advise governments and corporations globally.

Nick Fishwick served in the UK Foreign Office and HM Customs and Excise service for over twenty years and is a national security expert.

Stephen Gethins is a professor of practice in international relations at the University of St Andrews. He was formerly a spokesperson on international and European affairs for the SNP and spent two terms as a member of the House of Commons Foreign Affairs Committee.

Philip Ingram MBE served in British military intelligence for twenty-six years and is now a journalist and consultant in intelligence, counter-intelligence and security sectors.

Mahmud Khalili is an Afghan-American writer. He is the author of *Afghanistan Decoded: Perspectives in Domestic and Foreign Affairs.*

Masood Khalili is an Afghan diplomat, linguist and poet. He is the author of *Whispers of War: An Afghan Freedom Fighter's Account of the Soviet Invasion.*

Jill Suzanne Kornetsky is a Kabul-based scientist, social entrepreneur, consultant, researcher, analyst, guest speaker, guest lecturer, author, editor and company founder.

Hollie McKay is a foreign policy expert and war crimes investigator based in Afghanistan. She focuses on warfare, terrorism and crimes against humanity. She is the author of *Only Cry for the Living: Memos from Inside the ISIS Battlefield*.

Safa Mahdi is a professional and academic specialist in the field of international security, security risk management, intelligence and counter-terrorism.

Lord Purvis of Tweed is the Liberal Democrats' foreign affairs, international development and international trade spokesman in the House of Lords.

Dr Arun Sahgal is the director of the Forum for Strategic Initiatives, the founding director of the Office of Net Assessment, Indian Integrated Defence Staff, and senior fellow of Delhi Policy Group.

NOTES

INTRODUCTION

1   Virginia Woolf, *The Diary of Virginia Woolf, Volume 1: 1915–1919* (London: The Hogarth Press, 1977), p. 216.

AFGHAN WITNESS 1: ZARIFA: A POLICEWOMAN FACES A DANGEROUS FUTURE

1   Stories from the Afghan Witness project: https://www.afghanwitness.org/. Afghan Witness is a project to independently collect, preserve and verify information on human rights and current events in Afghanistan. Afghan Witness aims to provide a reliable source of information for international organisations, governments, the media and NGOs, and to raise awareness of the reality of everyday life for Afghans living in the country.

CHAPTER 1: WHAT NOW? THE FUTURE IN AFGHANISTAN

1   These and other figures that are not referenced to another source are based on the author's own extensive experience of living and working in Afghanistan.

2   'Afghanistan Unemployment Rate', Trading Economics, https://tradingeconomics.com/afghanistan/unemployment-rate

3   'Unemployment Rate Spikes in Afghanistan', Tolo News (2 October 2015), https://tolonews.com/afghanistan/unemployment-rate-spikes-afghanistan

4   'The employment rate in Afghanistan', Knoema, https://knoema.com/data/afghanistan+employment-rate

5   'Afghanistan Security: US-Funded Equipment for the Afghan National Defense and Security Forces', US Government Accountability Office, https://www.gao.gov/products/gao-17-667r

6   'Dukons' is a transliteration of a Dari word.

7   'Agriculture', USAID, https://www.usaid.gov/afghanistan/fact-sheets/agriculture

8   'What is a Food Forest?', Project Food Forest, https://projectfoodforest.org/what-is-a-food-forest/

CHAPTER 2: SOMEONE'S GOTTA SAY IT: UNSPOKEN GROUND TRUTHS AND MISTAKES NOT TO REPEAT

1   This is based on the author's own extensive experience of living and working in Afghanistan.

2   *Ibid.*

3   This estimate is based on the author's own extensive experience of living and working in Afghanistan. The last numbers were up to 90,000 people (20,000 in pipeline, 70,000 eligible), but this was before they dropped the time requirement from two years of work to one year of work, and everyone started applying in August and September using the new time limit. Daniel F. Runde and

Elena Méndez Leal, 'The Case for Expediting Special Immigrant Visas amid a Transition of Power in Afghanistan', Center for Strategic and International Studies (16 August 2021), https://www.csis.org/analysis/case-expediting-special-immigrant-visas-amid-transition-power-afghanistan; 'Special Immigrant Visas for Afghans – Who Were Employed by/on Behalf of the US Government', Travel.State.Gov, https://travel.state.gov/content/travel/en/us-visas/immigrate/special-immg-visa-afghans-employed-us-gov.html

4　This is based on the author's own extensive experience of living and working in Afghanistan.
5　*Ibid.*

CHAPTER 3: FROM TALIBAN TO TALIBAN: CYCLE OF HOPE, DESPAIR ON WOMEN'S RIGHTS

1　Sune Engel Rasmussen and Jalal Nazari, 'Afghanistan's Taliban Prohibit Girls From Attending Secondary School', *Wall Street Journal* (19 September 2021), https://www.wsj.com/articles/afghanistans-taliban-prohibit-girls-from-attending-secondary-school-as-boys-return-to-classrooms-11631951310

2　Hira Humayun and Helen Regan, 'About the only job women can do for the Kabul government is clean female bathrooms, acting mayor says', CNN (20 September 2021), https://edition.cnn.com/2021/09/19/asia/afghanistan-women-government-jobs-intl-hnk/index.html

3　Lulu Garcia-Navarro, 'The future of women's education in Afghanistan remains uncertain', NPR (3 October 2021), https://www.npr.org/2021/10/03/1042802598/the-future-of-womens-education-in-afghanistan-remains-uncertain; https://tolonews.com/index.php/afghanistan-174874

4　'Taliban Abuses Cause Widespread Fear', Human Rights Watch (23 September 2021), https://www.hrw.org/news/2021/09/23/afghanistan-taliban-abuses-cause-widespread-fear

5　Alissa J. Rubin, 'Threats and Fear Cause Afghan Women's Protections to Vanish Overnight', *New York Times* (4 September 2021), https://www.nytimes.com/2021/09/04/world/middleeast/afghanistan-women-shelter-taliban.html

6　Peter Beaumont, 'Afghan women to be banned from playing sport, Taliban say', *The Guardian* (8 September 2021), https://www.theguardian.com/world/2021/sep/08/afghan-women-to-be-banned-from-playing-sport-taliban-say

7　Heather Barr, 'For Afghan Women, the Frightening Return of "Vice and Virtue"', Human Rights Watch (29 September 2021), https://www.hrw.org/news/2021/09/29/afghan-women-frightening-return-vice-and-virtue

8　'Taliban Abuses Cause Widespread Fear', Human Rights Watch (23 September 2021), https://www.hrw.org/news/2021/09/23/afghanistan-taliban-abuses-cause-widespread-fear; Fereshta Abbasi, 'Afghan Women Protest Against Taliban Restrictions' (7 September 2021), https://www.hrw.org/news/2021/09/07/afghan-women-protest-against-taliban-restrictions

9　'Taliban Severely Beat Journalists', Human Rights Watch (8 September 2021), https://www.hrw.org/news/2021/09/08/afghanistan-taliban-severely-beat-journalists; Akhtar Mohammad Makoii, Peter Beaumont and Patrick Wintour, 'Taliban ban protests and slogans that don't have their approval', *The Guardian* (8 September 2021), https://www.theguardian.com/world/2021/sep/08/taliban-ban-protests-and-slogans-that-dont-have-their-approval

10　Heather Barr, 'The Fragility of Women's Rights in Afghanistan', Human Rights Watch (17 August 2021), https://www.hrw.org/news/2021/08/17/fragility-womens-rights-afghanistan

11　Megan K. Stack, 'The Inconsistency of American Feminism in the Muslim World', *New Yorker* (7 October 2021), https://www.newyorker.com/news/news-desk/the-inconsistency-of-american-feminism-in-the-muslim-world

12　John Sifton, 'Averting Afghanistan's Economic and Food Crises', Human Rights Watch (6 October 2021), https://www.hrw.org/news/2021/10/06/averting-afghanistans-economic-and-food-crises

13　'Closing the Gender Gap in Humanitarian Action', UN Women, https://interactive.unwomen.org/multimedia/infographic/humanitarianaction/en/index.html

14　'Afghanistan Food Security Update', World Food Programme (10 September 2021), https://docs.wfp.org/api/documents/WFP-0000131668/download/

15 'WFP committed to averting humanitarian crisis as one in three people go hungry', World Food Programme (17 August 2021), https://www.wfp.org/stories/afghanistan-wfp-committed-averting-humanitarian-crisis-one-three-people-go-hungry

16 'Afghanistan Humanitarian Situation Report No. 3', UNICEF (16 February 2021), https://reliefweb.int/report/afghanistan/unicef-afghanistan-humanitarian-situation-report-no-3-year-end-2020

17 Christina Wilkie, '1 million Afghan children are at risk of starvation, UNICEF director warns', CNBC (13 September 2021), https://www.cnbc.com/2021/09/13/1-million-afghan-children-at-risk-of-starvation-unicef-chief-warns-.html

18 '97 percent of Afghans could plunge into poverty by mid 2022, says UNDP', UNDP (9 September 2021), https://www.undp.org/press-releases/97-percent-afghans-could-plunge-poverty-mid-2022-says-undp

19 Tim Lister, '"Basic things are just not there": Health care collapse in Afghanistan threatens lives of millions as winter approaches', CNN (8 October 2021), https://edition.cnn.com/2021/10/08/asia/afghanistan-health-care-collapse-intl-cmd/index.html

20 Shadi Khan Saif, 'University teachers unpaid, academic activities stalled', University World News (2 December 2021), https://www.universityworldnews.com/post.php?story=20211202142134173

21 Deirdre Shesgreen, '"War rarely goes as planned": New report tallies trillions US spent in Afghanistan, Iraq', USA Today, https://www.usatoday.com/story/news/politics/2021/09/01/how-much-did-war-afghanistan-cost-how-many-people-died/5669656001/

22 'G7 Leaders Statement on Afghanistan', G7 (24 August 2021), https://www.g7uk.org/g7-leaders-statement-on-afghanistan/

23 'Resolution adopted by the Human Rights Council on 24 August 2021', Human Rights Council (26 August 2021), https://reliefweb.int/report/afghanistan/resolution-adopted-human-rights-council-24-august-2021-strengthening-promotion; John Fisher, Twitter (24 August 2021), https://twitter.com/JohnFisher_hrw/status/1430277574291337226?s=20

24 'UN: World Leaders Should Address Rights Crises', Human Rights Watch (17 September 2021), https://www.hrw.org/news/2021/09/17/un-world-leaders-should-address-rights-crises

25 'UN to appoint special rapporteur to monitor rights in Afghanistan', Al Jazeera (7 October 2021), https://www.aljazeera.com/news/2021/10/7/un-to-appoint-special-rapporteur-to-monitor-rights-in-afghanistan

26 Heather Barr, 'UN Should Investigate Deadly Attacks on Afghan Civilians', Human Rights Watch (2 July 2021), https://www.hrw.org/news/2021/07/02/un-should-investigate-deadly-attacks-afghan-civilians

27 'UN to appoint special rapporteur to monitor rights in Afghanistan', Al Jazeera (7 October 2021), https://www.aljazeera.com/news/2021/10/7/un-to-appoint-special-rapporteur-to-monitor-rights-in-afghanistan

28 'Afghanistan and the International Criminal Court', Human Rights Watch (20 November 2017), https://www.hrw.org/news/2017/11/20/afghanistan-and-international-criminal-court

29 Mike Corder, 'ICC prosecutor seeks to resume Afghanistan war crimes probe', AP News (27 September 2021), https://apnews.com/article/crime-courts-afghanistan-war-crimes-taliban-a758ac22703e13c37a58322f0c26c3f1

30 Alice Speri, 'How the US Derailed an Effort to Prosecute its Crimes in Afghanistan', The Intercept (5 October 2021), https://theintercept.com/2021/10/05/afghanistan-icc-war-crimes/

31 Amnesty UN Office, Twitter (7 October 2021), https://twitter.com/AmnestyUN/status/1446146181277564938?s=20

32 'Feminist Foreign Policy: Comparing France, Sweden and the United States', SciencesPo (18 March 2021), https://www.sciencespo.fr/en/news/news/feminist-foreign-policy-comparing-france-sweden-and-the-united-states/5453

33 'Handbook: Sweden's feminist foreign policy', Swedish Ministry for Foreign Affairs (2019), https://www.government.se/reports/2018/08/handbook-swedens-feminist-foreign-policy/

34 'Gender equality in German foreign policy and in the Federal Foreign Office', Germany Federal Foreign Office (2020), https://www.auswaertiges-amt.de/blob/2313976/c951f-0cbdbb084d38bafc8e65760fc43/geschlechtergerechtigkeit-engl-data.pdf

35 Rajiv Chandrasekaran, 'In Afghanistan, U.S. shifts strategy on women's rights as it eyes wider priorities', *The Washington Post* (5 March 2011), https://www.washingtonpost.com/world/in-afghanistan-us-shifts-strategy-on-womens-rights-as-it-eyes-wider-priorities/2011/03/02/ABkxMAO_story.html

36 Heather Barr, Twitter (7 October 2021), https://twitter.com/heatherbarr1/status/1445990415191220230?s=20

37 Martine van Bijlert, 'The Taleban's Caretaker Cabinet and other Senior Appointments', Afghanistan Analysts Network (7 October 2021), https://www.afghanistan-analysts.org/en/reports/political-landscape/the-talebans-caretaker-cabinet-and-other-senior-appointments/

38 Ayesha Tanzeem, 'Russia, China, Pakistan Push Taliban Toward Inclusivity', VOA News (22 September 2021), https://www.voanews.com/a/russia-china-pakistan-push-taliban-toward-inclusivity/6240971.html

39 'Afghan girls' school ban un-Islamic, says Imran', The News (22 September 2021), https://www.thenews.com.pk/print/894377-afghan-girls-school-ban-un-islamic-says-imran

40 'Qatar calls Taliban moves on girls education "very disappointing"', Al Jazeera (30 September 2021), https://www.aljazeera.com/news/2021/9/30/qatar-taliban-afghanistan-eu-borrell

41 'Global Fund and UNDP Join Efforts to Maintain Access to Essential Health Services in Afghanistan', UNDP (6 October 2021), https://www.undp.org/news/global-fund-and-undp-join-efforts-maintain-access-essential-health-services-afghanistan

42 Irwin Loy, 'For some NGOs, female staff guarantees are a red line for continuing Afghan aid', The New Humanitarian (17 September 2021), https://www.thenewhumanitarian.org/news/2021/9/17/Afghanistan-aid-groups-seek-Taliban-guarantees-for-female-humanitarian-staff

43 Rangita de Silva de Alwis and Melanne Verveer, '"Time Is A-Wasting": Making the Case for CEDAW Ratification by the United States', IPS (7 September 2021), http://www.ipsnews.net/2021/09/time-wasting-making-case-cedaw-ratification-united-states/

CHAPTER 4: STOLEN PROMISES: THE US RETREAT AND THE AFGHAN DIASPORA

1 Ibrahim Abraham and Rachel Busbridge, 'Afghan-Australians: Diasporic Tensions, Homeland Transformations and the "2014 Syndrome"', *Journal of Muslim Minority Affairs*, 34:3 (September 2014), p. 244; Tabasum Akseer, 'A View from the Afghan Diaspora', *Forced Migration Review*, 46 (May 2014), p. 30.

2 Ahmet İçduygu and Sibel Karadağ, 'Afghan migration through Turkey to Europe: seeking refuge, forming diaspora, and becoming citizens', *Turkish Studies*, 19:3 (2018), pp. 486–7.

3 James Weir and Rohullah Amin, 'The Journey to Europe: A Young Afghan's Experience on the Migrant Route', in Reece Jones and Md. Azmeary Ferdoush (eds), *Borders and Mobility in South Asia and Beyond* (Amsterdam: Amsterdam University Press, 2018), p. 171.

4 Abraham and Busbridge, p. 244.

5 Rahmatullah Amiri, 'Continuing conflict, continuing displacement in southern Afghanistan', *Forced Migration Review*, 46 (May 2014), pp. 7–8.

6 Cordaid, 'Diaspora Engagement in Afghanistan', MIND Project Policy Paper (April 2021), https://www.cordaid.org/en/wp-content/uploads/sites/11/2021/04/210330-Policy-Brief-Diaspora-Sustainable-Development-Afghanistan.pdf; Muhammad Abdul Wassay, 'Future of Afghan Refugees in the Post-US Withdrawal', Pak Afghan Youth Forum (26 June 2021).

7 Cordaid; Khalid Koser, 'Transition, Crisis and Mobility in Afghanistan: Rhetoric and Reality', International Organization for Migration (January 2014).

8 İçduygu and Karadağ, p. 482.

9   Jeanne Batalova, 'Afghan Immigrants in the United States', Migration Policy Institute (9 September 2021), https://www.migrationpolicy.org/article/afghan-immigrants-united-states

10 Ibid.

11 Carolin Fischer and Marieke van Houte, 'Dimensions of agency in transnational relations of Afghan migrants and return migrants', Migration Studies, 8:4 (2020), p. 557; Dave Braneck, 'How does Europe's largest Afghan diaspora view the crisis back home?', Euronews (16 September 2021), https://www.euronews.com/2021/09/15/how-does-europe-s-largest-afghan-diaspora-view-the-crisis-back-home

12 Ibid.

13 Fischer and van Houte, p. 557.

14 Laura Cretney, Interview with Gulwali Passarlay via Zoom (11 November 2021).

15 Cordaid.

16 Weir and Amin, p. 182.

17 Mikkel Rytter and Andreas Nielsen, 'Marriage in the Ruins of War: Intergenerational Hauntings in the Afghan Diaspora', Ethnicities, 20:5 (2019), p. 994.

18 Abraham and Busbridge, p. 245.

19 Sanmeet Kaur, 'Afghan Sikhs: persecution, resistance and life in diaspora', Media Diversified (17 April 2018), https://mediadiversified.org/2018/04/17/afghan-sikhs-persecution-resistance-and-life-in-diaspora/

20 Zuhra and Maryam, 'Ashamed of Me: Culture Shaming in the Afghan Diaspora', Chai Sabz podcast (16 August 2021).

21 Rytter and Nielsen, p. 995.

22 Ibid., p. 994.

23 Ibid., pp. 997–8

24 Sanaa Alimia, 'Violence and vulnerabilities: Afghans in Pakistan', Forced Migration Review, 46 (May 2014), p. 24; Christine Roehrs, 'The Refugee Dilemma: Afghans in Pakistan between expulsion and failing aid schemes', Afghanistan Analysts Network (9 March 2015), https://www.afghanistan-analysts.org/en/reports/migration/the-refugee-dilemma-afghans-in-pakistan-between-expulsion-and-failing-aid-schemes/

25 Roehrs.

26 Ibid.

27 Armando Geller and Maciej Latek, 'Returning from Iran', Forced Migration Review, 46 (May 2014), p. 26.

28 Thomas Ruttig, 'Pressure and Peril: Afghan refugees and Europe in 2017', Afghanistan Analysts Network (30 December 2017), https://www.afghanistan-analysts.org/en/reports/migration/pressure-and-peril-afghan-refugees-and-europe-in-2017/

29 Ibid.; Braneck.

30 Mostafa Rachwani, 2021, 'Australians with family in Afghanistan tell of despair, survivor guilt', The Guardian (16 August 2021), https://www.theguardian.com/world/2021/aug/16/australians-with-family-in-afghanistan-tell-of-despair-survivor-guilt

31 Weir and Amin, p. 182.

32 Ceri Oeppen, '"Leaving Afghanistan! Are You Sure?" European Efforts to Deter Potential Migrants Through Information Campaigns', Human Geography, 9:2 (2016), p. 57.

33 Abraham and Busbridge, pp. 247–8.

34 Cretney.

35 Weir and Amin, p. 182.

36 Kaur.

37 Zarlasht Halaimzai, '"I pleaded for help. No one wrote back": the pain of watching my country fall to the Taliban', The Guardian (30 September 2021), https://www.theguardian.com/world/2021/sep/30/i-pleaded-for-help-no-one-wrote-back-the-pain-of-watching-my-country-fall-to-the-taliban

38 Cordaid.

39 Cretney.

40 Cordaid.

41 Braneck.

42 'Homepage', Afghanistan and Central Asian Association, https://acaa.org.uk/

43 Jennifer Brinkerhoff, 'Digital diasporas and international development: Afghan-Americans and the reconstruction of Afghanistan', *Public Administration and Development*, 24:5 (December 2004), p. 400.

44 Fischer and van Houte, p. 557.

45 Said Sabir Ibrahimi, 'Conversation with Haris Tarin on Afghan American Diaspora role in building Afghanistan', *Afghan Affairs* podcast (31 October 2020).

46 Fischer and van Houte, p. 557.

47 Fatimah Hossaini, 'Photos: I dodged the Taliban to get out of Afghanistan. Here's what it was like – and what I lost along the way', Business Insider (28 August 2021), https://www.businessinsider.com/photos-how-i-left-kabul-and-what-i-lost-along-the-way-2021-8?r=US&IR=T

48 Cordaid.

49 *Ibid.*

50 Gabriel Piccillo and Mark Patterson, 'The Critical Role of the Afghan Diaspora in the Pursuit of Peace in Afghanistan', *CSR Journal* (1 June 2019), https://thecsrjournal.in/role-afghan-diaspora-peace-afghanistan/

51 Peymana Assad, 'About Peymana', Peymana Assad Website, https://www.peymanaassad.co.uk/about

52 Cretney.

53 Marie Zamecnikova, 'Afghan Diaspora in the Digital Age: A Grounded Theory', Royal Holloway, University of London (2019), https://marieolivie.com/afghan-diaspora-in-the-digital-age/

54 Rytter and Nielsen, p. 997.

55 Froher Yasin, 'Grief beyond borders: Afghan diaspora and the crisis in Afghanistan', *Varsity (University of Cambridge)* (7 September 2021), https://www.varsity.co.uk/features/21968

56 Halaimzai.

57 Cretney.

58 Halaimzai.

59 Rachwani.

60 Halaimzai; Cretney.

61 Cretney.

62 *Ibid.*

63 Sangar Paykhar, 'An Open Letter to the Afghan Diaspora', Afghan Eye (29 October 2021), https://afghaneye.org/2021/10/29/an-open-letter-to-the-afghan-diaspora/

64 'Afghanistan: How many refugees are there and where will they go?', BBC News (31 August 2021).

65 Secunder Kermani, 'Desperate Afghans turn to people smugglers for help fleeing the country', BBC News (9 November 2021), https://www.bbc.co.uk/news/av/world-asia-59213113

66 Halaimzai.

67 Hossaini.

68 Cretney.

69 Yasin.

70 Cretney.

CHAPTER 6: A CONVERSATION WITH FORMER MINISTER OF THE INTERIOR MASOUD ANDARABI

1   This chapter is based on a Zoom conversation with the editor.

NOTES

CHAPTER 7: DISPATCHES: EXTRACTS FROM THE JOURNALISM OF HOLLIE MCKAY IN AFGHANISTAN

1   You can subscribe to Hollie McKay's substack here: https://holliesmckay.substack.com/ and her website is here: http://holliemckay.com/journalism. Hollie McKay is a foreign policy expert, war crimes investigator and bestselling author of *Only Cry for the Living: Memos from Inside the ISIS Battlefield*. She was an investigative and international affairs/war journalist for Fox News Digital for over fourteen years, where she focused on warfare, terrorism and crimes against humanity. Hollie has worked on the frontlines of several major war zones and covered humanitarian and diplomatic crises in Iraq, Afghanistan, Pakistan, Syria, Iran, Turkey, Yemen, Saudi Arabia, Burma, Russia, Africa, Latin America and other areas. Her globally spanned coverage, in the form of thousands of print articles and essays, has included exclusive and detailed interviews with numerous captured terrorists, as well as high-ranking government, military and intelligence officials and leaders from all sides. She has spent considerable time embedded with US and foreign troops, conducted extensive interviews with survivors of torture, sex slavery and forced child jihadist training, refugees and internally displaced people to communicate the complexities of such catastrophes and war crimes on local populations. Hollie's columns have additionally been featured in and referenced in innumerable mainstream publications and academic journals, and she has won numerous foreign press and humanitarian awards.

In addition, Hollie serves as a board member for EMERGENCY USA. This non-governmental organisation endeavours to assist victims of conflict around the world. She is also the outreach director for Burnt Children Relief Foundation (BCRF) to bring severely bomb-burned Syrian children to the US for life-saving treatment.

2   Jeremy Beaman, 'Reporter reveals how she ended up being escorted by Taliban out of Afghanistan', *Washington Examiner* (27 August 2021), https://www.washingtonexaminer.com/news/reporter-details-fall-of-afghanistan/

3   Hollie McKay, 'Dispatches from Afghanistan: Returning to the Dungeon's Lair' (6 September 2021), https://holliesmckay.substack.com/p/dispatches-from-afghanistan-returning

4   *Ibid.*

5   Hollie McKay, 'US Exit Leaves Afghan Women's Education In Limbo Despite Taliban Promises – Special Report From Afghanistan', Deadline (31 October 2021), https://deadline.com/2021/10/afghanistan-women-education-taliban-repression-takeover-1234863863/

6   Hollie McKay, 'Dispatches from Afghanistan: The Taliban Air Force, Life in the Korengal Valley Now and Female Taekwondo Stars Abandoned post US Departure' (10 November 2021), https://holliesmckay.substack.com/p/dispatches-from-afghanistan-the-taliban

7   *Ibid.*

8   Hollie McKay, 'What Life Is Like Under the Afghan Taliban', *National Interest* (16 November 2021), https://nationalinterest.org/feature/what-life-under-afghan-taliban-196298

9   Hollie McKay, 'Dispatches from Afghanistan: Victims of US drone strike still have not received an apology, Taliban government luring tourists with glossy campaign and girls left behind battling depression' (12 November 2021), https://holliesmckay.substack.com/p/dispatches-from-afghanistan-victims

10 Hollie McKay, 'Dispatches from Afghanistan: The Taliban Air Force, Life in the Korengal Valley Now and Female Taekwondo Stars Abandoned post US Departure' (10 November 2021), https://holliesmckay.substack.com/p/dispatches-from-afghanistan-the-taliban

11 *Ibid.*

12 Hollie McKay, 'Relatives of Afghans killed in US drone strike still haven't heard from Washington', *New York Post* (11 November 2021), https://nypost.com/2021/11/11/afghan-family-of-us-drone-victims-havent-heard-from-washington/

13 Hollie McKay, 'Women And Girls Left Behind In Afghanistan Battling Depression And Hopelessness', KNEWZ (9 November 2021), https://knewz.com/knewz-exclusive-women-and-girls-left-behind-in-afghanistan-battling-depression-and-hopelessness/

14 Hollie McKay, 'Three Months Into The Taliban Rule Economic, Humanitarian And Security Catastrophe Exists', KNEWZ (10 November 2021), https://knewz.com/knewz-exclusive-three-months-into-the-taliban-rule-economic-humanitarian-and-security-ca-tastrophe-exists/

15 Hollie McKay, 'What Life Is Like Under the Afghan Taliban', *National Interest* (16 November 2021), https://nationalinterest.org/feature/what-life-under-afghan-taliban-196298

16 *Ibid.*

17 Hollie McKay, 'Dispatches from Afghanistan: Three Months of Life Under the Taliban Rule, How Scams Target Evacuation Efforts and Future of Mining' (17 November 2021), https://holliesmckay.substack.com/p/dispatches-from-afghanistan-three

AFGHAN WITNESS 2: GHULAM: A YOUNG MAN TRIES TO ESCAPE BEING RECRUITED BY THE TALIBAN

1 Stories from the Afghan Witness project: https://www.afghanwitness.org/

CHAPTER 8: ISLAM-INSPIRED WAYS OF AVOIDING THE RESOURCE CURSE IN AFGHANISTAN

1 Jeffrey D. Sachs and Andrew M. Warner, 'The curse of natural resources', *European Economic Review*, 45 (2001), pp. 827–38.

2 Michael L. Ross, 'What Have We Learned about the Resource Curse?', *Annual Review of Political Science*, 18 (2015), pp. 239–59.

3 Simeon Djankov, Jose G. Montalvo and Marta Reynal-Querol, 'The curse of aid', *Journal of Economic Growth*, 13:3 (2008), pp. 169–94.

4 Jonathan Lipow and Francois Melese, 'Can Afghanistan avoid the Natural Resource Curse?', *Defense & Security Analysis*, 28:4 (2012), pp. 316–25.

5 'Afghanistan GDP per capita PPP', Trading Economics, https://tradingeconomics.com/afghanistan/gdp-per-capita-ppp

6 'Afghanistan', CIA Factbook, https://www.cia.gov/the-world-factbook/countries/afghanistan/

7 'Afghanistan', Observatory of Economic Complexity, https://oec.world/en/profile/country/afg

8 Scott Montgomery, 'Afghanistan has vast mineral wealth but faces steep challenges to tap it', *The Conversation* (2021), https://theconversation.com/afghanistan-has-vast-mineral-wealth-but-faces-steep-challenges-to-tap-it-166484

9 Erica Downs, 'China buys into Afghanistan', *SAIS Review of International Affairs*, 32:2 (2012), pp. 65–84.

10 'Afghanistan: How much opium is produced and what's the Taliban's record?', BBC News (25 August 2021), https://www.bbc.com/news/world-asia-58308494

11 'Net official development assistance and official aid received (current US$) – Afghanistan', World Bank Data, https://data.worldbank.org/indicator/DT.ODA.ALLD.CD?locations=AF

12 Sarajuddin Isar, 'A Blessing or a Curse? Aid Rentierism and State-building in Afghanistan', E-International Relations (23 May 2014)

13 'Afghanistan Government Budget', Trading Economics, https://tradingeconomics.com/afghanistan/government-budget

14 Ross.

15 Djankov *et al.*

16 'Polity5: Regime Authority Characteristics and Transitions Datasets', Center for Systemic Peace, https://www.systemicpeace.org/inscrdata.html

17 Ross.

18 Isar.

19 'Corruption Perceptions Index', Transparency International, https://www.transparency.org/en/cpi/2020/index/nzl

20 Kevin Watkins, 'The Taliban are not the only threat to Afghanistan. Aid cuts could undo

20 years of progress', *The Guardian* (11 September 2021), https://www.theguardian.com/global-development/2021/sep/11/the-taliban-are-not-the-only-threat-to-afghanistan-aid-cuts-could-undo-20-years-of-progress

21 Derek Grossman, 'Chinese Recognition of the Taliban Is All but Inevitable', The RAND Blog (27 August 2021), https://www.rand.org/blog/2021/08/chinese-recognition-of-the-taliban-is-all-but-inevitable.html

22 Andrew Rosser, 'The Political Economy of the Resource Curse: A Literature Survey', IDS Working Paper, 268 (2006).

23 A. Kamarulzaman and S. M. Saifuddeen, 'Islam and harm reduction', *International Journal of Drug Policy*, 21:2 (2010), pp. 115–18.

24 Lipow and Melese.

25 Observatory of Economic Complexity.

26 M. H. Shayah, 'Economic diversification by boosting non-oil exports (case of UAE)', *Journal of Economics, Business and Management*, 3:7 (2015), pp. 735–8.

27 Rosser.

28 Kara Fox, 'Afghanistan is the world's opium king. Can the Taliban afford to kill off their "un-Islamic" cash cow?', CNN (29 September 2021), https://edition.cnn.com/2021/09/29/asia/taliban-afghanistan-opium-drug-economy-cmd-intl/index.html

CHAPTER 10: HOSTILE TAKEOVER OF AFGHANISTAN – REGIONAL APPROACH AND INDIA'S CONCERNS

1 Shreyas Deshmukh and Brig. Arun Sahgal, 'US Withdrawal from Afghanistan: Compromising the Peace', Delhi Policy Group (22 April 2021), https://www.delhipolicygroup.org/publication/policy-briefs/us-withdrawal-from-afghanistan-compromising-the-peace.html

2 House Hearing, 114 Congress, 'Assessing the Development of Afghanistan National Security Forces', US Government Publishing Office (2016), https://www.govinfo.gov/content/pkg/CHRG-114hhrg98960/html/CHRG-114hhrg98960.htm

3 'Gandhi Letter to Regan, August 3, 1988', US National Security Archive (27 February 2019), https://nsarchive.gwu.edu/document/18262-national-security-archive-doc-14-gandhi-letter

4 Shreyas Deshmukh, 'Mainstreaming Pashtun Tribal Areas: Pakistan's Strategy at a Critical Juncture', 9DashLine (8 June 2021), https://www.9dashline.com/article/mainstreaming-of-pashtun-tribal-areas?rq=Shreyas

5 *Ibid.*

6 'Pakistan's Support of the Taliban', Human Rights Watch (July 2001), https://www.hrw.org/reports/2001/afghan2/Afghan0701-02.htm#TopOfPage

7 'Direct Overt US Aid Appropriations for and Military Reimbursements to Pakistan, FY2002–FY2020', Congressional Research Service (12 March 2019), https://sgp.fas.org/crs/row/pakaid.pdf

8 'Statement by H.E. Sun Yuxi Deputy Head of the Chinese Delegation on Security, Rule of Law and Reforms-the Challenges Ahead at the International Conference on Afghanistan', Ministry of Foreign Affairs of the People's Republic of China (1 April 2004), https://www.fmprc.gov.cn/mfa_eng/wjb_663304/zzjg_663340/yzs_663350/gjlb_663354/2676_663356/2680_663364/200404/t20040401_509841.html

9 'Joint Declaration between The People's Republic of China and The Islamic Republic of Afghanistan on Establishing Strategic and Cooperative Partnership', Ministry of Foreign Affairs of the People's Republic of China (8 June 2012), https://www.fmprc.gov.cn/mfa_eng/wjdt_665385/2649_665393/201206/t20120608_679340.html

10 'Spokesperson on China's role in the future reconstruction of Afghanistan', Ministry of Foreign Affairs of the People's Republic of China (14 December 2001), https://www.fmprc.gov.cn/mfa_eng/wjb_663304/zzjg_663340/yzs_663350/gjlb_663354/2676_663356/2679_663362/200112/t20011214_509820.html; 'Wang Yi: China is Willing to Play Constructive Role in Peaceful Reconciliation Process of Afghanistan', Ministry of Foreign Affairs of the People's Republic of

China (1 November 2014), https://www.fmprc.gov.cn/ce/cgjb/eng/xwdt/zgyw/t1207127.htm; 'Foreign Minister Wang Yi Arrives in Kabul for a Visit to Afghanistan', Ministry of Foreign Affairs of the People's Republic of China (22 February 2014); Steve Holland, 'Obama plans to end U.S. troop presence in Afghanistan by 2016', Reuters (27 May 2014), https://www.reuters.com/article/us-usa-afghanistan-obama-idUSKBN0E71WQ20140527

11 'First Round of China-Afghanistan-Pakistan Trilateral Strategic Dialogue Held in Kabul', Ministry of Foreign Affairs of the People's Republic of China (20 February 2015).

12 'Joint Press Release of the China-Pakistan-Afghanistan Trilateral Meeting', Ministry of Foreign Affairs of the People's Republic of China (9 December 2015); 'Wang Yi Attends 2+2 Quartet Meeting on the Afghan Issue', Ministry of Foreign Affairs of the People's Republic of China (10 December 2015), https://www.fmprc.gov.cn/ce/cgbelfast/eng/zgxw_1/t1323369.htm; 'Wang Yi Talks about Shuttle Diplomacy towards Pakistan and Afghanistan', Ministry of Foreign Affairs of the People's Republic of China (25 June 2017), https://www.fmprc.gov.cn/mfa_eng/wjb_663304/zzjg_663340/yzs_663350/gjlb_663354/2757_663518/2759_663522/20170 6/t20170628_520493.html

13 'China offers $31m in emergency aid to Afghanistan', BBC News (9 September 2021), https://www.bbc.com/news/world-asia-china-58496867

14 Poulomi Ghosh, '"India's concern inappropriate": Taliban say nothing wrong in China helping Afghanistan', Hindustan Times (15 September 2021), https://www.hindustantimes.com/world-news/indias-concern-inappropriate-taliban-say-nothing-wrong-in-china-s-help-101631698510911.html

15 Ibid.

16 'China eyes investment opportunity in Taliban-controlled Afghanistan, to set up industry platform: Report', Hindustan Times (9 September 2021), https://www.hindustantimes.com/world-news/china-eyes-investment-opportunity-in-taliban-controlled-afghanistan-to-set-up-industry-platform-101631180993928.html

17 'China calls for lifting sanctions on Taliban-controlled Afghanistan, release of its forex reserves', Times of India (23 September 2021), https://timesofindia.indiatimes.com/world/china/china-calls-for-lifting-sanctions-on-taliban-controlled-afghanistan-release-of-its-forex-reserves/articleshow/86454154.cms

18 'US envoy Thomas West reacts to Taliban letter to US Congress', The News (20 November 2021), https://www.thenews.com.pk/print/910167-us-envoy-thomas-west-reacts-to-taliban-letter-to-us-congress

19 'Chinese Delegation Conducts Recce at Afghanistan's Bagram Airbase; India Concerned', News 18 (20 September 2021), https://www.news18.com/news/world/chinese-delegation-conducts-recce-at-afghanistans-bagram-airbase-india-concerned-4224605.html

20 Ibid.

21 'Taliban in Afghanistan: Will it be India–Russia–Iran vs China–Pakistan?', Times of India (14 September 2021), https://timesofindia.indiatimes.com/world/south-asia/afghan-crisis-will-it-be-india-russia-iran-vs-china-pakistan/articleshow/86191765.cms

22 Ibid.

23 'US–Russian Working Group on Afghanistan Joint Statement', The Ministry of Foreign Affairs of the Russian Federation (19 September 2001), https://www.mid.ru/en/web/guest/foreign_policy/international_safety/crime/-/asset_publisher/3F5lZsLVSx4R/content/id/572556

24 'Joint Press Statement by the US–Russia Working Group on Counterterrorism', US Department of State Archive (27 July 2002), https://2001-2009.state.gov/r/pa/prs/ps/2002/12224.htm

25 'Transcript of Russian Minister of Foreign Affairs Igor Ivanov's Al-Jazeera Interview, Moscow', The Ministry of Foreign Affairs of the Russian Federation (27 January 2003), https://www.mid.ru/en/web/guest/foreign_policy/news/-/asset_publisher/cKNonkJEo2Bw/content/id/534826

26 'Conversation with Russia's First Deputy Foreign Minister Vyacheslav Trubnikov', The

Ministry of Foreign Affairs of the Russian Federation (21 October 2003), https://www.mid.ru/en/web/guest/foreign_policy/international_safety/crime/-/asset_publisher/3F5lZsLVSx4R/content/id/500370

27 'NATO's once vital supply link to Afghanistan via Russia closes', *Stars and Stripes* (20 May 2015), https://www.stripes.com/news/nato-s-once-vital-supply-link-to-afghanistan-via-russia-closes-1.347249

28 'Comment by Foreign Ministry Spokeswoman Maria Zakharova on Washington's charges that Russia is complicit in the death of US soldiers in Afghanistan', The Ministry of Foreign Affairs of the Russian Federation (16 April 2021), https://www.mid.ru/en/web/guest/foreign_policy/international_safety/conflicts/-/asset_publisher/xIEMTQ3OvzcA/content/id/4688977

29 'Foreign Minister Sergey Lavrov's remarks at a joint press conference with Foreign Minister of the State of Qatar Mohammed bin Abdulrahman Al-Thani, Moscow', The Ministry of Foreign Affairs of the Russian Federation (11 September 2021), https://www.mid.ru/en/web/guest/maps/qa/-/asset_publisher/629HIryvPTwo/content/id/4856809

30 'Foreign Minister Sergey Lavrov's replies to media questions following participation in the international conference Central and South Asia: Regional Connectivity. Challenges and Opportunities, Tashkent', The Ministry of Foreign Affairs of the Russian Federation (16 July 2021), https://www.mid.ru/en/web/guest/foreign_policy/international_safety/conflicts/-/asset_publisher/xIEMTQ3OvzcA/content/id/4815366

31 'At Moscow Format meet, it seemed clear that neither Russia nor China is rushing to fill void after US exit', The Indian Express (22 October 2021), https://indianexpress.com/article/opinion/editorials/indian-delegation-taliban-afghanistan-moscow-7584012/

32 'Tajikistan Posthumously Awards Afghans Masud, Rabbani with One of Country's Highest Honors', Radio Free Europe/Radio Liberty (2 September 2021), https://www.rferl.org/a/tajikistan-masud-rabbani-awards/31440569.html

33 'Question No. 2019 Indian Projects in Afghanistan', The Ministry of External Affairs of India (5 August 2021), https://www.mea.gov.in/rajya-sabha.htm?dtl/34136/question+no2019+indian+projects+in+afghanistan

34 'Statement by Official Spokesperson in response to a question on the opening of the Taliban Office in Qatar', The Ministry of External Affairs of India (21 June 2013), https://www.mea.gov.in/media-briefings.htm?dtl/21849/statement+by+official+spokesperson+in+response+to+a+question+on+the+opening+of+the+taliban+office+in+qatar

35 'Statement by External Affairs Minister at the 9th Ministerial Conference of Heart of Asia – Istanbul Process (HoA-IP) on Afghanistan in Dushanbe', The Ministry of External Affairs of India (30 March 2021), https://www.mea.gov.in/Speeches-Statements.htm?dtl/33751/Statement_by_External_Affairs_Minister_at_the_9th_Ministerial_Conference_of_Heart_of_Asia__Istanbul_Process_HoAIP_on_Afghanistan_in_Dushanbe

36 'Joint Ministerial Statement of the Second Meeting of Foreign Ministers of Afghanistan's Neighboring Countries', Ministry of Foreign Affairs of the People's Republic of China (28 October 2021), https://www.fmprc.gov.cn/mfa_eng/zxxx_662805/202110/t20211028_10348756.html

37 'External Affairs Minister's remarks at the United Nations High-Level Meeting on the Humanitarian Situation in Afghanistan 2021', The Ministry of External Affairs of India (13 September 2021), https://www.mea.gov.in/Speeches-Statements.htm?dtl/34253/External_Affairs_Ministers_remarks_at_the_United_Nations_HighLevel_Meeting_on_the_Humanitarian_Situation_in_Afghanistan_2021

38 Snehesh Alex Philip, 'Gissar Military Aerodrome – India's first overseas base that came to the rescue in Afghan crisis', The Print (23 August 2021), https://theprint.in/defence/gissar-military-aerodrome-indias-first-overseas-base-that-came-to-the-rescue-in-afghan-crisis/720356/

39 Ambuj Sahu, 'US–China Relations Head into Uncharted Waters', Delhi Policy Group (2 October 2021), https://www.delhipolicygroup.org/publication/policy-briefs/us-china-relations-head-into-uncharted-waters.html

CHAPTER 11: 'NO END OF A LESSON': THE END OF LIBERAL INTERNATIONALISM AND THE NEW ISOLATIONISM

1   Anthony Nutting, *No End of a Lesson: The Story of Suez* (New York: C. N. Potter, 1967).
2   See Michael Anton, 'An insider explains the president's foreign policy', *Foreign Policy* (20 April 2019), https://foreignpolicy.com/2019/04/20/the-trump-doctrine-big-think-america-first-nationalism/
3   Norman Geras, *The Contract of Mutual Indifference: Political Philosophy After the Holocaust* (London: Verso, 1998).
4   Mary B. Anderson, *Do No Harm: How Aid Can Support Peace – or War* (Colorado: Lynne Rienner Publishers, 1999).
5   Prime Minister Tony Blair, 'The Doctrine of International Community', Speech to the Economic Club, Chicago (22 April 1999).
6   Conor Foley, *The Thin Blue Line: How Humanitarianism Went to War* (London: Verso, 2008).
7   'A More Secure World: Our Shared Responsibility: Report of the High-level Panel on Threats, Challenges and Change', United Nations (2004).
8   *Ibid.*, pp. 20–21
9   *Ibid.*, pp. 57–8.

AFGHAN WITNESS 3: SAKHI: LOSING MY CULTURE OVERNIGHT

1   Stories from the Afghan Witness project: https://www.afghanwitness.org/

CHAPTER 12: 'THE ENEMY IS IN KABUL'

1   US General Mark Milley, 'Testimony to United States Senate Committee on Armed Services' (28 September 2021), at 03:10:50. The Chairman of the Joint Chiefs of Staff argued that soldiers on the ground delivered an operational and tactical success with the evacuation, but 'strategically, the war is lost. The enemy is in Kabul.' He also stated 'an outcome that is a strategic failure. The enemy is in charge in Kabul. There's no way else to describe that' (at 02:37:39).
2   Lara Jakes, 'US Asks Taliban to Spare Its Embassy in Coming Fight for Kabul', *New York Times* (12 August 2021).
3   'Pentagon Press Secretary John F. Kirby Holds a Press Briefing', US Department of Defense (26 August 2021).
4   Yaroslav Trofimov and Vivian Salama, 'In Its Last Days in Kabul, US Turns to Taliban as a Partner', *Wall Street Journal* (27 August 2021).
5   As Gilles Kepel argued, in 1996 the Taliban 'did not so much take control of Afghan institutions as completely eviscerate them, erecting in their stead only three functions: morality, commerce and war'. See *Jihad: The Trail of Political Islam* (London: I. B. Tauris, 2002), p. 229.
6   'In Open Letter to Shanghai Summit, Taliban Urges Participants to Render Assistance in the Work of Liberating People!', MEMRI Special Dispatch No. 2599 (15 October 2009).
7   Jason Burke, *The 9/11 Wars* (London: Allen Lane, 2011), p. 307.
8   Gilles Dorronsoro, 'The Taliban's Winning Strategy in Afghanistan', Carnegie Endowment for International Peace (2009), p. 12.
9   Abdulkader Sinno, 'Explaining the Taliban's Ability to Mobilize the Pashtuns', in Robert D. Crews and Amin Tarzi (eds), *The Taliban and the Crisis of Afghanistan* (Boston: Harvard University Press, 2009), p. 88.
10 One study summarised the views of respondents in Wardak, Kandahar and Kabul: 'They reasoned that [NATO] objectives were clearly not to bring security to local populations, as their mere presence exacerbated violence and increased the numbers of civilians killed in air strikes … Democracy could not be an aim as the Afghan population had never been consulted about the occupation in the first place.' Sarah Ladbury, 'Testing Hypotheses on Radicalisation in Afghanistan', independent report for the UK Department for International Development (14 August 2009), pp. 5–6.
11 H. R. McMaster, *Battlegrounds: The Fight to Defend the Free World* (London: William Collins, 2020), p. 157.
12 'Remarks by President Biden on Afghanistan', The White House (16 August 2021).

13 Afghanistan Freedom Support Act of 2002, Public Law 107–327 (4 December 2002).

14 Ryan Crocker, 'Why Biden's Lack of Strategic Patience Led to Disaster', *New York Times* (21 August 2021).

15 Jonah Blank, 'The Original Sin of the War in Afghanistan', *The Atlantic* (20 April 2021).

16 Special Inspector General for Afghanistan Reconstruction, 'Quarterly Report to United States Congress' (30 January 2015), p. 65.

17 Marika Theros and Iavor Rangelov, 'Field Notes from Afghanistan', seminar at London School of Economics (15 February 2010).

18 Antonio Giustozzi, *Koran, Kalashnikov and Laptop: The Neo-Taliban Insurgency in Afghanistan* (London: C. Hurst & Co., 2007), p. 24.

19 Bruce Riedel, 'Pakistan and Terror: The Eye of the Storm', *The Annals of the American Academy of Political and Social Science*, 618 (July 2008), p. 38.

20 For example, in 2009, as Pakistan's continued sponsorship of the Taliban became a mainstream talking point in NATO policy circles, the US Congress authorised a tripling of economic and development assistance through the Enhanced Partnership for Pakistan Act. The Senate Committee on Foreign Relations made plain, 'There are no conditions on Pakistan attached to these funds.' See United States Senate Committee on Foreign Relations, 'Separating Myth from Fact on the Enhanced Partnership with Pakistan Act of 2009' (8 October 2009).

21 Henry R. Luce, 'The American Century', *Life Magazine* (17 February 1941), p. 64. Luce sketched a vision of America as a global powerhouse which was passionately devoted to the ideals of freedom and justice.

22 Mohammad Noureddine, 'The map of the north of Putin's table – Assad: Three challenges ahead of Damascus', *Al-Akhbar* (16 September 2021).

23 See Alia Brahimi, 'Twenty Years After 9/11, US Global Authority is Weaker Than Ever', *Foreign Policy* (8 September 2021).

24 The withdrawal was not dependent on important conditions like a successfully brokered peace agreement between the Taliban and the government in Kabul. A conditions-based approach was depicted by the Biden administration officials as 'a recipe for staying in Afghanistan forever'.

25 All the while, the Taliban leadership will seek to downplay the threat from ISIS in Afghanistan and mislead the international community about its strength. Even as its 'Khorasan Province' took responsibility for two bombings and a gun attack in Jalalabad in September, Taliban commander Sherullah Badri pronounced, 'There is no danger from Daesh.' In Saeed Shah and Yaroslav Trofimov, 'Islamic State Attacks in Eastern Afghanistan Challenge Taliban Rule', *Wall Street Journal* (22 September 2021).

26 On 14 April 2021, President Biden argued that the US had to focus on the challenges 'that are in front of us': disrupting terrorist networks beyond Afghanistan, meeting stiff competition from China and defeating the Covid-19 pandemic. On 16 August 2021, Biden stated, 'Our only vital national interest in Afghanistan remains today what it has always been: preventing a terrorist attack on American homeland.' On 31 August 2021, he repeated, 'To those asking for a third decade of war in Afghanistan, I ask: What is the vital national interest?'

27 Even the disastrous Soviet intervention in Afghanistan was, by 2004, reinvented as a heroic episode by a resurgent Russia under President Putin. See Rodric Braithwaite, *Afgantsy: The Russians in Afghanistan 1979–89* (London: Profile Books, 2011), p. 324.

CHAPTER 14: BATTLING FOR NARRATIVE ADVANTAGE IN AFGHANISTAN: NATO TV AND A DIGITAL-FIRST STRATEGY

1 There had been some academic analysis, for example: D. Betz, 'Communication Breakdown: Strategic Communications and Defeat in Afghanistan', *Orbis* (Foreign Policy Research Institute), 55:4 (2011), pp. 613–30; and J. Ringsmose and B. K. Børgesen, 'Shaping public attitudes towards the deployment of military power: NATO, Afghanistan and the use of strategic narratives', *European Security*, 20:4 (2011), pp. 505–28.

2   See assessments of NATO communications in previous campaigns, for example: A. Behnke, '"vvv.nato.int.": virtuousness, virtuality and virtuosity in NATO's representation of the Kosovo campaign', in P. van Ham and S. Medvedev (eds), *Mapping European Security After Kosovo* (Manchester: Manchester University Press, 2002).

3   Speech can be accessed here: https://www.nato.int/docu/speech/2007/s071008a.html

4   'NATO launches new TV channel', NATO (2 April 2008), https://www.nato.int/cps/en/natohq/news_7177.htm?selectedLocale=en

5   This was shown in documents leaked to the *New York Times*. See Stephen Castle, 'NATO Hires a Coke Executive to Retool Its Brand', *New York Times* (16 July 2008), https://www.nytimes.com/2008/07/16/world/europe/16nato.html?searchResultPosition=2

6   After the takeover, the Taliban issued new guidelines and rules for journalists, see Carlotta Gall, 'New Taliban Guidelines Stir Fear About the Future of Press Freedom', *New York Times* (23 September 2021), https://www.nytimes.com/2021/09/23/world/asia/taliban-media-guidelines-afghanistan.html

7   For example, 'Taliban kills Afghan gov't top media officer, US condemns', Reuters (6 August 2021), https://www.reuters.com/world/asia-pacific/taliban-says-it-has-killed-afghan-governments-top-media-officer-2021-08-06/

CHAPTER 15: THE INTELLIGENCE FAILURE AND THE CULTURAL FAILURE OF THE WEST TO THINK IN GENERATIONS

1   'Agreement for Bringing Peace to Afghanistan between the Islamic Emirate of Afghanistan which is not recognized by the United States as a state and is known as the Taliban and the United States of America' (29 February 2020).

2   'The UK's work in Afghanistan', UK Ministry of Defence (14 January 2014).

3   'The situation in Afghanistan and its implications for international peace and security – Report of the Secretary-General', A/67/354–S/2012/703 (13 September 2012).

4   Giulia Scalabrino, 'Afghanistan: a case study in IED harm', AOAV (15 October 2020), https://aoav.org.uk/2020/afghanistan-a-case-study-in-ied-harm/

5   'A decade of global IED harm reviewed', ReliefWeb (15 October 2020), https://reliefweb.int/report/world/decade-global-ied-harm-reviewed

6   'Afghanistan's Fight against Corruption: Crucial for Peace and Prosperity', United Nations Assistance Mission in Afghanistan (18 June 2020).

7   Vanda Felbab-Brown, 'Afghan National Security Forces: Afghan Corruption and the Development of an Effective Fighting Force', Brookings (2 August 2012), https://www.brookings.edu/testimonies/afghan-national-security-forces-afghan-corruption-and-the-development-of-an-effective-fighting-force/

8   Private information; Larisa Brown, 'Ministry of Defence cut back analysts before Afghanistan fell', *The Times* (14 September 2021).

9   'The UK and Afghanistan', House of Lords Select Committee on International Relations and Defence, 2nd Report of Session 2019–21 (13 January 2021), https://committees.parliament.uk/publications/4185/documents/43162/default/

10 Aimen Dean, Paul Cruickshank and Tim Lister, *Nine Lives: My Time As MI6's Top Spy Inside al-Qaeda* (London: Oneworld, 2018)

CHAPTER 16: AFGHANISTAN: A STRATEGIC FAILURE OF VISION, RESOURCE AND PATIENCE

1   Paul Cornish, 'The Rout of Kabul: its meaning and consequences for the West', *The Article* (3 September 2021), https://www.thearticle.com/the-rout-of-kabul-its-meaning-and-consequences-for-the-west

2   'How Biden's exit plan went wrong', *Financial Times* [Print Edition] (30 August 2021).

3   'Afghanistan after America: Peace out', *The Economist* [Print Edition] (10 July 2021).

4 Darryl Coote, 'Milley: Taliban takeover of Afghanistan "not a foregone conclusion"', UPI (22 July 2021).

5 'A humbled West still owes a huge debt to the Afghans', *Sunday Times* [Print Edition] (29 August 2021).

6 Ayaan Hirsi Ali, 'Joe Biden is deaf, dumb and blind to the chaos the US has unleashed', *Sunday Telegraph* [Print Edition] (29 August 2021).

7 Helen Warrell, Amy Kazmin and Andrew England, 'Escape from Kabul', *Financial Times* [Print Edition] (28–29 August 2021).

8 'Kabul evacuation "was planned and prepared for months", says Johnson', BBC News (2 September 2021), https://www.bbc.co.uk/news/av/uk-politics-58426588

9 H. R. McMaster, 'It is a delusion to believe the Taliban rebrand: these child abusers are a threat to humanity', *Sunday Times* [Print Edition] (12 September 2021).

10 David Charter and Michael Evans, 'Defiant Biden hails Afghan pullout as an extraordinary success', *The Times* [Print Edition] (1 September 2021).

11 Dominic Raab, 'The UK must face up to the new Afghan reality', *Sunday Telegraph* [Print Edition] (29 August 2021).

12 'Johnson praises exertions in Kabul airlift', *Financial Times* [Print Edition] (30 August 2021).

13 Jon Stone, 'We were not defeated in Afghanistan, UK defence secretary Ben Wallace says', *The Independent* [Print Edition] (27 October 2021), https://www.independent.co.uk/news/uk/politics/afghanistan-war-defeat-ben-wallace-uk-b1945721.html

14 Winston Churchill, 'We Shall Fight on the Beaches', House of Commons (4 June 1940), https://winstonchurchill.org/resources/speeches/1940-the-finest-hour/we-shall-fight-on-the-beaches/

15 Lawrence Freedman, 'Afghanistan was a 20-year distraction from the West's real troubles', *Sunday Times* [Print Edition] (5 September 2021).

16 Stephen Walt, 'The Biden doctrine will allow America to focus on bigger goals', *Financial Times* [Print Edition] (31 August 2021).

17 'President will "bear grudge" towards UK over suggestions he has gone "doolally"', *Sunday Telegraph* [Print Edition] (29 August 2021). Deolali was the site of a British Army transit camp and military sanatorium near Mumbai (then called Bombay) in late-nineteenth-century British India. Soldiers being repatriated after becoming mentally ill from fever were said to have gone 'doolally tap' – 'tap' being derived from the Hindustani *tapa* for fever.

18 Fraser Nelson, 'How the new Moscow–Beijing axis is already exploiting US exhaustion', *Daily Telegraph* [Print Edition] (27 August 2021).

19 'China's revealing Afghan strategy', *The Economist* [Print Edition] (29 May 2021).

20 Didi Tang and Marc Bennetts, 'China and Russia "ready to help the Taliban rebuild"', *The Times* [Print Edition] (27 August 2021).

21 'Where next for global jihad?', *The Economist* [Print Edition] (28 August 2021).

22 Raffaello Pantucci, 'Jihadis will remain a threat under the Taliban government', *Financial Times* [Print Edition] (6 September 2021).

23 Maleeha Lodhi, 'Pakistan has much to fear if Afghanistan descends into chaos', *Financial Times* [Print Edition] (26 August 2021).

24 'Rogue nations celebrate the "thunderous defeat" of US', *The Times* [Print Edition] (30 August 2021).

25 'Abandoning Afghanistan', *The Economist* [Print Edition] (10 July 2021).

26 Emile Simpson, 'Don't blame the Afghan army for what's happening now', *Financial Times* [Print Edition] (30 August 2021).

27 HM Government, 'Global Britain in a Competitive Age: The Integrated Review of Security, Defence, Development and Foreign Policy' (March 2021), pp. 14, 95.

28 Dominic Raab, 'The UK must face up to the new Afghan reality', *Sunday Telegraph* [Print Edition] (29 August 2021).

29 Arnold Toynbee, *The World and the West* (London: Oxford University Press, 1953).

AFGHAN WITNESS 4: ESIN: A HUMAN RIGHTS DEFENDER ATTEMPTS TO PROTEST PEACEFULLY
1   Stories from the Afghan Witness project: https://www.afghanwitness.org/

CHAPTER 20: GENERAL DANNATT, THE FOREVER WARS AND THE MILITARY ELITE'S THREAT TO DEMOCRACY
1   Ewen MacAskill and Ian Cobain, 'British forces' century of unbroken warfare set to end with Afghanistan exit', *The Guardian* (11 February 2014).
2   Theo Farrell, *Unwinnable: Britain's War in Afghanistan* (London: Bodley Head, 2017).
3   Simon Akam, *The Changing of the Guard: The British Army Since 9/11* (London: Scribe, 2021); Paul Dixon, 'The British Military, Democracy and the Limits of "Legitimate Debate"', Re-thinking Security (27 April 2021).
4   Paul Dixon, 'Frock Coats against Brass Hats? Politicians, the Military and the War in Afghanistan', *Parliamentary Affairs*, 73:3 (2020).
5   Richard Dannatt, *Leading from the Front: An Autobiography* (London: Bantam, 2011), p. 419.
6   Dannatt (2011), Chapter 8; Sarah Sands, 'Sir Richard Dannatt: A Very Honest General', *Daily Mail* (12 October 2006).
7   Paul Dixon, *Warrior Nation: War, Militarisation and British Democracy* (London: Forceswatch, 2018), p. 13–25.
8   Sands.
9   Dannatt (2011); Richard Dannatt, *Boots on the Ground* (London: Profile Books, 2016); Marco Giannangeli, 'UK must hold Chilcot-style inquiry into Afghanistan, says Gen Lord Dannatt', *Daily Express* (9 August 2021).
10 Dannatt (2016), p. 281.
11 Matthew Weaver and Hélène Mulholland, 'Sir Richard Dannatt and Sir Mike Jackson at the Iraq war inquiry – live', *The Guardian* (28 July 2010); Dannatt (2011), pp. 290–91.
12 Weaver and Mulholland; Giannangeli; Dannatt (2011), pp. 308–12; Dannatt (2016), pp. 297–8.
13 Mark Tran, 'Former army chief attacks government over Afghanistan troops request', *The Guardian* (6 October 2009).
14 Jasper Copping, 'Sir Richard Dannatt interview: Getting political help for Army was like pushing a rock up a steep hill', *Sunday Telegraph* (4 September 2010).
15 David Richards, *Taking Command* (London: Headline, 2014), pp. 210, 2.
16 Akam, p. 617 fn. 47.
17 C. Whitlock, *The Afghanistan Papers* (New York: Simon & Schuster, 2021).
18 Dannatt (2011), p. 419; Giannangeli; Dannatt (2016) rejects the idea of a bail out.
19 Farrell, pp. 262, 273.
20 Chilcot Inquiry, 'Executive Summary' (2016), para. 811, p. 120.
21 Richards, pp. 181, 186.
22 Dannatt (2016), p. 272.
23 Chilcot Inquiry, vol. 9.4, para. 536, p. 579 (2016); Jack Fairweather, *The Good War: Why We Couldn't Win the War or the Peace in Afghanistan* (London: Vintage, 2015), Chapter 12.
24 Dixon (2020), p. 676.
25 Dannatt (2016), pp. 295–6; Farrell, p. 159.
26 Dannatt (2016), p. 301.
27 *Ibid.*, p. 298; Giannangeli.
28 Dannatt (2016), p. 295.
29 Chilcot Inquiry (2016), pp. 687–91; Fairweather, pp. 147, 148.
30 Sands; Dannatt (2011), p. 395.
31 Dannatt (2016), pp. 281, 284, 310; Joe Shute, 'General Sir Lord Dannatt: "Going to Iraq was an error of near biblical proportions"', *Daily Telegraph* (1 October 2016).
32 Stuart Anderson, '"What we did was right": Ex-head of UK armed forces Lord Dannatt on legacy of the Iraq and Afghanistan wars', *Eastern Daily Press* (6 May 2019).

33 Frank Ledwidge, *Losing Small Wars* (London: Yale University Press, 2011), pp. 74, 78; Farrell, pp. 168–78.

34 Dannatt (2016), p. 314.

35 Dixon (2018), pp. 29–31.

36 Dannatt (2016), pp. 310–11.

37 Dannatt (2016), p. 310.

38 Fairweather, pp. 199–200, 320–21; Chilcot Inquiry, 'Executive Summary' (2016), para. 813, p. 122, para. 821, p. 126.

39 Anthony Seldon and Guy Lodge, *Brown at 10* (London: Biteback, 2010), p. 337; Farrell, pp. 269–70; G. Brown, *My Life, Our Times* (London: Bodley Head, 2017).

40 Anthony Seldon and Peter Snowdon, *Cameron at 10: The Inside Story 2010–2015* (London: William Collins, 2015), pp. 49, 56, 491; David Cameron, *For the Record* (London: William Collins, 2019), p. 166.

41 Akam, p. 388; Ledwidge.

42 David Runciman, *How Democracy Ends* (London: Profile Books, 2018), pp. 33, 35, 43, 46.

CHAPTER 21: THE POST-AFGHAN RESET AND THE CASE FOR REBUILDING EU-UK SECURITY COOPERATION

1 Nigel Walker and Tim Robinson, 'The Conflict in Afghanistan: A Reading List', House of Commons Library (2 November 2021).

2 Kirsty Hughes, 'European Union views of the UK post-Brexit and of the Future EU–UK Relationship', Scottish Centre on European Relations (25 November 2020).

3 House of Commons Foreign Affairs Committee, 'Global Britain: Sixth Report of Session 2017–19'.

4 Peter Jackson, 'Brexit's nostalgia-infused ideology is behind UK's new Aukus pact with US and Australia – Professor Peter Jackson', *The Scotsman* (21 September 2021).

5 'Nuclear subs deal a risk to NATO: UK former Ambassador', AFP News (20 September 2021).

6 Mark Stone, 'Biden signals end to "era of major military operations to remake other countries"', Sky News (1 September 2021).

7 Dominic Waghorn, 'US Betrayal of Kurds destroys the West's credibility for years to come', Sky News (16 October 2019).

8 Eleanor Beardsley, 'Anger and Consternation From Europeans Watching Afghanistan Fall to the Taliban', NPR (16 August 2021).

9 Samy Adghirni, 'European Leaders Point Fingers at the US After Fall of Kabul', Bloomberg (17 August 2021).

10 Ursula von der Leyen, State of the Union address to the European Parliament (15 September 2021).

11 David O'Sullivan, 'Europe back at heart of US global policy', BBC News (16 June 2021).

12 EU–US Summit 2021, 'Statement: Towards a Renewed Transatlantic Partnership'.

13 'Defence and security in Europe – Biden and Brexit as new parameters', Konrad Adenauer Foundation (9 March 2021).

14 Professor Rick Fawn, 'Not here for geopolitical interest or games: the EU's 2019 strategy and the regional and inter-regional competition for Central Asia', *Central Asian Survey* (17 August 2021).

15 Professor Phillips O'Brien, Twitter (22 September 2021).

AFGHAN WITNESS 5: GULNAZ: A MOTHER TURNS TO SEX WORK

1 Stories from the Afghan Witness project: https://www.afghanwitness.org/

INDEX